Foundations of Business Organizations for Paralegals

Foundations of Business Organizations for Paralegals

Margaret Bartschi

WEST

THOMSON LEARNING

Australia Canada Mexico Singapore Spain United Kingdom United States

WEST

THOMSON LEARNING

WEST LEGAL STUDIES

Foundations of Business Organizations for Paralegals
by Margaret Bartschi

Business Unit Director: Susan L. Simpfenderfer	**Editorial Assistant:** Lisa Flatley	**Executive Production Manager:** Wendy A. Troeger
Executive Editor: Marlene McHugh Pratt	**Executive Marketing Manager:** Donna J. Lewis	**Production Editor** Betty L. Dickson
Acquisitions Editor: Joan M. Gill	**Channel Manager:** Nigar Hale	**Cover Designer:** Dutton and Sherman Design

For permission to use material from this text or product, contact us by
Tel   (800) 730-2214
Fax   (800) 730-2215
www.thomsonrights.com

Library of Congress Cataloging-in-Publication Data

Bartschi, Margaret.
  Foundations of business organizations for paralegals / Margaret Bartschi.
     p.   cm.
  Includes index.
  ISBN 0-7668-1652-4
     1. Business enterprises—Law and legislation—United States.
2. Corporation law—United States. 3. Legal assistants—United States—Handbooks, manuals, etc. I. Title.

KF1355 .B37 2000
346.73'065—dc21   00-043416

NOTICE TO THE READER

Publisher does not warrant or guarantee any of the products described herein or perform any independent analysis in connection with any of the product information contained herein. Publisher does not assume, and expressly disclaims, any obligation to obtain and include information other than that provided to it by the manufacturer.

The reader is notified that this text is an educational tool, not a practice book. Since the law is in constant change, no rule or statement of law in this book should be relied upon for any service to any client. The reader should always refer to standard legal sources for the current rule or law. If legal advice or other expert assistance is required, the services of the appropriate professional should be sought.

The Publisher makes no representation or warranties of any kind, including but not limited to, the warranties of fitness for particular purpose or merchantability, nor are any such representations implied with respect to the material set forth herein, and the publisher takes no responsibility with respect to such material. The publisher shall not be liable for any special, consequential, or exemplary damages resulting, in whole or part, from the readers' use of, or reliance upon, this material.

TABLE OF CONTENTS

8 Limited Liability Partnership: Managers without Liability 76

SECTION FOUR: CORPORATIONS

9 Corporations: Ownership without Liability 90

10 Formation of a Corporation 99

TABLE OF FORMS

To my family
You are my foundation

LIABILITY - LEGAL RESPONSIBILITY

SEVERAL

~~SOLE~~ - ONLY ONE

JOINT - SHARED

AVOIDANCE/MINIMIZATION

INSURANCE

BY K

CHOICE OF ENTITY

XFER OWNERSHIP

INDEMNIFICATION

CONTRIBUTE ✓

WHAT DO YOU OWN?

" " WANT TO PROTECT?

" MUST YOU PROTECT?

AGENCY - DO YOU WANT TO BE RESPONSIBLE FOR THE

ACTS OF OTHERS? PARTNERS

EMPLOYEES

TAXATION - PASSTHRU OR

DOUBLE-TAXATION.

PREFACE

Foundations of Business Organizations is designed to provide the paralegal student with an overview of the law of business organizations. It is divided into five sections, beginning with Section 1, an introduction to the major organizational forms available for business owners today. Next, Section 2 discusses the most basic business form, the *sole proprietorship.* Section 3 is designed to familiarize the student with *partnerships,* business ventures with two or more associates. The most complex organizational form, *the corporation,* is considered in Section 4. Finally, Section 5 discusses an increasingly popular organizational form for many businesses today, the *limited liability company,* a hybrid of the partnership and corporation.

One of the main problems that I encountered as a paralegal instructor was the complexity of business organization materials available on the market. Most texts are geared toward the law student, rather than the paralegal, making the process of synthesizing the materials for the paralegal student arduous and cumbersome. This book is intended specifically for the paralegal student. It provides students with practical applications of the legal concepts associated with forming and creating a business organization.

Paralegals must become familiar with the various organizational forms, as well as the short- and long-term consequences of each. Therefore, the respective sections are divided into chapters that address formation considerations (e.g., document preparation and financing limitations), structure, liability issues, tax consequences, and methods for terminating or altering the organization of a chosen business form. To help students develop a working knowledge of the various organizational forms, each chapter provides study questions, case studies, and project applications to review the legal concepts presented within the chapter. The applications are intended to help the student put the concepts learned from the text into practice.

The text is supplemented by an Instructor's Manual that provides lecture outlines and test banks. The lecture outlines are designed to be reproduced on transparencies and used as overhead outlines to help students organize the lecture materials. Reading the text and attending lectures will help students to understand the legal concepts of choosing and forming a business entity. However, students need practical applications of the materials. These are provided at the end of each chapter in the case studies and project applications. Students should be provided opportunities to apply their knowledge to actual case situations and opportunities to complete projects, including the preparation of many of the business forms that paralegals will be expected to prepare when they enter the job market.

An important tool that will aid the student in succeeding as a paralegal is a working knowledge of the secretary of state's office, procedures, and forms. The project applications are designed, in part, to help students familiarize themselves with this office. A listing of each state's secretary of state or its corporation division is provided in Appendix A; websites, with state-specific business forms that can be downloaded, are provided for all of the offices. In addition, a comprehensive list of each state's business forms can be obtained at **www.westlegalstudies.com.** Paralegals who learn how to use these resources effectively will be well on their way to becoming a valuable asset to their law firm.

This text can be used nationally. Therefore, the presentation and discussion of partnerships, corporations, and limited liability companies are based upon the relevant uniform laws. Specifically, the Uniform Partnership Act, the Revised Uniform Partnership Act, the Revised Uniform Limited Partnership Act, the Revised Model Business Corporation Act, and the Uniform Limited Liability Company Act are referenced. Consideration of these uniform laws is helpful to understanding the development and rationale of the various organizational forms available for businesses today. However, while some states have adopted all or portions of the uniform laws, the business laws of other states vary substantially. A list of states that have adopted the respective uniform laws is provided in the Appendices. It is important for paralegals to become familiar with the statutory provisions of their state as well as those states in which their firms' clients may have business interests.

These materials are intended as a basic outline of organizational forms for students; however, paralegals will undoubtedly be presented with further client-specific considerations requiring independent research. The law of business organizations is extremely complex but a basic overview will provide students with the background that they will need to assist their reviewing attorney in assessing a client's most viable organizational option and preparing the information and documentation necessary to properly organize and maintain a client's business interests.

Margaret Bartschi
Missoula, Montana

ACKNOWLEDGMENTS

I am grateful for the contributions of many individuals who helped me develop this text. First and foremost I wish to express my gratitude to my father, Dean L. Flint, Esq., for his significant editing and research contributions. His legal expertise has been invaluable to me not only in the preparation of this book but also to my legal education and career as a whole. I am also thankful to my mother, Vena Flint, for encouraging all of my endeavors.

I am grateful for the patience and support of my husband Kent and the forbearance of our children, Stetson, Dean, Bailey Ann, and Kathleen, as I prepared this work. Without the support of my family, I would not have been able to complete this book.

This work as a whole is a culmination of not only my law practice and teaching experience but also the contributions of other authors, legal scholars, attorneys, business experts, companies, and government agencies whose work, expertise, and forms I referred to and relied upon in the preparation of this text. In particular, I am grateful for the willingness of Nancy K. Moe, of Dye & Moe, LLP, Missoula, Montana, for providing extensive sample documents for inclusion in the text; K.C. Sullivan, C.P.A., for clarifying the intricacies of the Internal Revenue Code; Thomas H. Stanton, Esq., of the University of Montana College of Technology, for his editorial comments and contributions; Miriam King for her organizational abilities; Shane C. Mason for his computer genius; Michelle Riley for her research assistance; Catherine and Donald Kipp for their editorial contributions; Katharine Whisler of the American Bar Association for her persistence in obtaining a partnership agreement for this text; Joan Gill and Lisa Flatley of West Legal Studies for their assistance in preparing the final manuscript for this project; West Group for granting permission to reprint their tables of adopted Uniform Laws; the secretaries of state of California, Texas, New York, Delaware, and Montana for sample forms for use throughout the text; and to my students who have used this text over the years and offered commentary on its application.

The text would not be complete without all of these contributions and I am grateful to all of those who willingly contributed to this effort.

Reviewers for Bartschi/Foundations of Business Organizations

Matthew Cornick
National Center for Paralegal Training

Michael Schneider
Denver Paralegal Institute

Thomas Gruenig
St. Mary's College

Anthony Piazza
David N. Myers College

Gary Ivanson
Roger Williams University

Susan Howery
Yavapai College

Ana Otero
Center for Advanced Legal Research

SECTION ONE
Introduction

CHAPTER 1

The Alternatives: A Basic Overview

Handwritten margin notes:
S.P. ONE OWNER
PERSONAL LIABILITY

P-SHIP - ASS'N OF
2 OR MORE
FOR PROFIT
PERSONAL LIABILITY

Paralegals must have a basic understanding of the law of business organizations. Familiarity with the various organizational forms, as well as the ramifications of each, will help paralegals to be aware of the options for each client's business, and knowledgeably and efficiently assist their reviewing attorney in preparing the legal documents necessary to structure a client's business interests. Many business owners may already be working as sole proprietors or in informal partnerships, unaware of the ramifications or availability of more advantageous alternatives.

Business organizations are based largely upon statute; therefore, the existence, formation, and ramifications of each may vary from state to state. However, the following are the basic forms with which you should be familiar.

SOLE PROPRIETORSHIP

A **sole proprietorship** is a business owned by one individual. The owner is personally liable for the debts and obligations of the business. This means that creditors of a business can and do look to the owner's personal assets, such as a family home and retirement savings, to pay the debts of the business.

PARTNERSHIP

A partnership is an association of two or more persons or entities who are in business together "for profit." Partnerships are relatively simple to create and offer business owners tax advantages not available to most businesses that incorporate.

A partnership is merely a group of owners working together in business. That is, the partnership is an extension of the individual partners and not a separate business entity. Therefore, the individual partners can be held personally responsible for the debts and obligations of the partnership. In order to protect partners and limit their **personal liability,** many states have adopted partnership forms that limit business owners' personal liability while maintaining the advantages of partnership organization.

General Partnership

A general partnership is the traditional and most common form of organization for a business owned by two or more people or entities. All partner-owners participate in management of the business and are, therefore, personally responsible for the debts and obligations incurred by the business.

Limited Partnership

A partnership may be designed to protect individuals and entities that invest in a business but do not participate in the management or control of the business from personal liability for the debts and obligations of the partnership; these are known as limited partnerships. In order to protect investors from personal liability, limited partnerships separate partners into two categories based on their rights and responsibilities: (1) **general partners,** who manage the partnership and are personally liable for the debts of the partnership and (2) **limited partners,** who invest in the partnership business but who have no right to participate in management and no personal responsibility for partnership debts.

Sole proprietorship A business owned by one person.

Personal liability An individual's responsibility to pay the debts and obligations of a business from personal assets (e.g., home, car, etc.).

General partner An individual or entity who manages a general or limited partnership.

Limited partner An investor in a limited partnership who has no management rights.

This partnership form recognizes that some business owners are merely investors in a business enterprise and do not participate in the business operation itself. Because these investors are not participating in management, they are not making decisions that cause the business to incur debt; therefore, they should not be responsible for the debts and obligations of the partnership.

Limited Liability Partnership

Limited liability partnerships operate like general partnerships but with the liability protections of limited partnerships. This partnership form offers all partners the right to participate in the management and the operation of a partnership business without subjecting themselves to unlimited personal liability.

CORPORATION

Corporations are legal entities that are separate and distinct from their owners; they are, in fact, "persons" created by state law. Corporations are owned by investors (shareholders) and generally managed by an elected **board of directors** and its appointed officers. Because **shareholders** do not have the right to participate in the management of the corporation's business, they are protected from personal liability for the debts and obligations of the corporation.

The main advantage to incorporation is that it offers investors protection from personal liability for the debts of the corporation and allows investors to sit back and wait for a return on their investment. Even if a corporation does not make money, the shareholders' risk is limited to the amount invested in the corporation.

Although corporations offer shareholders personal liability protections, they are not always the entity of choice of all business owners. Substantial formalities must be complied with to create and maintain a corporation. In addition, because a corporation is a separate "person" from its shareholders, corporate profits are taxed twice: (1) the corporation itself is taxed on its profits and (2) the shareholders are taxed on the corporate profits once they receive their share of the profits. For some business owners, these disadvantages override the extensive personal liability protections of the corporate form.

LIMITED LIABILITY COMPANY

The **limited liability company** is a hybrid of a corporation and a partnership. This business form offers its owners the limited liability protections of the corporation with the management rights and taxation advantages of general partnerships. A limited liability company is a separate legal entity from its members and must be created in accordance with state laws. All states as well as the District of Columbia authorize limited liability companies.

The law in most states is still developing with respect to limited liability partnerships and limited liability companies, both relatively new forms of business organization. However, the practical and legal advantages of both forms can be substantial. Many businesses are opting for the liability protections of these "simplified" business forms over the formalities of incorporation.

Corporation A legal business entity owned by shareholders and managed by an elected board of directors and appointed officers.

Board of directors The group elected to manage a corporation.

Shareholders Owners of a corporation.

Limited liability Investors' responsibility for the debts and obligations of a business is limited to the amount of their investment; when an investor is not responsible for paying the debts and obligations of a business from his or her personal assets.

Limited liability company An unincorporated entity that offers its members management rights, limited personal liability, and the taxation of partnerships.

THE ALTERNATIVES IN REVIEW

Sole Proprietorship
Business conducted by one person.

Partnership
♦ *General partnership:* Association of two or more persons or entities who operate a business as co-owners for profit.

♦ *Limited partnership:* Association of two or more persons or entities who operate a business as co-owners for profit with one or more general partners (managers) and one or more limited partners (investors).
    1. *General partners:* managers with personal liability
    2. *Limited partners:* investors with limited liability
♦ *Limited liability partnership:* General or limited partnership that registers as a limited liability partnership and protects its partners from vicarious liability for the negligence or malfeasance of other partners.

Corporation
Legal business entity owned by shareholders and managed by an elected board of directors and appointed officers.

Limited Liability Company
Unincorporated entity that offers its members management rights, limited personal liability and partnership taxation.

KEY TERMS

sole proprietorship	limited partner	shareholders
personal liability	corporation	limited liability company
general partner	board of directors	

STUDY QUESTIONS IN REVIEW

1. What is personal liability?
2. Identify the three forms of partnerships.
3. Who manages a limited partnership?
4. Are limited partners personally liable for the debts and obligations of a limited partnership?

5. Who owns a corporation?
6. Does a corporation pay taxes on its profits?
7. What is a limited liability company?

CASE STUDIES IN REVIEW

1. Cathy is a fifth grader who opens a lemonade stand on her block. Would Cathy's business be considered a sole proprietorship or a partnership? Why?

2. Frames 'R Us, Inc. is a local frame shop. Last year its corporate profits were $200,000 and each of its two shareholders received $100,000 in corporate profits. Will Frames 'R Us be taxed on its corporate profits, will the shareholders, or both? Explain.

Choosing a Business Entity

Each organizational form offers unique advantages and corresponding disadvantages. Your supervising attorney will consider the business and personal needs of each client in assessing which of the business structures best meets those needs. The key issues to consider in determining which organizational alternative would be most advantageous for a client are as follows:

Formalities
Management
Ownership restrictions
Taxation
Liability

Each issue is discussed briefly in this chapter.

FORMALITIES

Formalities vary significantly with each business form. Sole proprietorships and general partnerships may be automatically created when one or more individuals or entities simply begin a business, whereas limited partnerships, limited liability partnerships, corporations, and limited liability companies must be formally created by filing and drafting the appropriate documents.

The corporate form is well known for its extensive filing and reporting requirements. In order to form a corporation, **articles of incorporation** must be filed with the secretary of state or other appropriate state corporate division. **Bylaws** must then be drafted to organize the corporation. An organizational meeting of the incorporators and/or initial directors must be held in order to perform such formalities as electing directors, appointing corporate officers, approving the articles of incorporation, and adopting corporate bylaws. Even after the corporation is formed and organized, statutory formalities, such as holding required meetings, must be observed continually in order for the corporation to maintain its corporate status.

A client must be aware of the requirements necessary to form and operate his or her respective business choice. Failure to comply with the requisite filing and/or reporting requirements for an organizational form can result in a business losing its corporate status, thus exposing its owners to **personal liability** for the debts and other obligations of the business.

MANAGEMENT

Although many business owners want to actively participate in the management and operation of their enterprise, some owners merely want to invest in a business opportunity. The degree to which individuals want to be involved in management is a major consideration in determining which organizational form is best for them.

Owners who want to participate in the management of their business may choose to form sole proprietorships, general or limited liability partnerships, **S corporations** or limited liability companies, all organizational forms that allow owners to actively participate in management. However, individuals who merely want to invest in a business rather than manage its business affairs, may find limited partnerships or corporations more attractive alternatives; such business forms allow mere investors to simply wait for a return on their

Formalities The requirements for creating and maintaining a business.

Articles of incorporation The document that creates a corporation.

Bylaws Written guidelines and procedures for the operation and management of a corporation.

Personal liability An individual's responsibility to pay the debts and obligations of a business from personal assets (e.g., home, car, etc.).

S corporation Tax designation available to qualifying small corporations allowing corporate income to pass through the corporation to be taxed as personal income of the shareholders.

investment while avoiding personal liability for losses that the business might suffer or other business debts that might arise.

Owners who participate in management and control of a business and its enterprises must be cautioned that with decision making generally comes personal liability for the consequences of those decisions. Therefore, it is important to determine to what degree an owner intends to be involved in a business.

OWNERSHIP RESTRICTIONS

Some business forms impose restrictions on who may own and/or participate in the management of the business. Generally, businesses that allow their owners to participate in management, such as limited liability partnerships and limited liability companies, also restrict, to some degree, who may own an interest in the business. The purpose of such restrictions is to maintain some degree of harmony in management of the business and its interests. Without such ownership restrictions, disagreements and distrust in management could paralyze business operations.

Individuals who want to start their own business and/or participate in the management and operation of the business enterprise may appreciate the restrictions that partnerships and limited liability companies impose on ownership and management of the business. However, individuals and entities that are merely looking for an investment opportunity will not want to be bound by the ownership restrictions imposed by these types of business entities. Investors may instead be lured to corporations that provide investment opportunities while allowing investors to "cash out" their ownership interest without restrictions.

TAXATION

The tax consequences associated with the various business organizations should be considered when choosing a business entity. Business corporations suffer double taxation: once at the corporate level, and again in the hands of the shareholders when they receive corporate profits. Many business owners seek to escape these corporate tax rates by forming partnerships or limited liability companies, organizational forms that allow profits to "pass through" the business and be taxed directly as income of the individual owner(s).

However, an entity that elects not to incorporate in order to avoid double taxation may also require its owners to forfeit the extensive liability protections generally provided by the corporate form. Many states have realized this trade-off and, therefore, have adopted limited liability partnerships and limited liability companies, business forms that tend to offer corporate liability protections but with the partnership taxation advantage.

LIABILITY

Liability An individual's responsibility for the debts and obligations of a business.

Liability is one of the most significant considerations in selecting an appropriate business organization. Corporations and limited liability companies offer owners extensive personal liability protections; however, sole proprietorships and general partnerships leave owners virtually unprotected from personal liability for the debts and obligations of their business enterprises. This means that owners of sole proprietorships or general partnerships that fail or incur significant debt that cannot be paid, risk losing their personal property (house, cars, etc.) to pay business obligations. This is a risk that some business owners and their families are not willing to accept.

The extensive personal liability protections provided by the corporate form are significant. Thus, even with the adoption of other business forms that offer owners personal liability protections (e.g., limited liability partnerships and companies), the corporation will undoubtedly remain a popular organizational option for business owners in the future.

◆ CHOOSING A BUSINESS ENTITY IN REVIEW

Formalities
Filing and/or reporting requirements must be complied with to maintain organizational forms that offer limited liability protections.

Management
Participation in management creates personal liability.

Ownership Restrictions
Organizational forms that allow owners to participate in management may restrict ownership of business interests.

Taxation
Corporate (double) taxation vs. "pass through" taxation.

Liability
Personal liability vs. limited liability.

◆ KEY TERMS

formalities	bylaws	S corporation
articles of incorporation	personal liability	liability

◆ STUDY QUESTIONS IN REVIEW

1. What business forms are created simply by individuals or entities beginning business?
2. What document creates a corporation?
3. Identify two business forms that allow individuals to invest in a business without participating in its management.

4. Why do businesses that allow owners to participate in management restrict who may own an interest in the business?
5. What is liability and why is it important in choosing an organizational form for a business?

◆ CASE STUDIES IN REVIEW

1. Kent and his brother Craig manage their family's cattle ranch in Montana. They own the ranch as partners. Your supervising attorney recommends that they form a corporation to protect them from personal liability for any losses the ranch may suffer. Your supervising attorney asks you to briefly explain what personal liability is to Kent and Craig.

2. Laurie wants to open a small bakery in her hometown. Her parents are interested in financing her business. Can they invest in her business without participating in its management or day-to-day operations? Explain.

◆ PROJECT APPLICATION

Contact your state's secretary of state to obtain a form for filing a corporation's articles of incorporation.

CHAPTER 3

Agency in Business Organizations

Most business organizations are managed or operated to some extent by agents, people acting on behalf of another. Therefore, the law of agency is an integral part of understanding how businesses are organized and how they operate. Basically, an **agency** relationship is created when one person, an **agent,** acts on behalf of another, the **principal.** Agency is created by mutual agreement and may arise from an informal request or a written agreement.

Agency relationships exist in all aspects of human interactions. When an attorney is hired to represent a client and speak on the client's behalf, the attorney is the agent of the client, the principal. When a real estate agent represents an individual purchasing a home, the real estate agent is the agent of the individual, the principal. When an employer asks an employee to deliver merchandise to a customer, the employee is the agent of the employer, the principal. In all of these settings, the agent is acting on behalf of another person, the principal, with the principal's consent.

AGENCY

Most business enterprises need agents to conduct part or all aspects of the business. For example, in a partnership, each partner is an agent of the partnership and can bind the partnership to obligations within the scope of the partnership's business. Similarly, in a limited liability company, members or their managers may act as agents and may make commitments to third parties on behalf of the company, such as hiring employees to work in the company's offices. Finally, corporations are, of necessity, run entirely by agents, such as directors, officers, or corporate employees. Because agency relationships are a necessary part of operating any business, it is important to understand the principles of agency.

AUTHORITY OF AGENTS

Agency Relationship in which one person, an agent, acts on behalf of another, the principal.

Agent One who acts for the benefit of another.

Principal One who permits or directs another to act on his behalf.

Apparent authority When the principal's conduct makes it appear to a third party that an agent is authorized to act on behalf of the principal.

Ratify Retroactively accept/approve an obligation created by an agent who did not have authority to act on behalf of the principal at the time of the transaction.

Express actual authority Principal directs an agent to perform specified acts.

Agents are an arm or extension of their principal; when an agent acts on behalf of a principal, it is as though the principal acted. Therefore, principals can be held liable for the acts of their agents, if those actions are authorized or appear to be authorized by the principal. A principal authorizes an agent to act on his or her behalf when (1) the principal directs the agent to perform specified acts, thus granting the agent actual authority to perform those acts, (2) the principal's conduct makes it appear to third parties that the agent has the **apparent authority** to act on behalf of the principal, or (3) the principal retroactively accepts, or **ratifies,** the acts of an agent who acted beyond the agent's actual or apparent authority.

Actual Authority

When a principal asks someone to perform a task for him or her, an agency relationship is created and the principal has granted the agent the actual authority to act on the principal's behalf. The actual authority granted to the agent can be express or implied and continues until the principal revokes the agent's authority (e.g., "you're off the project" or "you're fired") or the agent terminates the relationship (e.g., "I quit").

An agent has the authority to act on behalf of a principal when the principal directs the agent to perform specified acts, either orally or in writing (e.g., a homeowner hires a real estate agent to sell his house); this is known as **express actual authority.** In addition to the agent's express actual authority, the agent has the **implied actual authority** to perform those acts necessary to carry out the principal's directives (e.g., the real estate agent may advertise the house for sale or show the house to potential buyers).

Apparent Authority

Even if an agent does not have the actual authority to act on behalf of the principal, the principal's conduct may cause a third party to reasonably believe that the agent has the authority to act for the principal. If the principal has made it appear that the agent has the authority to act on his or her behalf, the agent has the apparent authority to act for the principal and the principal will be bound to the actions of the agent.

> **Example:** Sports Fan is a local sporting goods store owned by Mark, a sole proprietor. Jason, a scuba diving expert is a purchaser for the store, authorized only to purchase scuba diving gear for the store. His official title is Purchasing Agent. This title appears on his business cards. During a purchasing trip, Jason finds several pieces of weight lifting equipment and charges the cost to Sports Fan. Mark, as the owner of Sports Fan, can be held responsible for the cost of the equipment, although Jason was not authorized to purchase it, because he has represented to the public that Jason is a general purchasing agent and has made no attempts to limit Jason's authority with the public.

Ratification

A principal can agree to accept an obligation created by an agent even if the agent did not have the authority to act on behalf of the principal at the time of the transaction. By ratifying the agent's action, the principal is retroactively granting the agent the authority to act.

> **Example:** Richard is a sales representative for Motors "R" Us. Motors "R" Us is exclusively a new or dealership, and sales representatives are not authorized to take used vehicles for trade-in credit. However, in order to make a sale, Richard agrees to take a trade-in from a customer purchasing a new car. The owner of Motors "R" Us learns of the trade-in and sells the car to another customer. The owner's actions in accepting and selling the car is a ratification of the agents unauthorized act.

DUTIES OF AGENTS AND PRINCIPALS

Agency creates a **fiduciary relationship** between the agent and the principal. A principal trusts an agent to be loyal, to act in good faith, and to use due care with respect to the principal's business. In return, an agent trusts that he or she will be paid by the principal and receive **indemnification** for any obligations incurred on behalf of the principal. These implied duties may be expanded by written agreement between the parties.

> **Example:** Kent, a sole proprietor, hires Megan, accountant, to manage the financial affairs of his business, including the company payroll. Kent trusts that Megan will use her professional knowledge and expertise to manage his business's finances and, further, that she will not embezzle funds from him. Megan trusts that she will be compensated for her services and reimbursed for any costs she has paid on behalf of Kent and his business (e.g., IRS filing fees).

Duties of Agents to Principals

Agents owe their principals three duties: (1) the duty of performance and obedience, (2) the **duty of care,** and (3) the **duty of loyalty**. Each of these duties is implied in the agency relationship and follows the general expectations of the public. That is, it is generally expected that an agent, such as an employee, will perform those tasks assigned by the principal with reasonable diligence and due care and, further, will be loyal to the principal in performing his or her duties.

Implied actual authority The authority necessary for an agent to carry out the express directives of a principal.

Fiduciary relationship A relationship of trust creating a duty to act in good faith.

Indemnification Reimbursement for payment of another's debt.

Duty of care The care a reasonably prudent person would use in similar circumstances.

Duty of loyalty Responsibility of an agent to act for the benefit of the principal.

The basic foundation of the agency relationship is that the agent will follow the instructions of the principal. Thus, if an employer hires an individual to clean tables and do dishes in the employer's restaurant, it is expected that the employee will follow the instructions. An agent who does not perform the duties assigned by the principal undermines the entire agency relationship and is of little value to the principal.

In addition to simply following directions, agents must perform their duties with reasonable diligence and due care. That is, an agent is expected to use the care that a reasonably prudent person would use in similar circumstances (e.g., the waitress should use care not to break the restaurant's dishes). If an agent is a professional or has other specialized knowledge or skills, the standard of care is higher (e.g., an attorney who is hired to prepare a will for a client is expected to use specialized knowledge and skills—professional expertise—on behalf of the client).

In addition to the duties of obedience and due care, agents must be loyal to their principals. The duty of loyalty requires that agents act solely for the benefit of their principals in performing their duties. Thus, agents cannot engage in transactions that create conflicts of interest with principals and their business affairs. For example, a real estate agent who is hired by a buyer to purchase a particular piece of property cannot negotiate to purchase the same property for him- or herself and then resell it at a profit. If an agent has a conflict of interest with his or her principal, the agent must disclose the conflict to the principal to avoid breaching the duty of loyalty.

In addition to an agent's duties of obedience, due care, and loyalty, an agent's duties to a principal can be, and often are, expanded by agreement of the parties.

> **Example:** Rita is a salesperson for Vann's Computer Store. Rita's employment contract requires her to sell $2,000 worth of electronic equipment each month. If Rita fails to fulfill this duty, she is in breach of her employment contract and can be terminated by Vann's.

Duties of Principals to Agents

Principals generally owe the following duties to their agents: (1) the duty to compensate, (2) the duty to indemnify and reimburse, and (3) the duty to facilitate agents in the performance of their duties. These duties are generally implied by law and may be expanded by written agreement of the parties.

In most agency relationships, it is generally understood that agents will be compensated for their services. For example, most attorneys expect to bill a client for their work; however, in specified circumstances, attorneys may offer their services on a *pro bono* basis. The circumstances under which agents do not expect to be paid should be established by the parties prior to forming an agency relationship, otherwise, it will be assumed that the agents are owed reasonable compensation for their services.

Pro bono Work performed without charge (literally, "for the public good").

In addition to receiving compensation, it is expected that the agent will be reimbursed and indemnified for any costs or other liabilities incurred on behalf of the principal. Since the agent is working for the principal, any obligations that the agent incurs are obligations of the principal. Thus, if an attorney's office pays filing fees to record documents for a client, the attorney is entitled to be reimbursed by the client for the amounts paid, since it is the client, and not the attorney, who benefits from the filing. In addition to reimbursements, an agent is also entitled to be indemnified for any losses suffered while acting within the course and scope of the employment.

In addition to the principal's obligation to compensate and indemnify an agent, the principal must also facilitate the performance of the agent's duties. For example, a principal must provide the equipment, office space, and other essentials that an agent needs to perform his or her duties. Thus, an employer who hires a telemarketer to work in the employer's office must provide the telemarketer with a telephone to make calls, a list of telephone numbers to call, and a space to sit while making the calls on the employer's behalf. Basically, the principal must make it possible for the agent to perform the job.

The agency relationship requires that both the agent and the principal perform their respective duties. If either one of them fails to do so, the fiduciary is breached and the agency relationship may be terminated.

LIABILITY OF THE PRINCIPAL FOR ACTS OF THE AGENT

In an agency relationship, the principal can be held responsible for the actions of the agent. Theoretically, the principal has the power to control the agent and is thus responsible for the agent's actions. When a father asks a child to run an errand for him, he is creating an agency relationship with the child; the child is becoming an agent of the parent. Thus, if the child is involved in an accident while driving the father's car, the father can be held responsible for his child's action because the father was in a position to know whether the child could safely operate a motor vehicle and obtain liability insurance on the car (that is, to insure the enterprise). This is known as **vicarious liability** and is based upon the doctrine of *respondeat superior,* literally, "let the master answer."

Although a principal may be held liable for the acts of an agent, this does not relieve the agent of responsibility, simply because the agent was acting on behalf of a principal. The agent remains personally liable for the injuries that he or she may cause. Thus, if a truck driver injures a pedestrian while making deliveries for an employer, the driver can be held personally liable for negligence. Practically speaking, however, the pedestrian may prefer the "deep pocket" of the principal (which includes the principal's business insurance) over that of the agent.

Generally, a principal can be held vicariously liable for the actions of an agent if (1) the agent is a servant of the principal, as opposed to being an independent contractor, and (2) the agent is acting within the course and scope of employment at the time of the injury/accident. A servant who is acting within the course and scope of employment is, theoretically, acting under the principal's direction and control, and is in furtherance of the business enterprise, therefore giving rise to the principal's liability for the agent's actions.

The ability of principals to control the actions of their agents is a determining factor in whether principals will be liable for the acts of their agents. Agents are either employees/servants or independent contractors of the principal. An employee/servant is one whose actions the principal can generally direct and control; therefore, it is presumed that the principal can prevent tortious acts by such agents. Thus, an accounting firm with in-house accountants can provide training for its employees and oversee their daily work. However, if a business hires an outside accountant to manage its financial affairs, the business is not in a position to directly oversee and control the accountant; the accountant is, therefore, generally considered to be an independent contractor. Because independent contractors are not under the direct supervision and control of a principal, the principal will not usually held liable for the contractor's torts.

Even when an agent commits a tort, however, the principal will be held liable only if the agent is acting within the course and scope of employment at the time of the wrongful action. It is fundamental that an agent must be working on the principal's behalf in order for the principal to be held liable for the agent's actions. However, the question of whether a principal will be held liable for the actions of an agent generally arises when the agent, while working for the principal, detours from the assigned task. The classic example is the truck driver who visits a friend while driving cross-country for the principal, the trucking company. If the friend's house is not on the assigned route and the driver is involved in an accident on the way to visit the friend, the court may still hold the principal liable because the driver was driving the truck as an employee of the trucking company. However, the driver's actions could also be seen as a personal "frolic"; that is, the driver was on a personal errand at the time of the accident and, therefore, was not acting within the course and scope of employment for the principal at the time of the accident. The distinction between a "detour" and a personal "frolic" has led to many court cases.

As a matter of public policy, principals must be held liable for the actions of their agents that cause injuries to others, when the principals have the authority to control their agents' actions and insure against the damages arriving from such injuries. The doctrine of vicarious liability helps to insure that principals act prudently in the selection and employment of their agents and obtain adequate **liability insurance** to protect both members of the public and the employer's business against the financial consequences of the agents' tortious acts.

Vicarious liability   Responsibility imposed on one person for the acts of another.

Respondeat superior   The doctrine that holds a master/superior responsible for the acts of a servant/agent.

Liability insurance   Insurance coverage intended to compensate third parties for losses.

◆ AGENCY IN BUSINESS ORGANIZATIONS IN REVIEW

Agency
Relationship created when one person, an agent, acts on behalf of another person, the principal.

Authority of Agents
1. actual authority
2. apparent authority
3. ratification

Duties of Agents and Principals
Duties of agents to principals:
1. duty of performance
2. duty of care
3. duty of loyalty

Duties of principals to agents:
1. duty to compensate
2. duty to indemnify and reimburse
3. duty to facilitate agent

Liability of Principal for Acts of Agent
Principal may be *vicariously liable* if (1) agent is servant of principal, and (2) agent is acting in course and scope of employment.

◆ KEY TERMS

agency	express actual authority	duty of loyalty
agent	implied actual authority	*pro bono*
principal	fiduciary relationship	vicarious liability
actual authority	indemnification	*respondeat superior*
apparent authority	duty of care	liability insurance
ratify		

◆ STUDY QUESTIONS IN REVIEW

1. What is an agent?
2. Why is an agency relationship necessary in a business?
3. What is apparent authority?
4. Are agents entitled to indemnification for expenses they pay on behalf of their principal?
5. Are principals responsible for the acts of their agents?

◆ CASE STUDIES IN REVIEW

1. Jason manages a flower boutique. As the store manager, Jason orders flowers each week for the store to use in its floral displays. He has done so for the past four years. Last month, the store owner refused to pay for the flowers Jason ordered because the owner did not like the new supplier. Can the owner refuse to pay for the flowers?

2. Stacy works as a cashier/bagger at a local supermarket. During her shift, she helps a customer out to her car with her groceries. While unloading the groceries from the shopping cart, Stacy lets go of the cart and it rolls into a moving car, causing a dent on the passenger side door. Can the driver hold the supermarket owner responsible for fixing the dent in the car?

◆ PROJECT APPLICATIONS

Identify two situations in which you have served as an agent of another.

SECTION TWO
Sole Proprietorships

CHAPTER 4

Sole Proprietorship: A "One-Person Operation"

[handwritten margin notes: BTS SIMPLE FORM TAX → P. INC LIAB → PERSONAL INVOL TERM UPON DEATH]

Sole proprietorships are the most common form of business organization, mainly because they are the simplest. The overriding characteristic of a sole proprietorship is, as the name appropriately indicates, the single **proprietor.** If two or more persons own a business together, they are generally considered a partnership.

Many business owners work as sole proprietorships by default, often because they cannot afford the legal costs of becoming informed about their various options or, in the case of your local teenage baby-sitter, they may not have the need for a more formal organization. The greatest benefits of sole proprietorships are the simplicity in formation and the informality in management. The greatest disadvantages are the personal liability of the sole proprietor and the involuntary termination of the business upon the proprietor's death. Despite these disadvantages, however, the majority of individuals conducting business are sole proprietors, often to their financial detriment.

FORMATION

Generally, no formal actions must be taken for a sole proprietorship to begin. Sole proprietorships are formed simply by beginning business. However, most states require that the proprietor register the name of the business if the business is operating under an **assumed business name,** also known as a **trade name** (e.g., Boston Market), rather than the owner's name (e.g., Denny's Copy Shop). Further, all businesses must comply with state and federal taxation requirements and, if the business is regulated, the owner must also comply with applicable licensing requirements.

Registration of Assumed Business Name

Most businesses operate under a name other than the owner's name. Although this practice provides for more appealing business names (e.g., Casa Pablos in lieu of Vasquez's Mexican Restaurant), most states require that the business name be registered with the secretary of state in order to avoid the use of deceptively similar names. Some states require further safeguards to avoid consumer confusion by directing that a notice of intent to operate under an assumed business name (also known as a trade name) be published prior to receiving approval by the secretary of state or other registering agent; this practice will, theoretically, notify other businesses with similar names to file objections with the registering department.

> **Example:** A local restaurant, known for its excellent quality of food, operates under the name Old Town Cafe. Undoubtedly the owner will not want another business to use the same name or a similar name (e.g., Old Town Cafe and Grill) which may cause customers to believe that the two restaurants are associated.

Proprietor Owner.

Assumed business name A name, other than the owner's name, under which a business operates.

Trade name Name used by a business.

Not only does registration of an assumed business name help to avoid consumer confusion, registration is also intended to provide the state with information about a business, including the name and address of the owner. This information, which becomes a public record, allows the state or a private individual who may be a creditor of the business, to locate the person who is responsible for the debts and obligations of the business.

> **Example:**   Jason owns an auto detailing business that operates under the name *Details Within*. After Jason finishes working on a new Porsche owned by an auto dealer, he drives the car back to the dealership, which is only two blocks away. As Jason is pulling in to the car lot, he skids out of control and causes substantial damage to the car. The dealer wants to sue for the damage to the car; however, the accounting department does not know Jason's last name. The dealer has always written the checks for Jason's work to *Details Within*. Therefore, the dealer contacts the secretary of state to find out the name of the owner of *Details Within* to begin action to recover its damages.

The requirements for registration and/or publication of an assumed business name are set forth by state statute. Generally, a business is required to provide the following in an assumed business name registration form: the name to be registered, the type of business to be transacted, the counties in which the business will operate, and the name and address of the applicant. (See Form 4.1, *Assumed Name Certificate for Filing with the Secretary of State*.) Once the secretary of state approves the use of the assumed business name, the applicant will have exclusive use of the name for a specified period of time.

In order to avoid possible consumer confusion, it is best to register all business names, even those using the owner's surname, with the secretary of state and, if required, with the county where the business operates. Even if a business has not yet begun operation but the prospective owner anticipates using a particular business name, it is advisable to reserve the name with the secretary of state. (See Form 4.2, *Application for Reservation of Name*.)

Licensing

Business Licenses

Most states and counties require certain businesses to be licensed in order to regulate the business. Although the secretary of state is the most common registration agency, many counties also require proprietors to obtain licenses.

Although licensing practices generate tremendous income for the governments, they also can and do provide safeguards for consumers. Most of us are aware that professions in the medical and legal fields require licensing in order to regulate the quality and standards of practice in those areas; however, many people are not aware that many other occupations are required to be licensed as well, particularly at the local level. For example, counties will often require the owners of residential cleaning businesses to be licensed in order to run a background check on the owners; this type of regulation is to protect the public from fraudulent enterprises.

Licensing requirements are designed not only to protect the consumer, but also to protect existing business interests. States, for example, often limit the number of liquor licenses granted; this reduces competition for the existing license owners while protecting the public from the dangers of the unregulated and unlimited sale of alcohol.

Be sure to contact your local and state licensing agencies to determine if a client's business requires a license. A surprising number of business operations do require both local and state licenses.

Sales Tax License

In addition to income tax requirements imposed on all businesses, those that sell goods must obtain a **sales tax permit.** This allows the state and local governments to impose and collect taxes assessed on the sale of goods.

Simply by contacting the secretary of state and the appropriate county licensing bureau in the jurisdiction in which a business is operating, you will generally be able to determine the licenses that must be obtained for a client's business.

Sales tax permit   Registration that allows state and local governments to impose and collect taxes assessed on the sale of goods.

Office of the Secretary of State
Corporations Section
P.O. Box 13697
Austin, Texas 78711-3697

ASSUMED NAME CERTIFICATE
FOR FILING WITH THE SECRETARY OF STATE

1. The name of the corporation, limited liability company, limited partnership, or registered limited liability partnership as stated in its articles of incorporation, articles of organization, certificate of limited partnership, application for certificate of authority or comparable document is

    _____

2. The assumed name under which the business or professional service is or is to be conducted or rendered is

    _____

3. The state, country, or other jurisdiction under the laws of which it was incorporated, organized or associated is_____and the

    address of its registered or similar office in that jurisdiction is

    _____

4. The period, not to exceed 10 years, during which the assumed name will be used is

    _____

5. The entity is a (check one):
    A.
    ☐ Business Corporation   ☐ Non-Profit Corporation
    ☐ Professional Corporation   ☐ Professional Association
    ☐ Limited Liability Company   ☐ Limited Partnership
    ☐ Registered Limited Liability Partnership

    B. If the entity is some other type business, professional or other association that is incorporated, please specify below (e.g., bank, savings and loan association, etc.)

    _____

6. If the entity is required to maintain a registered office in Texas, the address of the registered office is_____

    _____and the name of its registered agent

    at such address is_____

    The address of the principal office (if not the same as the registered office) is

    _____

FORM 4.1.
Application for Registration of Assumed Business Name

7. If the entity is not required to or does not maintain a registered office in Texas, the office address in Texas is_____

_____

and if the entity is not incorporated, organized or associated under the laws of Texas, the address of its place of business in Texas is _____

_____

and the office address elsewhere is _____

_____

8. The county or counties where business or professional services are being or are to be conducted or rendered under such assumed name are (if applicable, use the designation "ALL" or "ALL EXCEPT")

_____

_____

9. The undersigned, if acting in the capacity of an attorney-in-fact of the entity, certifies that the entity has duly authorized the attorney-in-fact in writing to execute this document.

By _____
Signature of officer, general partner, manager,
representative or attorney-in-fact of the entity

NOTE

This form is designed to meet statutory requirements for filing with the secretary of state and is not designed to meet filing requirements on the county level. Filing requirements for assumed name documents to be filed with the county clerk differ. Assumed name documents filed with the county clerk are to be executed and acknowledged by the filing party, which requires that the document be notarized.

Form No. 503
Revised 9/99

FORM 4.1. *continued*

Application for Reservation of Name
Under §303 of the Business Corporation Law

NYS Department of State
DIVISION OF CORPORATIONS, STATE RECORDS and UCC
41 State Street
Albany, NY 12231-0001

PLEASE TYPE OR PRINT

APPLICANT'S NAME AND ADDRESS

NAME TO BE RESERVED

RESERVATION IS INTENDED FOR (CHECK ONE)

G New domestic corporation

G Foreign corporation intending to apply for authority to do business in New York State*

G Proposed foreign corporation, not yet incorporated, intending to apply for authority to conduct business in New York State

G Change of name of an existing domestic or an authorized foreign corporation*

G Foreign corporation intending to apply for authority to do business in New York State whose corporate name is not available for use in New York State*

G Authorized foreign corporation intending to change its fictitious name under which it does business in this state*

G Authorized foreign corporation which has changed its corporate name in its jurisdiction, such new corporate name not being available for use in New York State*

X_____   _____
Signature of applicant, applicant s attorney or agent   *Typed/printed name of signer*
(If attorney or agent, so specify)

INSTRUCTIONS:
1. Upon filing this application, the name will be reserved for 60 days and a certificate of reservation will be issued.
2. The certificate of reservation must be returned with and attached to the certificate of incorporation or application for authority, amendment or with a cancellation of the reservation.
3. The name used must be the same as appears in the reservation.
4. A $20 fee payable to the Department of State must accompany this application.
5. Only names for business, transportation, cooperative and railroad corporations may be reserved under §303 of the Business Corporation Law.

*If the reservation is for an existing corporation, domestic or foreign, the corporation must be the applicant.

DOS-234 (Rev. 10/97)

FORM 4.2.
Application for Reservation of Name

MANAGEMENT

Sole proprietors have exclusive authority to manage their business operations without first obtaining the consent of partners or a board of directors. Although it is not uncommon to find sole proprietors who delegate duties such as bookkeeping, sales, and telemarketing to agents or employees, the proprietor has the ultimate responsibility for all management decisions and business operations.

[handwritten margin note: MAY DELEGATE NON-MANAGERIAL DUTIES]

LIABILITY

Sole proprietorships are considered an extension of the individual proprietor; thus, the proprietor is solely and personally responsible for all debts and obligations of the business. This means that creditors of a business that fails can and do look to the proprietor's personal assets such as a family home and retirement savings to satisfy the debts of the business. This is, of course, one of the most significant disadvantages of a sole proprietorship. Such unlimited liability often drives people to incorporate, especially if they are involved in a particularly risky business or have personal assets that they want to protect.

In considering a client's potential areas of liability, you must consider all possibilities; failure to do so can result in financial ruin for the proprietor, professionally as well as personally.

Example: Shiny and Bright Cleaning (S & B), a sole proprietorship owned by a widowed mother of four, cleans the windows of an exclusive furniture store once a month. Because the business needs to have the windows cleaned inside the store as well as outside, one of S & B's employees has a key to the store. The employee is always conscientious about locking the door after cleaning the windows inside; however, one morning the back door is found unlocked. It cannot be determined whether it was S & B's employee who failed to lock the door or if an employee of the furniture store entered the store after the windows were cleaned and forgot to lock up. During the night, $10,000 of furniture was stolen and the store was vandalized. The store sues S & B for the damages. S & B does not have the cash or assets to pay for the furniture; therefore the owner of S & B, whose only other asset is her family home, may have to sell her home to pay for the stolen goods if she is not insured.

Sole proprietors should attempt to limit their personal liability either by contract or through **bonding** and **insurance.**

Contract Liability Limitations

Contracts not only create the rights and duties of the contracting parties but they may also limit the parties' rights and duties. Therefore, sole proprietors may limit their liability for business debts and other obligations by including a provision in all business contracts which specifies that all obligations due on or created by the contract, or a breach thereof, will be limited to and payable solely from the business's assets. For purposes of clarification, such a provision should also include a statement that the personal assets of the proprietor shall not be liable for satisfaction of the specified obligations.

Although this type of provision may limit a sole proprietor's personal liability for the contractual obligations of the proprietor's business, it is not possible to anticipate and limit all potential business liabilities through contracts, especially those arising in tort (e.g., those arising from personal injury claims). Therefore, it is imperative that sole proprietors be appropriately bonded and insured.

Bonding and Insurance

A sole proprietor should be both bonded and insured. Bonding ensures the performance of a proprietor's contractual obligations; insurance protects the proprietor from unforeseen risks, including liability to third parties (e.g., property damage or theft by an employee). However, insurance is not available for all businesses, especially those with high risk factors or those that have not been operating for a minimum number of years. Furthermore,

Bonding Guarantee that an act will be performed.

Insurance Protection from unforseen losses.

because it is not possible to be insured for all potential business liabilities, business owners who want to protect their personal assets should consider alternative organizational forms that offer personal liability protections.

TAXATION CONSIDERATIONS

A sole proprietorship is an extension of the individual proprietor; therefore, all business profits and losses are taxed as the proprietor's personal income. Proprietors must report their business income to the Internal Revenue Service (IRS) as part of their personal income tax filing. (See Form 4.3, *IRS Form 1040, Schedule C, Profit or Loss from Business.*) A business owner who intends to hire employees must apply for a federal tax identification number from the IRS (IRS Form SS-4) and, if required, a state tax identification number from the state revenue department. Additionally, the sole proprietor hiring employees must comply with all state and federal withholding requirements (including Social Security and Medicare), as well as unemployment taxes and workers' compensation premiums.

Sole proprietors often benefit from the taxation structure for their businesses because individual tax rates are generally lower than corporate rates. Additionally, declaring business income as personal income allows a proprietor to offset other sources of personal income by losses from the business.

> **Example:** Mr. Smith owns a local printing business. His wife is a neurologist with substantial earnings. During 1996, Mr. Smith expanded his business to include six additional printing machines. Although Mr. Smith drew a comfortable monthly income during the taxable year, the amount the IRS allowed for depreciation of the new equipment offset his profits (gross income) and resulted in a business loss of $3,000. This loss, reported on the Smiths' personal income tax return, offset Mrs. Smith's yearly income and reduced the couple's overall tax liability for 1996.

Although most people do not intend to invest in a losing business, losses are not uncommon in the first few years of business. Therefore, the benefit of offsetting other sources of income with business income or losses makes sole proprietorships and partnerships appealing business forms in the first few years of business operations. However, as sole proprietorships expand and become more profitable, alternative business organizations often become more advantageous.

TERMINATION

Sole proprietorships may be terminated involuntarily (e.g., when the proprietor dies), or voluntarily by the proprietor (e.g., when the proprietor sells the business or forms a partnership or corporation). Upon the termination, the assets of the proprietorship may become the personal property of the proprietor or his or her heirs, may be sold, or may be contributed to a new business venture of the proprietor.

Termination by Death of Proprietor

Sole proprietorships are terminated upon the death of the proprietor. Until the business is assumed by a new owner, the business remains a part of the deceased proprietor's personal estate. As such, it can be managed by the estate's personal representative who will, hopefully, have some knowledge of the operation of the business. Once the business property is transferred to another individual, another sole proprietorship begins. Good estate planning can eliminate many of the uncertainties that would otherwise be caused by the death of the proprietor (e.g., will provisions that direct transfer and operation of the business after the proprietor's death).

SCHEDULE C
(Form 1040)

Department of the Treasury
Internal Revenue Service   (99)

Profit or Loss From Business

(Sole Proprietorship)

▶ **Partnerships, joint ventures, etc., must file Form 1065 or Form 1065-B.**

▶ **Attach to Form 1040 or Form 1041.**   ▶ **See Instructions for Schedule C (Form 1040).**

OMB No. 1545-0074

1999

Attachment
Sequence No. **09**

Name of proprietor | Social security number (SSN)

A Principal business or profession, including product or service (see page C-1) | **B** Enter code from pages C-8 & 9 ▶

C Business name. If no separate business name, leave blank. | **D** Employer ID number (EIN), if any

E Business address (including suite or room no.) ▶
City, town or post office, state, and ZIP code

F Accounting method: **(1)** ☐ Cash   **(2)** ☐ Accrual   **(3)** ☐ Other (specify) ▶

G Did you "materially participate" in the operation of this business during 1999? If "No," see page C-2 for limit on losses ☐ Yes ☐ No

H If you started or acquired this business during 1999, check here . . . . ▶ ☐

Part I   Income

1	Gross receipts or sales. **Caution:** If this income was reported to you on Form W-2 and the "Statutory employee" box on that form was checked, see page C-2 and check here . . . . ▶ ☐	**1**	
2	Returns and allowances	**2**	
3	Subtract line 2 from line 1	**3**	
4	Cost of goods sold (from line 42 on page 2)	**4**	
5	**Gross profit.** Subtract line 4 from line 3	**5**	
6	Other income, including Federal and state gasoline or fuel tax credit or refund (see page C-3) . .	**6**	
7	**Gross income.** Add lines 5 and 6 . . . . ▶	**7**	

Part II   Expenses. Enter expenses for business use of your home **only** on line 30.

8	Advertising	**8**	**19** Pension and profit-sharing plans	**19**	
9	Bad debts from sales or services (see page C-3) . .	**9**	**20** Rent or lease (see page C-4):		
10	Car and truck expenses (see page C-3)	**10**	**a** Vehicles, machinery, and equipment .	**20a**	
11	Commissions and fees . .	**11**	**b** Other business property . .	**20b**	
12	Depletion	**12**	**21** Repairs and maintenance . . .	**21**	
13	Depreciation and section 179 expense deduction (not included in Part III) (see page C-3) . .	**13**	**22** Supplies (not included in Part III) .	**22**	
			23 Taxes and licenses	**23**	
14	Employee benefit programs (other than on line 19) . . .	**14**	**24** Travel, meals, and entertainment:		
15	Insurance (other than health) .	**15**	**a** Travel	**24a**	
16	Interest:		**b** Meals and entertainment .		
a	Mortgage (paid to banks, etc.) .	**16a**	**c** Enter nondeductible amount included on line 24b (see page C-5) .		
b	Other	**16b**	**d** Subtract line 24c from line 24b	**24d**	
17	Legal and professional services	**17**	**25** Utilities	**25**	
			26 Wages (less employment credits) .	**26**	
18	Office expense	**18**	**27** Other expenses (from line 48 on page 2)	**27**	

28	**Total expenses** before expenses for business use of home. Add lines 8 through 27 in columns . . ▶	**28**	
29	Tentative profit (loss). Subtract line 28 from line 7	**29**	
30	Expenses for business use of your home. Attach **Form 8829**	**30**	
31	**Net profit or (loss).** Subtract line 30 from line 29.		
	• If a profit, enter on **Form 1040, line 12,** and A _SO on **Schedule SE, line 2** (statutory employees, see page C-6). Estates and trusts, enter on Form 1041, line 3.	**31**	
	• If a loss, you MUST go on to line 32.		
32	If you have a loss, check the box that describes your investment in this activity (see page C-6).		
	• If you checked 32a, enter the loss on **Form 1040, line 12,** and A _SO on **Schedule SE, line 2** (statutory employees, see page C-6). Estates and trusts, enter on Form 1041, line 3.	**32a** ☐ All investment is at risk.	
	• If you checked 32b, you MUST attach **Form 6198.**	**32b** ☐ Some investment is not at risk.	

For Paperwork Reduction Act Notice, see Form 1040 instructions.   Cat. No. 11334P   **Schedule C (Form 1040) 1999**

FORM 4.3.

IRS Form 1040, Schedule C, Profit or Loss from Business

Schedule C (Form 1040) 1999   Page **2**

Part III   Cost of Goods Sold (see page C-6)

33   Method(s) used to
       value closing inventory: **a** ☐ Cost   **b** ☐ Lower of cost or market   **c** ☐ Other (attach explanation)

34   Was there any change in determining quantities, costs, or valuations between opening and closing inventory? If
       "Yes," attach explanation . . . . ☐ **Yes**   ☐ **No**

35 Inventory at beginning of year. If different from last year's closing inventory, attach explanation . . .	**35**	
36 Purchases less cost of items withdrawn for personal use	**36**	
37 Cost of labor. Do not include any amounts paid to yourself	**37**	
38 Materials and supplies	**38**	
39 Other costs	**39**	
40 Add lines 35 through 39	**40**	
41 Inventory at end of year	**41**	
42 **Cost of goods sold.** Subtract line 41 from line 40. Enter the result here and on page 1, line 4 . . .	**42**	

Part IV   Information on Your Vehicle. Complete this part **ONLY** if you are claiming car or truck expenses on line 10 and are not required to file Form 4562 for this business. See the instructions for line 13 on page C-3 to find out if you must file.

43   When did you place your vehicle in service for business purposes? (month, day, year) ▶ ..../.........../........ .

44   Of the total number of miles you drove your vehicle during 1999, enter the number of miles you used your vehicle for:

a Business .... **b** Commuting .... **c** Other ....

45   Do you (or your spouse) have another vehicle available for personal use? . . . . ☐ **Yes**   ☐ **No**

46   Was your vehicle available for use during off-duty hours? . . . . ☐ **Yes**   ☐ **No**

47a Do you have evidence to support your deduction? . . . . ☐ **Yes**   ☐ **No**

   b If "Yes," is the evidence written? . . . . ☐ **Yes**   ☐ **No**

Part V   Other Expenses. List below business expenses not included on lines 8–26 or line 30.

--	
--	
--	
--	
--	
--	
--	
--	
--	
48 Total other expenses. Enter here and on page 1, line 27	**48**

Schedule C (Form 1040) 1999

✸

FORM 4.3. *continued*

Termination by Sale

A sole proprietorship may be terminated by the sale of the business assets. The relinquishment of the business to another terminates the existing proprietorship (ownership). However, an owner who seeks to sell a sole proprietorship is selling the tangible business assets and the intangible **goodwill** of the business, which is often based upon the ability and reputation of the proprietor.

Goodwill Reputation of a business and its goods and services.

   Although the value of the tangible assets such as desks, chairs, and merchandise can be objectively determined, it is difficult if not impossible to objectively value the reputation, known as the goodwill, of the business. Often, a professional can be hired to assess the dollar value of a company's reputation by comparing the sales price of similarly situated companies or, alternatively or conjunctively, considering the income of the sole proprietor in past years. Because many small businesses cannot afford these types of professional assessments, proprietors of such businesses often base the selling price upon the gross income of the business over a specified period of time. Such assessments are often inaccurate since any value assessments must, of necessity, assume that customers loyal to the original proprietor will also be loyal to the purchaser of the business; often, this is not the case. However, regardless of the method used for valuing the proprietorship, it will usually be worth less to a prospective purchaser than to the proprietor.

   Whether the business is transferred to a new owner after the original proprietor's death or is sold by the owner during his or her life, any value assessment must consider that the business may not be as profitable after the change in ownership.

◆ SOLE PROPRIETORSHIPS IN REVIEW

Definition
Business owned by one individual.

Advantages
♦ Simplicity of formation
♦ Flexibility of management

Disadvantages
♦ Involuntary termination upon proprietor's death
♦ Unlimited liability of sole proprietor

Key Considerations of the Paralegal:
Formation Procedures
1. File assumed business name/trade name with the secretary of state.
2. Publish notice of intent to operate under assumed business name, if required by the local jurisdiction.
3. Contact state and local licensing divisions to obtain required licenses and permits.
4. Apply for sales tax permit from state and local revenue agencies.
5. If the proprietor intends to hire employees:
   a. apply for a federal tax identification number (IRS Form SS-4),
   b. apply for a state identification number, if different from the IRS,
   c. contact the IRS to establish employee withholding procedures, and
   d. contact appropriate state agencies to make arrangements for unemployment and workers' compensation premium payments.

◆ KEY TERMS

proprietor
assumed business name
trade name

sales tax permint
bonding

insurance
goodwill

◆ STUDY QUESTIONS IN REVIEW

1. How is a sole proprietorship formed?
2. Are there any advantages to registering an assumed business name or trade name before a prospective business begins operation?
3. Why do some states and counties impose licensing requirements on businesses?
4. What is a sales tax permit?
5. What does the term "personal liability" mean?
6. Explain the difference between bonding and insurance.
7. Who pays the taxes due for the income earned by a sole proprietorship?

◆ CASE STUDIES IN REVIEW

1. Jeremy wants to open his own residential plumbing and heating business. He learns through an acquaintance that the county where his business is located requires residential plumbers to obtain a business license; the cost of the license is $250. Jeremy believes that the only purpose of the licensing requirement is simply to fill the government's pocket. Can you offer any other reason why the county would want to regulate a residential business such as Jeremy's?

2. Doreen is the sole owner of Doreen's Flowers, a local floral shop. While one of Doreen's drivers is delivering flowers in the business van to the local hospital, he hits a pedestrian at an intersection, severely injuring the pedestrian. Doreen is sued for the personal injury damages suffered by the pedestrian (medical expenses, pain and suffering, etc.). A jury awards the injured pedestrian $250,000, due from Doreen's Flowers. Doreen's Flowers has no insurance to cover the jury verdict. Who is responsible for paying the $250,000?

◆ PROJECT APPLICATIONS

1. Contact the secretary of state and obtain the forms required for registering an assumed business name/trade name. Complete the form for the following sole proprietorship:

   Copy Stop
   3444 Northwest Blvd.
   Georgetown, (your state) 55555

   Owner: George Denny
   55 Buckskin Way
   Savannah, (your state) 55555

2. Visit the county licensing bureau and determine what licenses and/or permits would be required for a residential cleaning business that intends to do business in your county and a neighboring county. Compile these forms and present them with a how-to manual for your supervising attorney.

SECTION THREE
Partnerships

CHAPTER 5

Partnerships: Associations for Profit

A **partnership** is an association of two or more persons or entities that operate a business for profit.[1] A partnership may be formed not only by individuals, but also by corporations, other partnerships, business trusts, estates, government agencies, and other associations. However, in most states, charitable and nonprofit organizations may not form partnerships because they are not "business[es] for profit," a limitation intended to protect philanthropists from being held personally liable for the debts and obligations of their charities.

The relative simplicity of partnerships, in addition to the flexibility of management and direct taxation of partners, attracts many business owners to this organizational form. However, as with sole proprietorships, partnerships are merely an extension of the individual partners; therefore, partners are personally liable for all debts and obligations of their partnerships, once the assets of the business are exhausted. This is the major disadvantage of partnerships, since each partner has the ability to bind the entire partnership to unwanted liability. In order to protect partners from potentially unlimited personal liability, many states have adopted partnership forms that limit partners' personal liability while maintaining the advantages of partnership organization. These partnership forms, the limited partnership and limited liability partnerships, are becoming increasingly popular.

Some states distinguish a partnership from a **joint venture** which is basically a partnership (association of two or more persons) for a particular undertaking (i.e., a single project). In contrast to a partnership, participants of a joint venture work together for a limited number of projects, after which they generally leave the association.

> **Example:** *Joint Venture.* The owners of two separate local engineering firms learn that the state is accepting plans for the design of its new capitol. The owners, who are friends, decide to collaborate and submit a proposal to the state, thus, they have entered into a joint venture for the purpose of designing a new state capitol.

> **Example:** *Partnership.* ABC Partnership, an engineering firm, learns that the state is accepting plans for the design of its new capitol. The engineers of the partnership collaborate their talents and ideas and submit a proposal to the state.

Because the practical effect between a joint venture and a partnership is minimal, some states have abandoned the distinction between the two.

Most partnerships are governed by the provisions of the Uniform Partnership Act (U.P.A.) and/or the Revised Uniform Partnership Act (R.U.P.A). These are uniform laws that the American Bar Association recommends states follow in adopting their laws. All states except Louisiana have adopted the U.P.A., the R.U.P.A., or substantially similar versions. See Appendix B.

PARTNERSHIP CHARACTERISTICS

Partnerships have traditionally been characterized by the following:

♦ Voluntary agreement
♦ Agency
♦ Equal management rights
♦ Personal liability

Partnership Association of two or more persons or entities who own a business for profit.

Joint venture Partnership for a limited duration.

♦ Equal rights to profits
♦ Personal taxation of business profits and losses
♦ Automatic dissolution upon the death, expulsion, or withdrawal of one or more of the partners

These traditional characteristics offer many advantages in the formation and management of a business. However, the potential personal liability of partners, as well as the logistical problems inherent in an automatic and often unexpected dissolution of a partnership, make traditional partnerships, known as general partnerships, impractical and inadvisable for many businesses.

PARTNERSHIP FORMS

Almost all states have adopted modified partnership forms that alleviate some of the burdensome elements of traditional partnerships. Therefore, a significant number of states provide for three forms of partnerships:

General partnerships
Limited partnerships
Limited liability partnerships

General and limited partnerships have, until recently, been the partnership forms available in almost every state. However, in 1991, Texas combined the benefits of the general partnership with those of a limited partnership and adopted a limited liability partnership.

Although each partnership form offers a business owner unique advantages, consideration must be given to the corresponding disadvantages. Therefore, a cost-benefit analysis of the various forms must be made for each client's business needs. The main distinctions between each partnership form are set forth in Table 5.1.

The limited liability partnership offers the benefits of general partnerships without the disadvantages. Limited liability partnerships operate like general partnerships but with the liability protections of limited partnerships. Because of this advantage, these new partnership forms will undoubtedly gain ever increasing popularity in the near future.

The partnership forms are addressed in the following chapters. In studying each, it is helpful to note how they build upon one another by offering increasingly limited personal liability to partners. Note initially that although general partnerships allow all partners the right to participate in management, all partners are also subject to unlimited personal liability. Limited partnerships were developed to limit the liability of those partners who do not participate in management (and do not make the decisions that subject the partners to liability). The newest partnership form, the limited liability partnership, combines the

---

TABLE 5.1.   Partnership Forms Compared

	Management Rights Allowed To:	Personal Liability Extends To:
General partnership:	All partners	All partners Partnership obligations Misconduct of all partners and agents
Limited partnership:	General partners only	General partners Partnership obligations Misconduct of all partners and agents Limited partners none
Limited liability partnership:	All partners	All partners Own misconduct only

General partnership An association of two or more persons or entities who operate a business as co-owners for profit and allow _all partners the right to manage business affairs._

Limited partnership An association of two or more persons or entities who operate a business as co-owners for profit with one or more general partners (managers) and one or more limited partners (investors).

Limited liability partnership A general or limited partnership that registers as a limited liability partnership and protects its partners from vicarious liability for the negligence or malfeasance of other partners.

general partners' advantage of management rights with limited liability protections somewhat reminiscent of limited partnerships.

However, do not automatically assume that limited liability partnerships are the partnership of choice for all business owners. Carefully consider the advantages and disadvantages of each partnership form in light of the potential needs of various businesses and their owners as you read the following chapters.

PARTNERSHIPS IN REVIEW

Partnership

An association of two or more persons or entities that operate a business for profit.

Partnership Forms

1. Generated partnership
2. Limited partnership
3. Limited liability partnership

KEY TERMS

partnership   general partnership   limited liability partnership
joint venture   limited partnership

STUDY QUESTIONS IN REVIEW

1. How is a partnership formed?
2. What type of organizations cannot enter into partnership arrangements?
3. Who is responsible for the debts and obligations of a partnership?

4. Name the three different forms of partnerships.
5. What is the major disadvantage to forming a partnership?

CASE STUDIES IN REVIEW

1. Dreams & Wishes is a nonprofit foundation organized for the purpose of making terminally ill children's dreams come true. Ninety percent of all of their "dream making" is providing terminally ill children and their families all-expense-paid trips to Disneyland. Because of the significant expense incurred by Dreams & Wishes, it approaches Disney with the idea of forming a business partnership; Dreams & Wishes would organize the trips for the children and their families, and Disneyland would provide hotel accommodations and entrance tickets to the park free of charge. Disneyland's officers are very interested in the idea of contributing to Dreams & Wishes' cause. They submit the proposal to their attorneys, for whom you work. Can Disney participate in a business partnership with Dreams & Wishes? Explain your answer.

2. Darcy is a prominent local architect and his friend Jerry is a building contractor. Their friend Jason wants to develop a piece of property that he owns in the downtown area. He discusses his plans with his friends Darcy and Jerry and the three decide that the location is perfect for an office building. The trio agree that Darcy will design the building, Jerry's company will build the building, and Jason will contribute his property to the project. In exchange for their respective contributions, Darcy will receive 10 percent of the profits and losses upon the sale of the property to a third party, Jerry will receive 50 percent of the profits, and Jason will receive 40 percent. After the property is sold, they will divide the profits and their association will end. Is this association a partnership?

◆ PROJECT APPLICATIONS

1. Review your state's statutory provision that sets forth the legal definition of a partnership. Prepare a brief legal memorandum, applying the statutory definition of partnership to Case Study in Review #1, above.

2. Research your state's statutes to determine whether limited liability partnerships have been adopted in your state. Provide the statutory provision for limited liability partnerships if your state has adopted these business forms.

◆ ENDNOTES

1. See Uniform Partnership Act § 6(1).

CHAPTER 6

General Partnership: The Traditional Partnership Form

General partnerships are the most common type of partnership because no formalities are required for their formation. The association of two or more persons operating a business for profit is, in many states, sufficient to form a general partnership. Therefore, general partnerships serve as the basis for the formation of all partnerships. Thus, the topics addressed with respect to general partnerships generally also apply to limited partnerships and limited liability partnerships, with the noted exceptions of formation requirements, management rights, and liability considerations. In order to understand these subsequent developments in partnership law, you must first understand how general partnerships are formed and operated.

FORMATION

Voluntary Agreement

In conformity with the Uniform Partnership Act (U.P.A.), many states provide that a partnership is formed only when there is an agreement by the parties to form a partnership, written or oral. This protects business associates from unintentionally entering into a "general partnership" arrangement simply because they are operating a business for profit, unaware of the ramifications of their association. However, the Revised Uniform Partnership Act (R.U.P.A.), adopted in a growing number of jurisdictions, provides that two or more persons who co-own a business for profit create a partnership whether or not they intend to. Thus, many business associates involuntarily and unknowingly become partners, subject to the statutory regulations imposed on partnership businesses.

Registration of Partnership and Assumed Business Name

Some states require that all partnerships register with the secretary of state or other designated state agency, as well as the appropriate local licensing agent. Even if partnership registration is not required, all businesses that operate under a name other than the owner's full name must register the assumed business name (also known as a trade name) with the appropriate state agency; this reserves use of the name for the registering business. The secretary of state of the operating jurisdiction generally provides a form for registration of the partnership and/or an assumed business name. (See Form 6.1, *Application for Registration of Assumed Business Name.*)

Businesses using an assumed name should promptly register the name with the secretary of state. However, registration does not affect the form of the partnership; that is, the partnership continues to exist as a business even if it has not properly registered its name. However, failure to register a partnership (if required) and an assumed business name can result in fines being imposed upon a business and the business being denied the right to bring suit in the state.

Foreign Registration

If a partnership is operating in a **foreign jurisdiction,** the partnership may need to register there as a **foreign partnership.** This allows states to regulate partnerships transacting business in their state and to impose a fee for the privilege of operating business within the jurisdiction. Although most states do not require such registration, if a partnership is operating a

Foreign jurisdiction A state other than the one in which a business is registered.

Foreign partnership A partnership organized and/or registered in another state.

FORM 6.1.
Application for Registration
of Assumed Business Name

Certificate of Assumed Name
Pursuant to General Business Law, §130

NYS Department of State
Division of Corporations, State Records and UCC
41 State Street, Albany, NY 12231-0001
www.dos.state.ny.us

1. NAME OF ENTITY

2. BUSINESS FORMED UNDER (CHECK ONE):

G Business Corporation Law   **G** Limited Liability Company Law

G Education Law   **G** Not-for-Profit Corporation Law

G Insurance Law   **G** Revised Limited Partnership Act

G Other (specify law): _____

3. ASSUMED NAME

4. PRINCIPAL PLACE OF BUSINESS IN NEW YORK STATE (MUST BE NUMBER AND STREET. IF NONE, INSERT OUT-OF-STATE ADDRESS)

5. COUNTIES IN WHICH BUSINESS WILL BE CONDUCTED UNDER ASSUMED NAME

G ALL COUNTIES (if not, circle county[ies] below)

Albany	Clinton	Genesee	Monroe	Orleans	Saratoga	Tompkins
Allegany	Columbia	Greene	Montgomery	Oswego	Schenectady	Ulster
Bronx	Cortland	Hamilton	Nassau	Otsego	Schoharie	Warren
Broome	Delaware	Herkimer	New York	Putnam	Schuyler	Washington
Cattaraugus	Dutchess	Jefferson	Niagara	Queens	Seneca	Wayne
Cayuga	Erie	Kings	Oneida	Rensselaer	Steuben	Westchester
Chautauqua	Essex	Lewis	Onondaga	Richmond	Suffolk	Wyoming
Chemung	Franklin	Livingston	Ontario	Rockland	Sullivan	Yates
Chenango	Fulton	Madison	Orange	St. Lawrence	Tioga	

6. NUMBER AND STREET ADDRESS(ES) AND COUNTY OF EACH BUSINESS LOCATION WITHIN NEW YORK STATE (USE CONTINUOUS SHEET, IF NEEDED)

G No New York State Business Location

INSTRUCTIONS FOR SIGNATURE: If corporation, by an officer; if limited partnership, by a
general partner; if limited liability company, by a member or manager or by an attorney-in-fact
or authorized person for such corporation, limited partnership, or limited liability company.

Name and Title   Signature

DOS-1338(7/99)

business in more than one state, a review of the foreign state's statutes is necessary to determine whether the partnership has complied with state and local registration requirements.

Licenses

All business owners must obtain the necessary state and local licenses and permits to operate a business. The state licensing agent (*e.g.,* department of commerce) and local agencies (county licensing division) will generally provide information on the requisite licensing of particular business enterprises.

Partnership Agreement

All partnerships should be governed by a partnership agreement that addresses the rights, duties, and interests of the partners and sets forth specific provisions regulating the operation of the partnership. If the partners do not have a formal agreement, the partnership will be governed by state statute, that is, the state laws regulating the formation and operation of partnerships.

In order to understand the basic parameters of a partnership agreement, you must first have a working knowledge of general partnerships. Therefore, a detailed discussion of the basics of a partnership agreement, including a checklist, is provided at the end of this chapter.

AGENCY

Once a partnership is created, each partner becomes an agent of the partnership, with the authority to act on behalf of the partnership in all partnership matters. This agency relationship allows each partner to bind the partnership to any obligations within the scope of the partnership business. This can and does create problems for general partners who are personally liable for all obligations of the partnership, including those that they did not approve or have knowledge of. To avoid the potential liability which can be incurred by partners acting as agents of the partnership, the partners should have a partnership agreement which specifies each partner's authority.

Apparent Authority

By virtue of the law of agency, a partnership may create the appearance that a partner has the authority to bind the partnership to acts within the scope of the partnership's business. This authority, known as apparent authority, is intended to provide protection to third parties who reasonably assume that a partner may participate in the operation of the partnership business, including entering into contractual or other business arrangements on behalf of the partnership.

Example: One of the partners of Joyrides, a mobile amusement park partnership, contracts with the Mayor of Charlo, a small Mississippi town, to have Joyrides set up its amusement park rides and booths in the small town on the Fourth of July weekend. The other partners of Joyrides do not want to honor the contract because they had hoped to work in a larger town, and increase their profits over the holiday weekend. Although the partners are upset, they must comply with the contract. The partner entering into the contract had apparent authority to enter into such agreements, which are within the scope of the partnership's business.

If a partner does not have the actual authority to act on behalf of the partnership (i.e., the act is beyond the scope of the partnership's business or the partnership agreement limits the partner's authority), and the person contracting with the partner is or should be aware of this fact, then the partner's authority is not "apparent" and the partnership will not be required to fulfill the obligation created by the unauthorized partner.[1]

Example: A partner in a landscaping business agrees to build a home for a customer of the business, who is a friend of all the partners. Undoubtedly, the partnership will not be bound by the partner's agreement, because home-building is not within the general scope of a landscaping business, thus the partner lacked the apparent authority to enter into the contract. The customer who is a friend of all of the partners, acting as a reasonably prudent person presumably would, should have known that the partner of a landscaping business lacked the authority to bind the business to a home-building contract.

Limiting Apparent Authority

Statement of partnership authority   Document filed with the secretary of state that identifies the partners authorized to act for the partnership and describes the extent of the partners' authority.

A partner's apparent authority can and should be restricted by, or at least addressed in, a partnership agreement. In addition to restrictions in the partnership agreement, partnerships can protect themselves from unauthorized acts of partners by filing a **statement of partnership authority** which sets forth the rights of each partner to act for the partnership (e.g., obtain partnership financing).[2] By specifying the duties and limitations of partners' individual authority, the partnership and partners can protect themselves from improper actions by unauthorized partners.

Actual Authority

In addition to a partner's apparent authority, partnerships can grant partners specific rights and duties, either through the partnership agreement or by majority vote; this authority is known as express authority.

> **Example:** *Actual authority granted by partnership agreement.* The partnership agreement of Baby Talk, a picture postcard business, delegates each partner specific duties in the operation of the partnership's business. The partners are given exclusive authority to operate in the area delegated to them. Pursuant to the partnership agreement, partner A is responsible for marketing, partner B is responsible for production, and, partner C is assigned accounting duties. Each partner has actual authority by virtue of the partnership agreement to engage in the delegated duties.

> **Example:** *Actual authority granted by partnership vote.* The partners of General Business Cleaners, a commercial cleaning business, decide to expand their business to include residential cleaning. They vote to authorize partner Z to enter into residential cleaning contracts for the partnership.

All businesses should be advised to include provisions regarding partners' duties and limitations in partnership agreements. Although the partnership agreement may not, in itself, protect the partnership from liability to third parties for a partner's unauthorized acts (e.g., if the third party was not aware of the partner's lack of authority, the partnership may be obligated to perform the contract), the agreement can serve as a basis for expulsion of the partner from the partnership or an action by the partnership against the unauthorized partner for damages incurred in performing the unauthorized contract (e.g., profits lost). Even if issues are not contemplated or addressed in a partnership agreement, they can subsequently be decided by vote of the partners, thus affording similar protections to the partnership.

In addition to the express authority granted to partners, partners have the *implied authority* necessary to exercise their express authority. For example, a partner who manages a local shoe store for a partnership has the implied authority to order shoes for the store on behalf of the partnership.

Whether actual authority is granted to partners pursuant to a partnership agreement or vote, the partnership should file a statement of partnership authority with the appropriate state and/or local agency. A statement of authority is generally filed with the secretary of state. Although most individuals and businesses dealing with a partnership will generally not have actual knowledge of the provisions of a statement of partnership authority, the information contained in the statement is imputed (charged) to them because they could, with diligence, obtain it. Partnerships should take advantage of such available opportunities to protect both the partnership and partners from liability for the acts of unauthorized partners.

Do not forgo the preparation of partnership agreements or statements of partnership authority because the partners have trust and confidence in each other. This spirit of cooperation is present at the inception of most partnerships and serves as an excellent basis for drafting a comprehensive partnership agreement. Clients must understand that disagreements in management, operation, and accounting will inevitably result even in the most amiable partnerships. Partnership agreements can help partners resolve minor management disagreements or major marketing issues, thereby preserving a productive partnership.

MANAGEMENT

All participants in a general partnership have the right to participate in the management of the business. Because of the logistical problems this can create, partnership agreements often delegate managerial responsibilities to a specified group of partners; however, because management rights are an inherent characteristic of general partnerships, all partners must agree to delegate these rights to other partners.

If partners do not waive their management rights, all partners have equal participation rights.[3] That is, regardless of a partner's interest in the partnership, the partner has an equal vote in all management decisions.

Example: A, B, and C are general partners in a movie production company. No partners have waived their management rights. Partner A has a 60 percent interest in the partnership, B has a 20 percent interest, and C has a 20 percent interest. The partners have the option of expanding their production company to include producing dramas for public television. In voting on the issue, each partner has one vote.

Voting Practices

Decisions regarding partnership business are generally made by majority vote of the partners, unless an alternative scheme is provided for by agreement.[4] If a partner waives the right to participate in management, the partner's voting rights will ordinarily be modified to reflect his or her involvement in management decisions (because decision making is a function of the managers); such modifications, if any, should be specified in the partnership agreement.

Although most decisions are made by majority vote, acts that would jeopardize the continuation of a partnership's business generally require unanimous consent of all of the partners, unless the partnership agreement provides otherwise.[5] Such acts include assigning the partnership's property to creditors, selling or otherwise destroying the goodwill of the business, acting to interfere with the ordinary course of business, consenting to a judgment against the partnership, or submitting a partnership dispute to arbitration. Additionally, acts beyond the scope of the partnership agreement (e.g., engaging in business other than that specified in the partnership agreement) or amendments to the agreement must be unanimous. Surprisingly, however, a partner generally has the authority to transfer property held in the name of the partnership to a third party without the consent of all of the partners, unless the partnership agreement provides otherwise.

FIDUCIARY DUTIES

Fiduciaries Those in a relationship of trust.

Partners are considered **fiduciaries** of one another because they hold positions of trust and confidence with each other. As fiduciaries, the law imposes special duties on partners to prevent them from being disloyal and dishonest with their business partners. Partners who do not act in good faith with each other will be liable to the other partners for their failure to do so.

Historically, partners' fiduciary duties to one another have not been statutorily defined. As a result, courts have often been called upon to determine the duties partners owe to one another and the partnership; this has led to inconsistency and confusion in determining partners' obligations. The R.U.P.A. attempts to eliminate the inconsistency in the fiduciary duties imposed upon partners by defining and limiting partners' fiduciary duties to the duty of loyalty and the duty of care; implicit in each of these duties is the additional duty of good faith and fair dealing.

Duty of Loyalty

A partner is obligated to be loyal to the partnership and to act solely for its benefit, refraining from activities that would or could be adverse to the partnership's interest. In order to accomplish this, the R.U.P.A. prevents partners from taking advantage of or competing with the partnership. Specifically, the R.U.P.A. specifies that partners must

1. disclose and hold for the partnership all benefits received from the partnership without the partnership's consent,
2. refrain from using partnership property or appropriating a business opportunity from the partnership,

3. refrain from holding, or acting on behalf of one holding, an interest adverse to the partnership, without the consent of the partnership, and

4. refrain from competing with the partnership without the consent of the partners.[6]

Partners do not violate their duty of loyalty to the partnership merely because they gain a personal benefit from the partnership business. With proper disclosure, they may lend money to or transact other business with the partnership; the partners' rights and obligations in such circumstances are the same as those who are not partners.[8]

In drafting a partnership agreement, be aware that because the duty of loyalty is often imperative to the success or failure of a partnership, the duty cannot be eliminated in a partnership agreement.

Failure by a partner to properly disclose a personal interest to a partnership clearly violates a partner's duty of loyalty. The following examples illustrate the impact that a violation of a partner's duty of loyalty can have on a partnership's business:

Example: Bonneville is a movie production partnership which is in the process of producing a western film entitled "Real Cowboys Aren't Urban." Each of the three partners of Bonneville, A, B, and C, are actively involved in the production which is being filmed in Wyoming.

1. *Duty to disclose benefits received from partnership.* The movie is being shot on property owned by A; however, A has not disclosed his ownership interest to his partners, who believe they are leasing the property from a local Wyoming resident. This is a clear violation of A's duty of loyalty to disclose and account for the benefits which he derives from the partnership. Partner A should not have entered into the lease without first informing the other partners of his interest in the property and receiving their consent. Had A disclosed his ownership of the land and the benefit he received from the lease to Bonneville, he would not be violating his duty of loyalty.

2. *Duty to refrain from using partnership property or appropriating partnership opportunity.* Partner B is responsible for obtaining props for the movie. While searching for five horses to lease for use in the movie, he learns that a local rancher is selling six horses at a bargain price. Partner B's family has always wanted horses but B has never had the money to buy them. However, he determines that he could buy all six horses from the rancher for less than the partnership had budgeted for the five horses that it needed. Therefore, feeling like he is getting a great deal, B uses the partnership's funds to buy all six horses. He delivers four to the production set and has the rancher haul the other two to his vacation home in a neighboring state; he tells his partners that he could only find four horses. In this instance, Partner B has violated his duty of loyalty to the partnership because he has used partnership funds for personal gain. Furthermore, he has appropriated the partnership's opportunity to purchase all of the horses which it needed for production at a bargain price.

3. *Duty to refrain from holding, or acting on behalf of one who holds, an interest adverse to the partnership, without the consent of the partnership.* Partner C has an ownership interest in the company which is providing the camera and crews for Bonneville's production; his partners are unaware of his interest. During filming, C feels that the partnership is not paying the crew enough to compensate them for the unusually hot working conditions and long hours. Therefore, he contacts the president of the filming company and tells them to go strike for higher wages; he knows that Bonneville must complete production within the month and cannot afford to stop production. The filming crew goes on strike and C encourages Bonneville's partners to meet the workers' demands so that production will not be held up. Partner C clearly holds an interest adverse to the partnership and his failure to disclose his interest violated his duty of loyalty. The mere fact that he has an interest in the filming company would not violate his duty of loyalty if he disclosed his interest to his partners.

4. *Duty to refrain from competing with the partnership.* Partner A holds a large interest in a failing theater company in the town in which Bonneville is filming. He encourages the company to produce a stage version of the movie that Bonneville is filming in order to take advantage of the advertising which Bonneville will do for its movie. The theater opens its production of "Real Cowboys Aren't Urban" on the same night that the movie opens at the local movie theater. The local stage production sells all of its seats while the movie theater has a very small turnout. Partner A's actions were clearly improper.

Duty of Care

Partners should use ordinary and reasonable care in conducting partnership business and are generally liable for "engaging in grossly negligent or reckless conduct, intentional misconduct, or a knowing violation of the law."[9] This statutory definition of a partner's violation of the duty of due care imposes only minimal obligations upon partners to act with ordinary and reasonable care.

Therefore, in order to protect partnerships and their business enterprises from any degree of negligence by the partners, it is advisable to insert a provision in the partnership agreement that requires partners to act with ordinary and reasonable care in the course of their partnership duties. Such a provision is consistent with the partners' duty of loyalty, which requires them to act in the best interests of the partnership.

Duty of Good Faith and Fair Dealing

Partners must exercise good faith and fair dealing in discharging their duties to the partnership, including the duty of loyalty and the duty of due care.[10] Partners act in good faith if they do not intend to seek an unfair advantage over the partnership or defraud the partnership.[11] Simply speaking, a partner must be honest with the partnership. This component of a partner's basic fiduciary duties is a codification of the expectations that partners generally have of one another.

LIABILITY

Personal Liability

Each partner is personally liable for all contractual obligations of the partnership and all damages for tortious actions (e.g., personal injuries caused) by a partner or an employee of the partnership. Thus, if the partnership cannot pay its debts or other obligations, the individual partners must pay them from their own personal funds or property.

> **Example:** An employee of The Flower Shop, a partnership owned by A and B hits a pedestrian while making a flower delivery. The pedestrian is severely injured and sues the Flower Shop for $100,000. A and B carry liability insurance; however, the limits of the policy are $50,000. A jury awards the victim $100,000. After the insurance company pays $50,000 to the victim, A and B liquidate The Flower Shop in an attempt to pay the remaining $50,000. The proceeds from the sale of the assets of The Flower Shop are $25,000, leaving $25,000 still due to the victim. A and B are personally liable for the remaining $25,000; therefore, they each take $12,500 out of their personal bank accounts to pay the remainder due to the victim.

Joint and several liability Doctrine of shared responsibility allowing creditors to sue individuals separately (severally) or together (jointly) to satisfy a debt.

All partners are equally liable for the obligations of the partnership, unless the partnership agreement provides otherwise. However, partners hold **joint and several liability** for the debts and other obligations of the partnership. Therefore, a plaintiff can choose to hold a wealthy partner responsible for all damages caused by the partnership. For example, the pedestrian in the preceding example could have sued B for the entire amount of his damages, $100,000, without naming A as a defendant. However, a partner who pays more than his or her proportionate share of partnership debts or other liabilities may be entitled to indemnification (reimbursement) from the other partners for their pro rata share(s). This, of course, assumes that the other partners have the money to pay their respective share of the partnership obligations.

> **Example:** Using the preceding example, if B were forced to pay the entire $25,000 due to the victim after A refused to pay her portion, B could sue A for her one-half, $12,500.

Contract Liability vs. Tort Liability

[handwritten: π must sue all p's]

All partners hold **joint liability** for the contractual obligations of the partnership. This means that if the partnership breaches a contract, the other party to the contract must sue all of the partners together (jointly) to recover damages caused by the partnership's breach. In contrast, each partner may be held individually responsible for all damages arising from the wrongful acts or omissions (torts) of the partners or their employees acting in the ordinary course of business. Thus, if a person is injured by one of the partners or an employee of the partnership acting within the ordinary course of business (e.g., a stockbroker steals money from a stock account), the injured party can sue one partner (severally) or all of the partners (jointly) to recover any losses. If the injured party sues the partners individually, he or she can collect all of the damages from one partner; that partner can then sue the other partners to collect their share of the amount paid (indemnification). This scheme puts wealthier partners at risk for the obligations of the partnership.

In an attempt to hold accountable partners who improperly incur partnership obligations, partnership agreements should contain a provision that allows nonculpable partners to seek indemnification (reimbursement) from partners who have acted improperly. Although such a provision will not protect an innocent partner from suits by those seeking to collect an obligation of the partnership, it will give the wronged partner the right to recoup losses from the personal assets of the partner who acted without authority. Of course, one of the reasons a creditor may seek recovery from a nonculpable partner is because the culpable partner may not have the personal assets to satisfy the obligation; in such a case, a wronged partner may end up bearing the brunt of the loss.

Personal liability is the most significant disadvantage of a general partnership. Limited partnerships and limited liability partnerships developed in order to limit such liability. However, business associates continue to form general partnerships, and accept the inherent risk of personal liability, often because of the simplicity in organization. Therefore, it is imperative to understand the potential liabilities of general partners and be aware of mechanisms to limit partners' personal risk.

Contract Liability

If a partnership breaches a contract (e.g., fails to perform a contract), the partners are jointly responsible for the damages/losses due for the breach. This means that a creditor must sue all of the partners together to recover any losses incurred because of the partnership's breach of contract. If the assets (property, accounts receivable, etc.) of the partnership are insufficient to pay the debts and liabilities of the business, business creditors can look to the partners' personal assets (home, cars, etc.) to satisfy these obligations. Thus partners risk their business as well as personal assets in all of their business ventures.

The R.U.P.A. offers some protections to partners' personal assets by requiring that judgment debts (court-ordered obligations) of a partnership be satisfied from partnership assets before a creditor can look to the partners' personal assets. Only when a partnership's assets are exhausted can a creditor require the partners to personally pay amounts due on the judgment; this is known as the **"exhaustion rule."**[12] Unfortunately, the R.U.P.A. has not yet been adopted in all jurisdictions. Even in those where it has, partners are still exposed to some personal liability.

However, because contracts can create, specify, and limit the rights and duties of contracting parties, it is possible and advisable to limit a partner's personal liability for contractual obligations of the partnership through the partnership's contracts. In order to do this, all partnership contracts should include a provision that specifies that all obligations due on or liabilities created by the contract, or a breach thereof, will be limited to and payable solely from the partnership's assets. Such a provision should also clearly, though redundantly, state that the personal assets of the partners shall not be liable for satisfaction of such obligations.

Joint liability   Shared responsibility; requires that all individuals be sued together to recover a debt.

Exhaustion rule   Requires that business assets be used to pay partnership debts before a creditor can look to partners' personal assets.

Although such provisions can significantly limit a partner's personal liability, not all potential partnership liabilities can be anticipated and limited by agreement. Therefore, partners should be appropriately bonded and insured.

Tort Liability

Torts Wrongful acts.

Partners are jointly and severally liable for the **torts** committed by a partner, employee, or other agent of the partnership in the ordinary course of business. Therefore, a tort victim can sue each partner separately (severally) to recover damages caused by the negligence or other wrongful act of an agent of the partnership; however, the victim can only receive one recovery for any losses.

> **Example:**   Stuart is an employee stockbroker for Stocks "R" Us, a general partnership. He is short on cash to pay his bills for several months and takes $25,000 from a client's stock account. The client learns of Stuart's actions and sues the partnership. The partnership doesn't have the money to pay the obligation. Therefore, the client decides to sue the partners personally to get his money back. Because the client knows that Partner Alice has a nice home, nice cars, and takes expensive vacations, he sues her for the $25,000. Partner Alice can only pay $15,000 of the obligation. Then, the client decides to sue Partner Betty. The client can only recover the unpaid $10,000, thus receiving one recovery. The client cannot sue each partner for $25,000 and recover that amount from each partner.

A partner's personal responsibility for torts committed by a partner or employee of the partnership includes liability for fraud, even if the partner is unaware of the fraudulent activity. This liability is imposed on partners because theoretically they are in a position to know of and monitor the activities of their agents.

> **Example:**   Clean and Bright, a housekeeping partnership of partners A and B, cleans the Smith house every Wednesday. While cleaning the home one week, E, an employee of Clean and Bright, steals Mrs. Smith's diamond necklace. Clean and Bright and its partners, A and B, are jointly and seperately liable to the Smiths for E's action.

Imposing joint and several liability on partners for tortious acts committed by a partner or employee of the partnership makes it easier for a tort victim to sue for damages. With joint liability, a tort victim would have to find and serve each partner. Several liability, in contrast, allows the victim to sue one partner at a time, thus reducing the cost and complexity of a suit, especially if one or more partners cannot be located.

The potential personal liability of one partner for all partnership obligations is the major disadvantage of a general partnership. Even if partnership liabilities are apportioned among the partners, a partner's pro rata share of the partnership's obligations can be financially devastating. Thus, individuals with personal assets of any value should be advised to consider limited partnerships, limited liability partnerships, corporations, or limited liability companies.

PARTNERSHIP PROPERTY

Partnership property, which generally consists of (1) contributions by the partners, (2) property purchased with partnership profits, and (3) property otherwise acquired by the partnership (e.g., through loans), has, traditionally, been owned by the individual partners rather than the partnership itself. However, increasingly, states are simplifying the ownership of partnership property and allowing the partnership as a separate entity to own property.[13]

It is important to know the source of partnership property and understand the attendant ownership rights in order to safeguard the individual partner's interest in and to partnership property.

Capital Investments

Partners contribute all of the property or money necessary to begin the partnership's business; these contributions are known as **partnership capital.** The capital investments of the partners become property of the partnership, in addition to subsequent contributions by the partners, property purchased with partnership profits, or property otherwise acquired by the partnership (e.g., through business loans). Partners do not have the right to withdraw their capital investment until the partnership is dissolved.

A partner's interest in the partnership is initially based upon his or her **capital contribution.** Therefore, a well-drafted partnership agreement should set forth in detail the capital contributions of the partners in order to establish each partner's interest. If a partner's investment is property (buildings, land, office supplies, etc.) rather than money, a dollar value should be assigned to the contribution. In the absence of an agreement allocating the profits and losses of the partnership, the U.P.A. and the R.U.P.A. provide that the partners share the profits and losses equally.

Rights to Partnership Property

Traditionally, partners have held partnership property as tenants in partnership.[14] As such, partners are considered co-owners of partnership property, with the right to possess partnership property only for partnership purposes, unless the other partners consent to a nonpartnership use.

Example: A partner in a local florist shop cannot use the business's delivery van for moving into her new home, unless she first receives the consent of the other partners.

Because of the contradiction created by "**tenancy in partnership**" the R.U.P.A. provides that partnership property is owned by the partnership, as an entity.[15] This structure eliminates the cumbersome requirements for tenancies in partnership, particularly in the transfer of partnership property.

Partnership Interests

An individual's partnership interest is based upon the partner's proportionate share of the assets and liabilities of the partnership as well as the business profits. Initially, the capital contributions of the respective partners establish each partner's interest; as the business grows and becomes more profitable, each partner's share of partnership profits is added to his or her initial contribution to determine that partner's partnership interest. Therefore, in order to protect a partner's investments, all contributions should be set forth in the partnership agreement and be assigned a reasonable value.

After establishing the value of each partner's capital contribution, the partners should then establish their future interests in the partnership by determining how the assets and liabilities of the partnership will be divided. The U.P.A. and the R.U.P.A. both provide that the profits and losses of a partnership will be shared equally, unless the partners agree to an unequal allocation.

Example: Gerry and Gina decide to work as partners in the snowcone business; they intend to set up at the local park. They draw up a partnership agreement that provides that Gerry will buy a refrigerated cart for $450 for the business and Gina will buy the ice shaver, cone cups, straws, and flavoring gels at a cost of $200. The first summer in business, the profits from the partnership are $30,000; each partner receives one-half of the profits. The partnership capital remains $650; the partners have not discussed how profits and losses will be divided. Therefore, the partners' respective interest in the business are their initial capital contributions plus their share of the profits. Thus, Gerry's interest is $15,450 and Gina's is $15,200.

Partnership capital The contribution of property or money to a partnership.

Capital contribution The initial investment of property or money by a partner to a partnership.

Tenancy in partnership Co-ownership of property by partners.

It is not uncommon to find partnership arrangements in which one partner contributes capital while another partner contributes experience. In such a case, the interest of the partner contributing capital is the capital investment plus his or her share of the profits; the interest of the partner contributing experience is his or her share of the profits.

> **Example:** Joe and Jerry are partners in BSM, a building service and maintenance company. Joe agrees to buy the supplies at a cost of $2,000, which the business needs to start cleaning offices. Although Jerry does not have any money to invest in the business, he has twenty years of janitorial experience. The first year of business, the partnership earns profits of $20,000. Joe's interest in the partnership is $12,000 (his capital investment plus profits). Jerry's interest is $10,000.

In order to assure smooth sailing in partnership ventures, partners should determine how their respective interests in the business will be determined, both initially and as the business continues. In the absence of an agreement between the partners, the default provisions of the U.P.A. and the R.U.P.A. will provide for equal allocation of partnership profits and losses, an arrangement with which not all partners will be satisfied.

Assignment of Partnership Interest

A partner may assign his or her interest in the partnership to a third party without the consent of the other partners. However, such an **assignment of interest** passes only the partner's right to receive profits from the partnership; it does not entitle the assignee (the person to whom the profits are assigned) the right to participate in the management or operation of the partnership, nor does it entitle the assignee to information (i.e., access to partnership books) regarding partnership transactions. If an assignee were granted such participatory rights, the assignee would essentially become a partner in the partnership and a new partnership would be formed, without the consent of the other partners; this cannot be done.

Attachment of Partnership Interest

Creditors of an individual partner may not **attach** or execute against property of the partnership to satisfy a partner's personal obligations. Creditors can seek a court judgment against the individual partner and execute against the partner's interest in the partnership. However, executing against a partner's partnership interest only gives the creditor the right to receive the debtor-partner's pro rata share of partnership profits; as with a voluntary assignment by a partner of his or her partnership interest, creditors have no right to participate in or oversee operation of the partnership business.

TAXATION CONSIDERATIONS

Partnerships are taxed in the same manner as sole proprietorships, with the profits or losses of the partnership apportioned to the partners individually. The partnership itself is not taxed separately; instead, each partner reports his or her share of the partnership profits or losses as personal income. (See Form 6.2, *IRS Form 1040, Schedule E, Supplemental Income and Loss.*) Each partner pays taxes on his or her pro rata share of all partnership profits, regardless of whether or not the profits were actually distributed to the partners. This taxation scheme benefits partners in several ways: (1) partnership profits are taxed only once (in contrast to corporate profits that are taxed twice), (2) partnership profits are taxed at the lower individual tax rates (as opposed to the relatively higher corporate tax rates), and (3) in the event of partnership losses, a partner may offset the losses against other sources of income to reduce his or her overall tax liability.

Although partnerships are not taxed directly, all partnerships must file an informational tax return with the Internal Revenue Service in order to verify the individual partners' tax liability. (See Form 6.3, *IRS Form 1065, U.S. Partnership Return of Income; and* Form 6.4, *IRS Form 1065, Schedule K-1, Partner's Share of Income, Credits, Deductions, etc.*)

Assignment of interest   Transfer of ownership interest to another.

Attach   Take property for the payment of debts.

SCHEDULE E
(Form 1040)

Department of the Treasury
Internal Revenue Service   (99)

Supplemental Income and Loss

(From rental real estate, royalties, partnerships,
S corporations, estates, trusts, REMICs, etc.)

▶ **Attach to Form 1040 or Form 1041.**   ▶ **See Instructions for Schedule E (Form 1040).**

OMB No. 1545-0074

1999

Attachment
Sequence No. **13**

Name(s) shown on return

Your social security number

Part I   **Income or Loss From Rental Real Estate and Royalties**   Note: *Report income and expenses from your business of renting personal property on* **Schedule C** *or* **C-EZ** *(see page E-1). Report farm rental income or loss from* **Form 4835** *on page 2, line 39.*

1	Show the kind and location of each **rental real estate property:**		2	For each rental real estate property listed on line 1, did you or your family use it during the tax year for personal purposes for more than the greater of: • 14 days, **or** • 10% of the total days rented at fair rental value? (See page E-1.)	Yes	No
A	....		A			
B	....		B			
C	....		C			

		Properties			Totals
Income:		**A**	**B**	**C**	(Add columns A, B, and C.)
3 Rents received	3				3
4 Royalties received	4				4
Expenses:					
5 Advertising	5				
6 Auto and travel (see page E-2) .	6				
7 Cleaning and maintenance . . .	7				
8 Commissions	8				
9 Insurance	9				
10 Legal and other professional fees	10				
11 Management fees	11				
12 Mortgage interest paid to banks, etc. (see page E-2)	12				12
13 Other interest	13				
14 Repairs	14				
15 Supplies	15				
16 Taxes	16				
17 Utilities	17				
18 Other (list) ▶................	18				
19 Add lines 5 through 18	19				19
20 Depreciation expense or depletion (see page E-3)	20				20
21 Total expenses. Add lines 19 and 20	21				
22 Income or (loss) from rental real estate or royalty properties. Subtract line 21 from line 3 (rents) or line 4 (royalties). If the result is a (loss), see page E-3 to find out if you must file **Form 6198** . .	22				
23 Deductible rental real estate loss. **Caution:** *Your rental real estate loss on line 22 may be limited. See page E-3 to find out if you must file* **Form 8582**. *Real estate professionals must complete line 42 on page 2*	23	(	)(	)(	)
24 **Income.** Add positive amounts shown on line 22. **Do not** include any losses				24	
25 **Losses.** Add royalty losses from line 22 and rental real estate losses from line 23. Enter total losses here				25	( )
26 Total rental real estate and royalty income or (loss). Combine lines 24 and 25. Enter the result here. If Parts II, III, IV, and line 39 on page 2 do not apply to you, also enter this amount on Form 1040, line 17. Otherwise, include this amount in the total on line 40 on page 2				26	

For Paperwork Reduction Act Notice, see Form 1040 instructions.   Cat. No. 11344 .   **Schedule E (Form 1040) 1999**

FORM 6.2.

IRS Form 1040, Schedule E, Supplemental Income and Loss

Schedule E (Form 1040) 1999   Attachment Sequence No. **13**   Page **2**

Name(s) shown on return. Do not enter name and social security number if shown on other side.	Your social security number

Note: *If you report amounts from farming or fishing on Schedule E, you must enter your gross income from those activities on line 41 below. Real estate professionals must complete line 42 below.*

Part II   **Income or Loss From Partnerships and S Corporations**   Note: *If you report a loss from an at-risk activity, you MUST check either column (e) or (f) on line 27 to describe your investment in the activity. See page E-5. If you check column (f), you must attach* **Form 6198.**

27	(a) Name	(b) Enter P for partnership; S for S corporation	(c) Check if foreign partnership	(d) Employer identification number	Investment At Risk? (e) All is at risk	(f) Some is not at risk
A						
B						
C						
D						
E						

	Passive Income and Loss		Nonpassive Income and Loss		
	(g) Passive loss allowed (attach **Form 8582** if required)	(h) Passive income from **Schedule K-1**	(i) Nonpassive loss from **Schedule K-1**	(j) Section 179 expense deduction from **Form 4562**	(k) Nonpassive income from **Schedule K-1**
A					
B					
C					
D					
E					
28a Totals					
b Totals					

29	Add columns (h) and (k) of line 28a	29	
30	Add columns (g), (i), and (j) of line 28b	30	( )
31	Total partnership and S corporation income or (loss). Combine lines 29 and 30. Enter the result here and include in the total on line 40 below	31	

Part III   **Income or Loss From Estates and Trusts**

32	(a) Name	(b) Employer identification number
A		
B		

	Passive Income and Loss		Nonpassive Income and Loss	
	(c) Passive deduction or loss allowed (attach **Form 8582** if required)	(d) Passive income from **Schedule K-1**	(e) Deduction or loss from **Schedule K-1**	(f) Other income from **Schedule K-1**
A				
B				
33a Totals				
b Totals				

34	Add columns (d) and (f) of line 33a	34	
35	Add columns (c) and (e) of line 33b	35	( )
36	Total estate and trust income or (loss). Combine lines 34 and 35. Enter the result here and include in the total on line 40 below	36	

Part IV   **Income or Loss From Real Estate Mortgage Investment Conduits (REMICs)—Residual Holder**

37	(a) Name	(b) Employer identification number	(c) Excess inclusion from Schedules Q, line 2c (see page E-6)	(d) Taxable income (net loss) from Schedules Q, line 1b	(e) Income from Schedules Q, line 3b

38	Combine columns (d) and (e) only. Enter the result here and include in the total on line 40 below	38	

Part V   **Summary**

39	Net farm rental income or (loss) from **Form 4835**. Also, complete line 41 below	39	
40	TOTAL income or (loss). Combine lines 26, 31, 36, 38, and 39. Enter the result here and on Form 1040, line 17 ▶	40	

41	**Reconciliation of Farming and Fishing Income.** Enter your **gross** farming and fishing income reported on Form 4835, line 7; Schedule K-1 (Form 1065), line 15b; Schedule K-1 (Form 1120S), line 23; and Schedule K-1 (Form 1041), line 14 (see page E-6)	41	
42	**Reconciliation for Real Estate Professionals.** If you were a real estate professional (see page E-4), enter the net income or (loss) you reported anywhere on Form 1040 from all rental real estate activities in which you materially participated under the passive activity loss rules . . .	42	

Schedule E (Form 1040) 1999

FORM 6.2. *continued*

Form **1065**		U.S. Partnership Return of Income		OMB No. 1545-0099

Form **1065**
Department of the Treasury
Internal Revenue Service

U.S. Partnership Return of Income

For calendar year 1999, or tax year beginning ...., 1999, and ending ...., ...
▶ See separate instructions.

OMB No. 1545-0099

1999

A Principal business activity	Use the IRS label. Other-wise, please print or type.	Name of partnership	**D** Employer identification number
B Principal product or service		Number, street, and room or suite no. If a P.O. box, see page 12 of the instructions.	**E** Date business started
C Business code number		City or town, state, and ZIP code	**F** Total assets (see page 12 of the instructions) $

G Check applicable boxes: **(1)** ☐ Initial return **(2)** ☐ Final return **(3)** ☐ Change in address **(4)** ☐ Amended return
H Check accounting method: **(1)** ☐ Cash **(2)** ☐ Accrual **(3)** ☐ Other (specify) ▶ ....
I Number of Schedules K-1. Attach one for each person who was a partner at any time during the tax year ▶ ....

Caution: *Include **only** trade or business income and expenses on lines 1a through 22 below. See the instructions for more information.*

Income

1a Gross receipts or sales	**1a**		
b Less returns and allowances.	**1b**		**1c**
2 Cost of goods sold (Schedule A, line 8)			**2**
3 Gross profit. Subtract line 2 from line 1c.			**3**
4 Ordinary income (loss) from other partnerships, estates, and trusts *(attach schedule)*. . ..			**4**
5 Net farm profit (loss) *(attach Schedule F (Form 1040))*			**5**
6 Net gain (loss) from Form 4797, Part II, line 18.			**6**
7 Other income (loss) *(attach schedule)*.			**7**
8 **Total income (loss).** Combine lines 3 through 7			**8**

Deductions (see page 14 of the instructions for limitations)

9 Salaries and wages (other than to partners) (less employment credits)			**9**
10 Guaranteed payments to partners			**10**
11 Repairs and maintenance			**11**
12 Bad debts			**12**
13 Rent			**13**
14 Taxes and licenses			**14**
15 Interest			**15**
16a Depreciation (if required, attach Form 4562)	**16a**		
b Less depreciation reported on Schedule A and elsewhere on return	**16b**		**16c**
17 Depletion **(Do not deduct oil and gas depletion.)**			**17**
18 Retirement plans, etc.			**18**
19 Employee benefit programs			**19**
20 Other deductions *(attach schedule)*			**20**
21 **Total deductions.** Add the amounts shown in the far right column for lines 9 through 20 .			**21**

| **22** Ordinary income (loss) from trade or business activities. Subtract line 21 from line 8 . . | | | **22** |

Please Sign Here

Under penalties of perjury, I declare that I have examined this return, including accompanying schedules and statements, and to the best of my knowledge and belief, it is true, correct, and complete. Declaration of preparer (other than general partner or limited liability company member) is based on all information of which preparer has any knowledge.

▶ Signature of general partner or limited liability company member	▶ Date

Paid Preparer's Use Only

Preparer's signature ▶	Date	Check if self-employed ▶ ☐	Preparer's SSN or PTIN
Firm's name (or yours if self-employed) and address ▶		EIN ▶	
		ZIP code ▶	

For Paperwork Reduction Act Notice, see separate instructions. Cat. No. 11390Z Form **1065** (1999)

FORM 6.3.
IRS Form 1065, U.S. Partnership Return of Income

SCHEDULE K-1
(Form 1065)
Department of the Treasury
Internal Revenue Service

Partner's Share of Income, Credits, Deductions, etc.

▶ See separate instructions.

For calendar year 1999 or tax year beginning , 1999, and ending ,

OMB No. 1545-0099

1999

Partner's identifying number ▶

Partnership's identifying number ▶

Partner's name, address, and ZIP code

Partnership's name, address, and ZIP code

A This partner is a ☐ general partner ☐ limited partner
 ☐ limited liability company member
B What type of entity is this partner? ▶ ....
C Is this partner a ☐ domestic or a ☐ foreign partner?
D Enter partner's percentage of: **(i)** Before change or termination **(ii)** End of year
 Profit sharing . . . . % .... %
 Loss sharing . . . . % .... %
 Ownership of capital . . . . % .... %
E IRS Center where partnership filed return:

F Partner's share of liabilities (see instructions):
 Nonrecourse . . . . $ ....
 Qualified nonrecourse financing . . $ ....
 Other . . . . $ ....
G Tax shelter registration number . ▶ ....
H Check here if this partnership is a publicly traded partnership as defined in section 469(k)(2) . . . . . ☐
I Check applicable boxes: **(1)** ☐ Final K-1 **(2)** ☐ Amended K-1

J **Analysis of partner's capital account:**

(a) Capital account at beginning of year	(b) Capital contributed during year	(c) Partner's share of lines 3, 4, and 7, Form 1065, Schedule M-2	(d) Withdrawals and distributions	(e) Capital account at end of year (combine columns (a) through (d))
			( )	

	(a) Distributive share item		(b) Amount	(c) 1040 filers enter the amount in column (b) on:
	1 Ordinary income (loss) from trade or business activities . . .	**1**		See page 6 of Partner's Instructions for Schedule K-1 (Form 1065).
	2 Net income (loss) from rental real estate activities	**2**		
	3 Net income (loss) from other rental activities	**3**		
	4 Portfolio income (loss):			
	a Interest	**4a**		Sch. B, Part I, line 1
	b Ordinary dividends	**4b**		Sch. B, Part II, line 5
Income (Loss)	**c** Royalties	**4c**		Sch. E, Part I, line 4
	d Net short-term capital gain (loss)	**4d**		Sch. D, line 5, col. (f)
	e Net long-term capital gain (loss):			
	(1) 28% rate gain (loss)	**e(1)**		Sch. D, line 12, col. (g)
	(2) Total for year.	**e(2)**		Sch. D, line 12, col. (f)
	f Other portfolio income (loss) (attach schedule)	**4f**		Enter on applicable line of your return.
	5 Guaranteed payments to partner	**5**		See page 6 of Partner's Instructions for Schedule K-1 (Form 1065).
	6 Net section 1231 gain (loss) (other than due to casualty or theft) .	**6**		
	7 Other income (loss) (attach schedule)	**7**		Enter on applicable line of your return.
Deduc-tions	**8** Charitable contributions (see instructions) (attach schedule) . .	**8**		Sch. A, line 15 or 16
	9 Section 179 expense deduction	**9**		See pages 7 and 8 of Partner's Instructions for Schedule K-1 (Form 1065).
	10 Deductions related to portfolio income (attach schedule) . . .	**10**		
	11 Other deductions (attach schedule).	**11**		
Credits	**12a** Low-income housing credit:			
	(1) From section 42(j)(5) partnerships for property placed in service before 1990	**a(1)**		Form 8586, line 5
	(2) Other than on line 12a(1) for property placed in service before 1990	**a(2)**		
	(3) From section 42(j)(5) partnerships for property placed in service after 1989	**a(3)**		
	(4) Other than on line 12a(3) for property placed in service after 1989	**a(4)**		
	b Qualified rehabilitation expenditures related to rental real estate activities	**12b**		
	c Credits (other than credits shown on lines 12a and 12b) related to rental real estate activities.	**12c**		See page 8 of Partner's Instructions for Schedule K-1 (Form 1065).
	d Credits related to other rental activities	**12d**		
	13 Other credits.	**13**		

For Paperwork Reduction Act Notice, see Instructions for Form 1065. Cat. No. 11394R Schedule K-1 (Form 1065) 1999

FORM 6.4.

IRS Form 1065, Schedule K-1, Partner's Share of Income, Credits, Deductions, etc.

Schedule K-1 (Form 1065) 1999   Page **2**

(a) Distributive share item		(b) Amount	(c) 1040 filers enter the amount in column (b) on:
Investment Interest	**14a** Interest expense on investment debts	14a	Form 4952, line 1
	b (1) Investment income included on lines 4a, 4b, 4c, and 4f	b(1)	See page 9 of Partner's Instructions for Schedule K-1 (Form 1065).
	(2) Investment expenses included on line 10	b(2)	
Self-employment	**15a** Net earnings (loss) from self-employment	15a	Sch. SE, Section A or B
	b Gross farming or fishing income	15b	See page 9 of Partner's Instructions for Schedule K-1 (Form 1065).
	c Gross nonfarm income	15c	
Adjustments and Tax Preference Items	**16a** Depreciation adjustment on property placed in service after 1986	16a	See page 9 of Partner's Instructions for Schedule K-1 (Form 1065) and Instructions for Form 6251.
	b Adjusted gain or loss	16b	
	c Depletion (other than oil and gas)	16c	
	d (1) Gross income from oil, gas, and geothermal properties	d(1)	
	(2) Deductions allocable to oil, gas, and geothermal properties	d(2)	
	e Other adjustments and tax preference items *(attach schedule)*	16e	
Foreign Taxes	**17a** Type of income ▶		Form 1116, check boxes
	b Name of foreign country or possession ▶		
	c Total gross income from sources outside the United States *(attach schedule)*	17c	Form 1116, Part I
	d Total applicable deductions and losses *(attach schedule)*	17d	
	e Total foreign taxes (check one): ▶ ☐ Paid ☐ Accrued	17e	Form 1116, Part II
	f Reduction in taxes available for credit *(attach schedule)*	17f	Form 1116, Part III
	g Other foreign tax information *(attach schedule)*	17g	See Instructions for Form 1116.
Other	**18** Section 59(e)(2) expenditures: **a** Type ▶		See page 9 of Partner's Instructions for Schedule K-1 (Form 1065).
	b Amount	18b	
	19 Tax-exempt interest income	19	Form 1040, line 8b
	20 Other tax-exempt income	20	See pages 9 and 10 of Partner's Instructions for Schedule K-1 (Form 1065).
	21 Nondeductible expenses	21	
	22 Distributions of money (cash and marketable securities)	22	
	23 Distributions of property other than money	23	
	24 Recapture of low-income housing credit:		
	a From section 42(j)(5) partnerships	24a	Form 8611, line 8
	b Other than on line 24a	24b	

Supplemental Information

25 Supplemental information required to be reported separately to each partner *(attach additional schedules if more space is needed)*:

Schedule K-1 (Form 1065) 1999

FORM 6.4. *continued*

Partnerships must file both forms with the IRS and provide a copy of each to the partners. The partners use Schedule K-1 to complete their personal tax returns (e.g., Schedule E, 1040). Because of the required informational filings, all partnerships must apply for a federal tax identification number with the IRS. (See Form 6.5, *Application for Employer Identification Number.*) In addition, if the partnership hires employees, it must comply with all employee withholding requirements, including Social Security and Medicare as well as unemployment and workers' compensation laws. A partnership should be advised to contact a certified public accountant to prepare all the necessary documents to comply with all state and federal requirements.

The direct taxation scheme of the general partnership, in addition to the flexibility of management, are generally the two most appealing characteristics of a general partnership. However, these advantages must be weighed against the unlimited personal liability of general partners. Given the alternative organizational forms that offer the benefits of direct taxation, management rights, and limited liability (limited liability partnerships, limited liability companies, and S corporations), business owners are wise to consider their options.

TERMINATION OF A PARTNERSHIP

Dissolution of a Partnership

Dissolution Termination of business association.

The **dissolution** of a partnership is caused by a change in the legal relationship of the partners and occurs when a partner ceases to be associated with the partnership.[16] A dissolution does not automatically terminate the partnership business or distribute partnership assets; rather, the partnership form technically dissolves and the remaining partners generally continue to operate the partnership business until the business is wound up (terminated by the liquidation and distribution of business assets).

A partnership may dissolve for a variety of reasons, which include but are not limited to the following:

♦ Expiration of the partnership agreement (the terms of the partnership agreement provide that the partnership will terminate on a specified date or upon the completion of a specified partnership project);
♦ Mutual agreement of the partners;
♦ Expulsion of a partner pursuant to the partnership agreement (e.g., for a breach of the duty of loyalty);
♦ Election: Termination of the partnership by a partner (if the termination violates the partnership agreement, the departing partner may be liable for damages caused by the election);
♦ Operation of law:
    Illegality of partnership business (e.g., a casino partnership will automatically terminate if gambling becomes illegal);
    Death of a partner; or
    Bankruptcy of a partner.
♦ Court decree when it is not reasonably practical to carry on the partnership business (i.e., the business is consistently unprofitable or a partner becomes unable to participate in the partnership).

The R.U.P.A. recognizes that partnerships and their businesses do not automatically terminate when one partner leaves the partnership. Therefore, the R.U.P.A. provides for the reorganization, rather than the termination, when one or more partners leave the partnership. The reorganization is accomplished by allowing the remaining partners to purchase the departing partner's interest at a buyout price (i.e., the value of the departing partner's share of the partnership's assets and liabilities) or at a value previously established in the partnership agreement.[17] This statutory scheme more accurately reflects the practicalities of the need for continuity in a partnership's business.

Form **SS-4** (Rev. February 1998) Department of the Treasury Internal Revenue Service	**Application for Employer Identification Number** (For use by employers, corporations, partnerships, trusts, estates, churches, government agencies, certain individuals, and others. See instructions.) ▶ **Keep a copy for your records.**	EIN OMB No. 1545-0003

Please type or print clearly.

1 Name of applicant (legal name) (see instructions)

2 Trade name of business (if different from name on line 1)	**3** Executor, trustee, "care of" name
4a Mailing address (street address) (room, apt., or suite no.)	**5a** Business address (if different from address on lines 4a and 4b)
4b City, state, and ZIP code	**5b** City, state, and ZIP code

6 County and state where principal business is located

7 Name of principal officer, general partner, grantor, owner, or trustor—SSN or ITIN may be required (see instructions) ▶ _____

8a Type of entity (Check only one box.) (see instructions)

Caution: *If applicant is a limited liability company, see the instructions for line 8a.*

- ☐ Sole proprietor (SSN) _____
- ☐ Partnership
- ☐ REMIC
- ☐ State/local government
- ☐ Church or church-controlled organization
- ☐ Other nonprofit organization (specify) ▶ _____
- ☐ Other (specify) ▶
- ☐ Personal service corp.
- ☐ National Guard
- ☐ Farmers' cooperative
- ☐ Estate (SSN of decedent) _____
- ☐ Plan administrator (SSN) _____
- ☐ Other corporation (specify) ▶ _____
- ☐ Trust
- ☐ Federal government/military

(enter GEN if applicable) _____

8b If a corporation, name the state or foreign country (if applicable) where incorporated | State | Foreign country

9 Reason for applying (Check only one box.) (see instructions)
- ☐ Started new business (specify type) ▶ _____
- ☐ Hired employees (Check the box and see line 12.)
- ☐ Created a pension plan (specify type) ▶
- ☐ Banking purpose (specify purpose) ▶ _____
- ☐ Changed type of organization (specify new type) ▶ _____
- ☐ Purchased going business
- ☐ Created a trust (specify type) ▶ _____
- ☐ Other (specify) ▶

10 Date business started or acquired (month, day, year) (see instructions) | **11** Closing month of accounting year (see instructions)

12 First date wages or annuities were paid or will be paid (month, day, year). **Note:** *If applicant is a withholding agent, enter date income will first be paid to nonresident alien. (month, day, year)* . . . . ▶

13 Highest number of employees expected in the next 12 months. **Note:** *If the applicant does not expect to have any employees during the period, enter -0-. (see instructions)* . . . . . ▶	Nonagricultural	Agricultural	Household

14 Principal activity (see instructions) ▶

15 Is the principal business activity manufacturing? . . . . ☐ Yes ☐ No
If "Yes," principal product and raw material used ▶

16 To whom are most of the products or services sold? Please check one box. ☐ Business (wholesale)
☐ Public (retail) ☐ Other (specify) ▶ ☐ N/A

17a Has the applicant ever applied for an employer identification number for this or any other business? . . . . . ☐ Yes ☐ No
Note: *If "Yes," please complete lines 17b and 17c.*

17b If you checked "Yes" on line 17a, give applicant's legal name and trade name shown on prior application, if different from line 1 or 2 above.
Legal name ▶ Trade name ▶

17c Approximate date when and city and state where the application was filed. Enter previous employer identification number if known.
Approximate date when filed (mo., day, year) | City and state where filed | Previous EIN

Under penalties of perjury, I declare that I have examined this application, and to the best of my knowledge and belief, it is true, correct, and complete. | Business telephone number (include area code)

Fax telephone number (include area code)

Name and title (Please type or print clearly.) ▶

Signature ▶ Date ▶

Note: *Do not write below this line. For official use only.*

Please leave blank ▶	Geo.	Ind.	Class	Size	Reason for applying

For Paperwork Reduction Act Notice, see page 4. | Cat. No. 16055N | Form **SS-4** (Rev. 2-98)

FORM 6.5.

IRS Form SS-4, Application for Employer Identification Number

Continuation of Partnership after Dissolution

Once a partnership dissolves, the remaining partners are stripped of their authority to act on behalf of the partnership, except for purposes of **winding up** the partnership. Because of the obvious difficulties this creates for partners who desire and need to continue the partnership business, the U.P.A. provides that a business may continue if (1) the dissolution was wrongful or (2) the partnership agreement provides for the continuation of the partnership.[18]

Wrongful Dissolution

If a partner is expelled from the partnership for improper conduct or withdraws from the partnership in violation of the partnership agreement, the resulting dissolution of the partnership is wrongful. To protect the remaining partners from the losses that could result from winding up the business, the U.P.A. authorizes the remaining partners to continue the business without liquidating the assets. However, in electing to continue the business, the remaining partners must compensate the expelled partner for his or her interest in the partnership.

Partnership Agreement

The partnership agreement can circumvent the automatic termination of the partnership business by authorizing the continuation of the business upon the retirement, withdrawal, death, disability, or bankruptcy of one or more of the partners. Such a provision must provide that the withdrawing partner or his or her representative will receive the value of the partner's interest in the partnership, determined as of the date of the dissolution. The agreement should provide the method of determining the value of the withdrawing partner's interest.

Once again, the importance of a comprehensive partnership agreement is evident. Without foresight of the potential issues that a partnership might face, partners can suffer tremendous business and personal financial losses.

Deferred Dissolution

Although a partnership agreement authorizing the continuation of the partnership is ideal, in the absence of such an agreement, the R.U.P.A. provides for a **deferred dissolution** of the partnership. This is a ninety-day grace period, during which the partnership business continues and the withdrawing partner has the option of waiving the right to have the partnership business wound up. If the partner does not elect to waive this right, the partnership is automatically terminated after the ninety-day period. Regardless of whether the partnership is dissolved after the deferred dissolution period, the withdrawing partner is entitled to compensation for the value of his or her partnership interest. While the R.U.P.A. attempts to provide for a smooth transitory period, the grace period gives the withdrawing partner tremendous power to negotiate a high price for his or her partnership interest in exchange for waiving the right to formally terminate the partnership (thus, terminating or at least interrupting what may be, for the other partners, their only source of income).

Winding Up

After a partnership is dissolved, the partnership must be wound up, unless the partnership agreement provides otherwise. The remaining partners have the authority necessary to terminate the business of the partnership; this authority includes completing existing partnership contracts, collecting obligations due to the partnership, settling the accounts of the partnership, and **liquidating** its assets. After the partnership assets are liquidated, the funds are used to pay the partnership's liabilities and, if any funds remain, the individual partners receive distributions of their capital contributions or share of profits.

The liquidated proceeds of the partnership are paid in the following order of priority: (1) obligations of the partnership owed to creditors who are not partners, (2) loans or advances made to the partnership by individual partners, (3) reimbursements to partners

Winding up The process of liquidating assets, paying debts, and distributing surplus to partners.

Deferred dissolution Ninety-day grace period allowing partnership business to continue when a partner withdraws.

Liquidation Process of turning assets into cash ("liquid assets").

for capital contributions (contributions of working capital made by the partner to the partnership), and (4) distributions to partners, which are generally based upon the partners' respective contributions to capital or upon the partnership agreement.[19] Once the partnership assets are distributed, the partnership is wound up and ceases to exist.

PARTNERSHIP AGREEMENT

Throughout the discussion of general partnerships, the paramount importance of a partnership agreement has been a recurring theme. Although a partnership can be formed by an oral or implied agreement, it is advisable for the business associates to have a **partnership agreement,** also known as the *articles of partnership.* A partnership agreement should be specifically tailored to the particular business enterprise and should address, at a minimum, the partnership purpose, the relative contributions of the partners and their ownership interests in partnership property, the distribution of profits and losses, management responsibilities, compensation of partners, partnership accounting procedures, methods of dispute resolution, personal liability of partners, dissolution procedures and valuations (including valuation of partnership assets and purchase of partnership interests), and the term of the partnership agreement.

Partnership agreement A contract among partners that addresses the rights, duties, and interests of the partners and governs the operation of the partnership; also known as the *articles of partnership.*

A partnership agreement must be designed specifically for each partnership and its business enterprise. In preparing a partnership agreement, it is beneficial to refer to legal form books such as *American Jurisprudence,* state legal forms, statutory provisions (in order to include statutorily required language), and any other form books offered at the local law library. A combination of sources will provide the best and most comprehensive listing of issues to consider in preparing an agreement. A sample partnership agreement is offered in Appendix C. Of course, all standard forms must be modified to conform to the needs of each partnership. In addition to standard forms, potential problems of a partnership must be brainstormed and addressed in the partnership agreement.

Although a form partnership agreement cannot address all of the needs of an individual partnership, the following checklist illustrates basic provisions that all partnership agreements should contain:

1. *Statement* of partnership agreement.
2. *Date* of partnership agreement.
3. *Names and addresses* of partners.

Example:
Partnership Agreement
This partnership agreement is entered into on this 4th day of October, 1996, by and between George Washington, of 33 Cherry Lane, Hamilton, Montana, and Harold Moosman, of 445 Bitterroot Way, Stevensville, Montana (hereinafter referred to as "partners") for the purpose of setting forth the organizational requirements of Business Breather, a partnership.

These elements can generally be combined in an introductory paragraph:
4. *Name of partnership.*
5. *Purpose of partnership.* In addition to setting forth the specific purposes of the partnership, this section often sets forth a statement that the business may engage in any lawful purpose. This allows the partners to expand their business to include other areas of interest. However, the partners' authority to develop additional business enterprises not associated with the initial ordinary course of business, should be limited by a provision that permits expansion of the partnership's activities only upon the written consent of all or a majority of partners. Although it is common to have an expansive purpose clause, this provision may also be seen as granting partners the expansive authority to act for or on behalf of the business. The disadvantages of the potential liability which could be incurred by a partner unilaterally expanding the partnership business should be weighed against the advantage of allowing reasonable business growth.

6. *Principal place of business,* expressly allowing the establishment of additional offices/distributors.
7. *Term of partnership.*

These particulars set forth general organizational provisions for the partnership.

Example:

Organization

The partnership shall be organized on the following basis:
1. **Name.** The name of the partnership shall be Business Breather.
2. **Purpose.** The partnership shall be formed for the purpose of manufacturing spas and accessories and any other lawful purpose mutually agreed upon in writing by the partners.
3. **Place of business.** The principal place of business of Business Breather shall be 113 Spa Lane, Stevensville, Montana, with independent distributors throughout the state of Montana, as agreed by the partners.
4. **Termination.** This partnership agreement shall govern the relationship of the partners and the partnership business until such time as it is terminated by written notice of one or more of the partners.

---

8. *Partners' capital contributions.* Specify in detail the partners' capital contribution, including the value of noncash contributions (e.g., property or services). If each partner's share of the profits of the partnership will be based upon the percentage of his or her capital contributions, this should be noted.
9. *Additional capital contributions.* Provision should be made for additional capital contributions should this be necessary at any time for the continued operation of the partnership business. The terms under which additional contributions must be made should be specified.
10. *Partners' compensation,* if any.

Example:

Financial Considerations

1. **Capital contributions.** Each partner's capital contribution to the partnership is as follows:
   Partner A   Cash, $4,000
   Partner B   Spas with a fair market value of $3,000
   Partner C   Managerial experience
2. **Reservation of profits for partnership capital.** Before partners receives their proportionate share of the partnership profits, 25 percent of all partnership profits will be reserved by the partnership as working capital. These amounts will be held in a separate account in the name of the partnership. Each partner will be allocated his or her pro rata share of all profits reserved in the event a distribution of capital is made upon the termination of the partnership.
3. **Additional capital contributions.** In the event that the partnership business is operating at a loss, the partners may determine by majority vote whether additional capital contributions will be required to be made by the partners. In such event, the partnership will determine the minimum amount of additional capital needed to maintain the business's operations and will require each partner to make an additional contribution based upon the percentage of partnership profits allocated to the partner, as set forth *supra* at para 1. If a partner does not provide his or her pro rata share of the necessary additional capital, the partner's proportionate share of the partnership profits will be reallocated based upon each partner's total capital investment
4. **Profit sharing.** Partner A and Partner B will each be entitled to 35 percent of all partnership profits. Partner C will be entitled to 30 percent of all partnership profit. No partner shall be entitled to remuneration for service rendered to the partnership other than his or her distributive share of the partnership profits.

11. *Accounting procedures.* The accounting procedures of the partnership should be set forth. Most partnerships will either have an in-house bookkeeper or certified public accountant who should be consulted to establish the firm's accounting procedures (fiscal year, method of accounting, etc.).

12. *Partnership books.* The location of the partnership's books should be provided. Typically, this is the partnership's office or its accountant's.

13. *Partnership bank.* The name and location of the partnership's bank should be specified.

14. *Financial officers.* The partner(s) authorized to transact the financial business of the partnership should be identified. The specific transactions each partner is authorized for should be specified (issue/sign checks, deposit and/or withdraw funds, apply for and receive partnership credit/loans). It is advisable for all partners to be notified of any loans or credit lines that are extended to the partnership; this can be accomplished by requiring the consent of all partners for such transactions.

15. *Financial reports.* In order to avoid fraud on the partners or on the partnership, the agreement should require that periodic financial reports of the partnership be issued to each partner. The reports should at least include a list of the partnership capital, assets, liabilities to third parties and partners, credit lines, and loans.

Example:

Accounting Procedures

1. **Fiscal year.** The fiscal year of the partnership shall be the calendar year.
2. **Financial records.** The partnership's financial books will be maintained at the partnership's principal place of business.
3. **Banking/deposit accounts.** All funds and accounts of the partnership shall be held on deposit with First Interstate Bank, 101 East Front St., Missoula, Montana. All partners are authorized to make deposits for and on behalf of the partnership.
4. The signatures of two partners are required for all checks issued by the partnership.
5. **Loans.** The consent of all partners is necessary for the partnership to receive a loan or line of credit.
6. **Financial report.** A financial report of the partnership capital, assets, liabilities, loans, and credit lines will be issued to each partner semiannually. The first report shall be due January 15th of each year and the second shall be issued to the partners no later than June 15th of each year.

---

16. *Management authority.* The management responsibilities of the partners should be set forth. In small partnerships, it is feasible for all partners to participate in the management of the partnership business. However, partnerships of four of more should consider allocating management responsibilities between the partners. If responsibilities are allocated, the duties of each partner should be listed (financial record keeping, marketing, property acquisition, etc.).

17. *Partnership meetings.* Partnership meetings should be scheduled on a regular basis as stated in the agreement. The agreement should also provide for special meetings to consider extraordinary or urgent matters.

18. *Partner duties.* The rights and duties of each partner should be specified. The agreement should provide that partners are authorized to perform all acts necessary to perform their duties. The agreement should recite that the respective authority of the partners will be set forth in a statement of partnership authority, to be filed with the appropriate state and/or local agency. This provision should also provide that if a partner acts without authority and improperly binds the partnership to an obligation which must be satisfied by the partnership or the individual partners, the non-culpable partners shall have the right to seek indemnification from the personal assets of the unauthorized partner for their losses as well as those suffered by the partnership.

19. *Fiduciary duties.* Partners' fiduciary duties should be addressed. Although statutory standards are imposed on the partners, they do not, in themselves, provide the part-

nership sufficient safeguards against improper or negligent acts by a partner (e.g., partners are not statutorily required to use ordinary and reasonable care and are liable only for "gross negligence"). At the very least, it is advisable to require all partners to act with reasonable care in the performance of their duties.

Example:

Management and Business Operations

1. **Management.** All partners shall have the right to participate in management decisions of the partnership equally. Each partner shall have one vote on management decisions, and decisions shall be made by majority vote.
2. **Partnership meetings.** All partners shall meet on the first Monday of each month at 2:00 P.M. at the partnership's offices for the purpose of addressing partnership matters including operations.
3. **Partners' duties.**
   a. Partner A shall be responsible for marketing all products of Business Breather, including but not limited to contracting for the sale of products to third parties.
   b. Partner B shall be responsible for the research and development as well as production of all partnership products. Partner B may delegate this responsibility to others, including hiring employees to complete development and/or production.
   c. Partner C shall be responsible for maintaining the financial records of the partnership and issuing the requisite semiannual partnership reports. Partner C may delegate this responsibility to a third party approved by the partnership.
4. **Authority and indemnification.** Each partner shall have the authority to perform all acts necessary or incident to the performance of that partner's enumerated partnership duties. If a partner, acting outside of the scope of his or her authority, incurs an obligation due by the partnership, the other partners shall have the right to seek indemnification from the personal assets of the unauthorized partner for the losses which the partnership or the innocent partners incur as a result of the improper acts.
5. **Statement of partnership authority.** The authority granted to each partner by the provisions of this agreement shall be set forth in a statement of partnership authority, to be filed with the secretary of state.
6. **Duty of care.** Partners shall use ordinary and reasonable care in the performance of their duties and shall be liable to the partnership for their failure to do so.
7. **Duty of loyalty.** No partner shall gain a personal benefit, including appropriating a business opportunity, from the partnership, directly or indirectly, without the express written consent of the other partners.

---

20. *Changes in partnership.* Provision should be made for changes in the partnership association, including the sale of a partner's interest, the admission of a new partner, withdrawal of a partner, retirement of a partner, death of a partner, and other conditions under which the partnership would dissolve.
21. *Right of first refusal.* In the event of an intended sale of a partner's interest in the partnership, the partnership should reserve the right to purchase the partner's interest.
22. *Valuation of partnership interests.* A valuation should be placed upon a withdrawing partner's interest in the partnership, including reimbursement for the partner's capital contributions as well as a proportionate share of the partnership's goodwill. The agreement should specify that the valuation of a partner's interest shall apply in the event of the voluntary withdrawal, retirement, expulsion, bankruptcy, disability, death of a partner, or other conditions resulting in the voluntary and involuntary withdrawal of a partner.
23. *Continuation of partnership after dissolution.* The business should be expressly permitted to continue after the dissolution of a partnership, and all partners should be given the authority to continue to transact business after a dissolution.
24. *Winding up procedures and distribution of assets.* The agreement should authorize the remaining partners to dissolve the partnership and complete those tasks necessary to wind up the business. A separate provision should address how assets and/or liabilities will be distributed or assessed.

Example:

Dissolution and Winding Up

1. **Dissolution.**
   a. **Withdrawal.** A partner shall be permitted to withdraw from the partnership at any time. However, in the event the partnership suffers losses as a direct result of a partner's withdrawal, the withdrawing partner shall be liable for all damages caused thereby.
   b. **Expulsion.** A partner shall be expelled from the partnership if he or she knowingly and intentionally violates any provision of this agreement, including but not limited to the duties of loyalty and care.
   c. **Court decree.** A court may, upon motion of a partner, dissolve the partnership if conditions exist which make it impractical to continue the partnership business.
2. **Sale of partnership interest.** In the event one or more partners intends to sell or otherwise transfer his or her partnership interest, the partnership shall be given the right of first refusal to purchase the interest. If the partnership does not elect to purchase the withdrawing partner's interest, each partner shall individually be offered the opportunity to purchase the interest, or a portion thereof. If an election to purchase is made either by the partnership or an individual partner, the interest shall be purchased pursuant to the valuation provisions of this agreement.
3. **Valuation of partnership interest.** In the event of the voluntary withdrawal, retirement, expulsion, bankruptcy, disability, death of a partner, or other conditions resulting in the withdrawal of one or more partners from the partnership, or the sale of a partner's partnership interest, the withdrawing partner's interest may be purchased by the partnership or an individual partner. In such event, the withdrawing partner shall be paid the following as consideration for his or her interest in the partnership:
   a. return of the withdrawing partner's capital contributions,
   b. payment of the withdrawing partner's proportionate share of undistributed profits not held in reserve accounts pursuant to this agreement,
   c. $2,500 for the withdrawing partner's portion of the goodwill of the partnership business, and
   d. two percent of all net profits earned by the partnership for the four years immediately preceding the voluntary or involuntary withdrawal of the partner from the partnership.
4. **Admission of new partners.** The admission of new partners into the partnership shall be permitted upon a two-thirds vote of the partners. A new partnership agreement or an addendum hereto, shall be executed prior to the new partner's admission. The new agreement or addendum shall set forth the capital contributions of the new partner, his or her interest in the partnership as well as the relative interests of the other partners, and the new partner's rights and duties in the partnership business.
5. **Continuation of partnership business.** In the event of the dissolution of the partnership, the partners may determine based upon a two-thirds vote to continue the partnership business until such time as a new partnership is formed. If such an election is made, the partners shall continue to have all authority necessary for the operation of the partnership business, as specifically set forth herein or as otherwise required to maintain the ordinary course of business.
6. **Winding up.**
   a. **Authorized acts.** In the event the partners determine, by two-thirds vote, to dissolve the partnership upon the voluntary or involuntary withdrawal of one or more of the partners, each partner shall be authorized to do the following:
      (1) complete or authorize completion of all existing partnership contracts,
      (2) liquidate all business assets,
      (3) pay all obligations of the partnership due to creditors or other third parties,
      (4) make distributions of any remaining funds to partners as reimbursement for their respective capital contributions, and
      (5) pay all remaining proceeds to partners based upon their proportionate partnership interests.
   b. **Distribution of pro rata assets.** If the partnership assets/funds are not sufficient to make payment of all or a portion of the listed distributions, the assets/funds will first be used to satisfy creditors' claims in full, then applied to reimburse partners for their capital contributions, and then distributed to the partners based upon their respective partnership interests. In the event the assets cannot pay each class listed, the remaining assets shall be prorated among the first class which cannot be paid in full.

25. *Dates and signatures.* The partnership agreement must be dated and signed by all partners.

Example:

This partnership agreement is entered into this _____ day of November, 1996, by the undersigned.

_____   _____

Partner A   Partner B

The foregoing checklist offers a skeletal outline of basic provisions which should be included in partnership agreements. This list is by no means exhaustive and additional references must be consulted during the drafting of any partnership agreement. In addition, you must consider and address potential problems which will be unique to your partnership clients. Be careful and be thorough in drafting the agreement; failure to prepare a comprehensive agreement can be financially devastating to partnerships and their partners.

◆ GENERAL PARTNERSHIPS IN REVIEW

Definition

An association of two or more persons (individuals, corporations, other partnerships, business trusts, estates, government entities, or other associations) carrying on business as co-owners for profit.

Advantages

♦ Simplicity of organization
♦ Flexibility of management

Disadvantages

♦ Unlimited personal liability of partners
♦ Involuntary termination upon the death, withdrawal, or bankruptcy of one or more partners, absent agreement for continuation

Key Considerations of the Paralegal:
Formation Procedures

1. File assumed business name/trade name with the secretary of state.
2. File notice of partnership association (if required).
3. Contact state and local licensing divisions to determine required licenses and permits.
4. If goods will be sold through the partnership business, apply for a sales tax permit from the state and local revenue agencies.
5. Apply for a tax identification number with the IRS (Form SS-4) and, if required, with the state revenue department.
6. If the partnership intends to hire employees:
   a. contact the IRS to establish employee withholding procedures, and
   b. contact appropriate state agencies to make arrangements for premium payments for unemployment and workers' compensation.
7. Draft a comprehensive partnership agreement.
8. File a statement of partnership authority with the secretary of state.

◆ KEY TERMS

foreign jurisdiction	statement of partnership authority	joint and several liability
foreign partnership	fiduciaries	joint liability

exhaustion rule

torts

partnership capital

capital contribution

tenancy in partnership

assignment of interest

attach

dissolution

winding up

deferred dissolution

liquidation

partnership agreement

◆ STUDY QUESTIONS IN REVIEW

1. What formalities are required to form a general partnership?
2. Are general partnerships required to register an assumed business name with the secretary of state?
3. What is the effect of failing to register an assumed business name with the secretary of state?
4. What is agency?
5. Distinguish between the apparent authority of a partner and the actual authority of a partner.
6. How can a partnership limit the seemingly unlimited apparent authority of its partners?
7. What is actual authority and how is it granted?
8. Who has management rights in a general partnership?
9. What are the fiduciary duties imposed on partners?
10. Are partners personally liable for the debts and obligations of the partnership?
11. What is the exhaustion rule?
12. What are capital investments and why are they necessary for partnerships?
13. Can a partner withdraw his or her capital investments at any time?
14. How are partnerships taxed?
15. How does a partnership terminate?

◆ CASE STUDIES IN REVIEW

1. Cary, Kent, and Dean are partners of *Flywings,* a small aircraft charter service. They are all pilots and each contributed their personal plane to the partnership when they first started it. Their comprehensive partnership agreement prevents any one of them from purchasing a plane for the partnership without the consent of the other partners. Kent believes that the partners need a new plane to polish their image; Cary and Dean disagree. Nonetheless, Kent buys an upgraded plane from another charter company that is in bankruptcy. When Cary and Dean find out about the purchase, they are both very upset. They tell Kent that the partnership will not make the payments on the plane and tell him that he will be personally responsible for any obligations under the purchase contract. Kent tells them that the partnership is stuck with the plane and that he is not going to be stuck with the payments. Cary and Dean ask your advising attorney for legal advice. What would be your initial response to your attorney regarding Cary and Dean's rights?

2. Shane, Stetson, and Kilee own a cattle ranch in Montana. Shane's parents own an adjoining cattle ranch, which Shane will inherit on his parents' death. The partners want to expand the partnership's ranch. Shane learns that a neighbor wants to sell 500 acres; one-half of the acreage adjoins the partnership's property and one-half of it adjoins his parents' property. The neighbor is offering all 500 acres for $250,000. Shane, who still helps his father out with the ranch and earns 20 percent of the earnings from his parents' ranch, wants his parents to buy the property. He does not tell Stetson or Kilee that the neighbor is offering the property for sale. Has Shane violated his fiduciary duty to the partnership? Explain.

3. Mary and Bill own Mystic Mountain Retreat and operate it as a partnership. At the beginning of their partnership, Mary contributed the property and buildings for the retreat. Bill came to the partnership with eighteen years of hotel management experience, but he did not contribute any money or property to the venture. A friend of Mary's told her that she and Bill should have a partnership agreement to make sure that all of her contributions (i.e., property) return to her if the partnership is dissolved. Her friend also told her that since she contributed all of the assets of the partnership, she should get more than half of the earnings. Mary visits your office and asks the attorney you work with to make sure that the property that she contributed to the partnership remains hers if the partnership dissolves. She would also like to know if she is entitled to ask for more than 50 percent of the partnership's income based on her initial contributions. What opinion would you give your advising attorney regarding Mary's situation? How would you protect her property and insure that she will receive more than 50 percent of the partnership's income?

◆ PROJECT APPLICATIONS

Studio Records is operated as a general partnership by Marie and Kent. The two began Studio Records in 1997 to help lesser-known artists to have a recording of their work. Throughout their partnership, they have had issues arise which could have destroyed their professional relationship because they did not have a partnership agreement, which would have addressed many of the issues that have arisen. They ask your law firm to draft a partnership agreement; the task is assigned to you. You have been given minimal information for your task. The firm's file provides the following information:

Marie Call
728 Roomie Drive
Los Angeles, CA 91340
(310) 471-3588

Kent Earl
285 Laurie Drive
Woodland Hills, Ca 91306
(818) 509-1134

TO: File
FROM: Karen Black
DATE: February 14, 1999
RE: Call/Earl Partnership

Met with client, Marie Call, on this date. She and Kent Earl began a computer consulting business January 28, 1998, in Ms. Call's home office. Both Ms. Call and Mr. Earl are computer programmers who worked for IBM; they have extensive programming experience and have built their small business rapidly. Their partnership now earns $100,000.00 per year.

When they started their business, Ms. Call agreed to provide the office space rather than having to spend $2,000 a month for office space. She also provided most of the computer equipment, although Mr. Call intended to use their own personal laptop for his work. The two agreed that regardless of their respective contributions to the partnership, they would share partnership profits equally, but would keep 14 percent of the net income in reserve at their bank, First Interstate, 500 Capital Highway, Los Angeles, CA 91340. They do their own accounting and have never had a professional accountant.

They intend to continue their business, but as it expands, they want to solidify their business relationship and have asked the firm to prepare a partnership agreement.

First draft has been assigned to a paralegal of the firm.

1. Contact your secretary of state to determine if general partnerships are required to be registered. If your state requires registration, obtain the necessary forms and complete them for the above partnership.
2. Obtain and complete the forms required by your secretary of state for registration of an assumed business name/trade name for the above described partnership.
3. Draft a partnership agreement for the Call/Earl partnership based upon the above memorandum. Supply reasonable terms if sufficient information has not been provided via the above inter-office memorandum.

◆ ENDNOTES

1. See R.U.P.A. § 301(1).
2. See R.U.P.A. § 303.
3. See U.P.A. § 18(e) and R.U.P.A. § 401(f).
4. See U.P.A. § 18(h) and R.U.P.A. § 401(j).
5. See U.P.A. § 9(3).
6. R.U.P.A. § 404.
7. Ibid.
8. Ibid.
9. Ibid.
10. Ibid.
11. See *Black's Law Dictionary* 623 (5th ed. 1979).
12. See R.U.P.A. § 307(d).
13. See also R.U.P.A. § 20.
14. See U.P.A. § 25.
15. See R.U.P.A. § 203.
16. See U.P.A. § 29.
17. See R.U.P.A. § 701.
18. See U.P.A. § 38(1).
19. See U.P.A. § 50. The R.U.P.A. varies the distribution priority slightly, essentially by omitting the distinctions between third-party creditors and partner creditors. See R.U.P.A. § 808.

CHAPTER 7

Limited Partnership: Managers and Investors Working Together

Limited partnerships are designed to protect investors from personal liability for the obligations of a partnership business, thereby encouraging investments in business ventures. This form of partnership recognizes that although many businesses require financial investments from several sources, investors do not want to bear any risk beyond their investments. In order to protect investors from personal liability, limited partnerships separate partners into two categories based on their rights and responsibilities: (1) general partners, who manage the partnership and are personally liable for the obligations of the partnership and (2) limited partners, who invest in the partnership business but have no right to participate in management and have no personal responsibility for partnership debts. The rights and duties of general partners are governed by all of the provisions and regulations of general partnerships. Limited partners, however, are governed by separate provisions that restrict their participation rights and limit their liabilities.

Most state laws on limited partnerships are governed by the Uniform Limited Partnership Act of 1916 (U.L.P.A.) or the Revised Uniform Limited Partnership Act of 1976 (R.U.L.P.A., hereafter referred to as the Revised Act) with 1985 amendments. (See Appendix D.) The Revised Act made several substantive changes to the U.L.P.A. and has been adopted by most states. However, not all states have adopted the 1985 amendments which clarify the rights and obligations of limited partners; nonetheless, because they "modernize" partnership law, the amendments will undoubtedly be considered in some form by all states in the future.

Limited partnerships are particularly suitable for businesses that require substantial investment backing, such as real estate. However, in order for investors to receive the liability protections that can be afforded by limited partnerships, the partnership must comply with the statutory requirements for formation and operation of a limited partnership. Only if these are satisfied, may a limited partnership provide investors protection from personal liability.

LIMITED PARTNERSHIP STATUS

Limited partners are merely investors in a partnership. They have no management rights and their liability for partnership obligations is limited to their investment in the partnership, the value of which should be set forth in the partnership agreement. The Revised Act provides that if limited partners participate in the control of the partnership business, they lose their limited liability and become personally liable for the debts and other obligations of the partnership.[1]

Traditionally, limited partners were permitted to contribute only cash and property to their partnership business; no contribution of services was allowed.[2] This limitation was intended to prevent limited partners from participating in the management of the partnership business. However, the Revised Act recognizes that limited partners may contribute services to the partnership business without participating in management or control of the business.[3] Under the Revised Act, the following activities will not jeopardize a limited partner's liability protections: (1) acting as an employee, agent, or contractor of the limited partnership or as an officer, director, or shareholder of a general partner that is a corporation; (2) acting as a consultant to the partnership or its general partners; (3) acting as a surety, guarantor, or endorser of the limited partnership's obligations; (4) calling or participating in meetings of the partners; (5) voting, proposing, approving, or disapproving matters effecting a change in the partnership association or business; (6) winding up the limited partnership; (7) bringing a derivative action (a lawsuit filed by a partner on behalf of the limited partnership to recover damages for the partnership); or (8) serving on a committee of the limited partnership. Despite these exceptions, limited partners must always be cautious to avoid the appearance of management participation. Failure to do so will result in a loss of their protected status.

FORMATION

As with general partnerships, limited partners may be natural persons, partnerships, limited partnerships, corporations, trusts, estates, or other associations.[4] Limited partnerships are formed in much the same way as general partnerships and must do the following:

♦ Register an assumed business name/trade name
♦ File a notice of partnership association, if required by state law
♦ Obtain the required business and/or professional licenses and permits
♦ Draft a comprehensive partnership agreement
♦ Investigate taxation considerations
♦ Apply for a sales tax permit, if goods will be sold
♦ Apply for a tax identification number with the IRS and/or state
♦ Establish employee withholding as well as unemployment and workers' compensation coverage

In addition to these basic partnership formation requirements, a limited partnership must also do the following:

♦ Make sure that the partnership name includes the designation "limited partnership"
♦ File a certificate of limited partnership with the secretary of state and, if required, the appropriate local (county) agency
♦ Include provisions addressing the nature of the limited partnership in the partnership agreement (e.g., specifying the general versus limited partners)
[*Note:* Limited partnerships are not required to have written partnership agreements; however, they should always be recommended to the client.]

Only if these provisions are complied with, will a limited partnership, with its attendant advantages, be created. It is important to make sure that associations seeking to form a limited partnership conform to the state and local statutory provisions.

Limited Partnership Name

The name of a limited partnership must contain the words *limited partnership,* without abbreviation.[5] The limited partnership designation notifies third parties who deal with the partnership (e.g., vendors, advertisers, creditors) that not all of the partners will be personally liable for obligations incurred by the partnership. This is particularly important to those who extend credit to the partnership, often in reliance on the credit of individual partners.

In addition to the limited partnership designation, the name of the limited partnership may not contain the surname of a limited partner unless (1) a general partner has the same name and (2) the partnership had carried on under the limited partner's name before he or she became a limited partner (e.g., a general partner becomes a limited partner). If a limited partner's name is included in the limited partnership name, the named partner may lose limited liability for obligations of the partnership. These restrictions are intended to prevent limited partners from having the apparent authority to act on behalf of the partnership.

Example:

1. The limited partnership Kipp, Flint, and Holt, Limited Partnership, has as its general partners: Cathy Kipp, Margaret Flint, and Vena Holt; its limited partners are Don Kipp, Dean Roy, and Betty Ken. This limited partnership name is permissible although a limited partner's surname is used in the partnership name because it is also the name of a general partner.

2. In the preceding example, Vena Holt withdraws as a general partner and becomes a limited partner. Her name may remain in the limited partnership's name in order to maintain the name recognition of the partnership's business.

Although most states impose these basic requirements and restrictions on partnership names, you must review the applicable state statutes to determine if these general provisions, or others, must be complied with before the limited partnership may register its name and business. Once the limited partnership complies with the statutory name requirements, it may then file a certificate of limited partnership with the secretary of state, thus creating its limited partnership status.

Certificate of Limited Partnership

A **certificate of limited partnership** must be filed with the secretary of state for limited partners to have protection from personal liability. This provides the state as well as the general public with information about the partnership and its partners. It has also traditionally served as a basic partnership agreement for the partners by defining their respective financial interests and participatory rights.

> **Certificate of limited partnership** Document filed with the secretary of state registering for limited partnership status.

The U.L.P.A. requires the partnership to provide substantial information about the partnership and its business in order to receive the designation of a limited partnership.[6] The Revised Act greatly simplifies the requirements for a certificate of limited partnership.[7]

Most states have adopted a combination of the U.L.P.A. and the Revised Act. The requirements for each state vary and the state statutes must be consulted before preparing the certificate. The secretary of state may provide a form for filing the certificate of limited partnership; if so, this should serve as the basis for a partnership's filing. (See Form 7.1, *Certificate of Limited Partnership.*) Once the certificate of limited partnership is filed, the limited liability of limited partners is established. At this point, the world has been put on notice of the limited partnership status and the corresponding limited liability which partners may have.

Requirements for Certificate of Limited Partnership
Uniform Limited Partnership Act

1. The name of the limited partnership
2. The type of business
3. The address of the principal place of business
4. The name and residence address of the partners, with general and limited partners appropriately designated
5. The term of the partnership
6. The contributions of the limited partners, including the amount of cash contributed or a description and agreed value of noncash property (land, computers, etc.) contributed by limited partners
7. Additional contributions to be made by the limited partners, including the time at which such contributions are to be made
8. When the limited partners' contributions will be returned
9. The share of profits or other compensation which the limited partners are to receive for their investment

State of California
Secretary of State

CERTIFICATE OF LIMITED PARTNERSHIP

A $70.00 filing fee must accompany this form.
IMPORTANT— Read instructions before completing this form

This Space For Filing Use Only

1. NAME OF THE LIMITED PARTNERSHIP (END THE NAME WITH THE WORDS "LIMITED PARTNERSHIP" OR THE ABBREVIATION "L.P.")

2. STREET ADDRESS OF PRINCIPAL EXECUTIVE OFFICE   CITY AND STATE   ZIP CODE

3. STREET ADDRESS OF CALIFORNIA OFFICE WHERE RECORDS ARE KEPT   CITY   ZIP CODE
    CA

4. COMPLETE IF LIMITED PARTNERSHIP WAS FORMED PRIOR TO JULY 1, 1984 AND IS IN EXISTENCE ON THE DATE THIS CERTIFICATE IS EXECUTED.

    THE ORIGINAL LIMITED PARTNERSHIP CERTIFICATE WAS RECORDED ON _____ 19 _____ WITH THE RECORDER

    OF _____ COUNTY.   FILE OR RECORDATION NUMBER _____

5. NAME THE AGENT FOR SERVICE OF PROCESS AND CHECK THE APPROPRIATE PROVISION BELOW:

    _____ WHICH IS

    [   ] AN INDIVIDUAL RESIDING IN CALIFORNIA. PROCEED TO ITEM 6.
    [   ] A CORPORATION WHICH HAS FILED A CERTIFICATE PURSUANT TO SECTION 1505. PROCEED TO ITEM 7.

6. IF AN INDIVIDUAL, CALIFORNIA ADDRESS OF THE AGENT FOR SERVICE OF PROCESS:

    ADDRESS:

    CITY: STATE: **CA**   ZIP CODE:

7. NAMES AND ADDRESSES OF ALL GENERAL PARTNERS: (ATTACH ADDITIONAL PAGES, IF NECESSARY)

    A. NAME:

        ADDRESS:

        CITY: STATE: ZIP CODE:

    B. NAME:

        ADDRESS:

        CITY: STATE: ZIP CODE:

8. INDICATE THE NUMBER OF GENERAL PARTNERS' SIGNATURES REQUIRED FOR FILING CERTIFICATES OF AMENDMENT, RESTATEMENT, MERGER, DISSOLUTION, CONTINUATION AND CANCELLATION.

9. OTHER MATTERS TO BE INCLUDED IN THIS CERTIFICATE MAY BE SET FORTH ON SEPARATE ATTACHED PAGES AND ARE MADE A PART OF THIS CERTIFICATE BY CHECKING THIS BOX. OTHER MATTERS MAY INCLUDE THE PURPOSE OF BUSINESS OF THE LIMITED PARTNERSHIP E.G. GAMBLING ENTERPRISE.

10. TOTAL NUMBER OF PAGES ATTACHED, IF ANY:

11. I CERTIFY THAT THE STATEMENTS CONTAINED IN THIS DOCUMENT ARE TRUE AND CORRECT TO MY OWN KNOWLEDGE. I DECLARE THAT I AM THE PERSON WHO IS EXECUTING THIS INSTRUMENT, WHICH EXECUTION IS MY ACT AND DEED.

SIGNATURE	POSITION OR TITLE	PRINT NAME	DATE
SIGNATURE	POSITION OR TITLE	PRINT NAME	DATE

SEC/STATE (REV. 11/98)   FORM LP-1 – FILING FEE: $70.00
                                Approved by Secretary of State

FORM 7.1.
Certificate of Limited Partnership

10. The right, if given, of a limited partner to assign his or her interest in the partnership to another, thereby substituting the limited partner
11. The right, if given, of partners to admit additional limited partners
12. The priorities, if any, of the limited partners to contributions (profits) or compensation
13. The right of general partners to continue the business after the death, retirement, or insanity of a general partner
14. The right, if given, of limited partners to demand and receive noncash property in return for their contribution[8]

Requirements for Certificate of Limited Partnership
Revised Uniform Limited Partnership Act

1. The name of the limited partnership
2. The address of the business office and the name and address of the agent for service of process (i.e., the name of the person who should be served in the event the partnership is sued)
3. The name and business address of each general partner
4. The latest date upon which the limited partnership is to dissolve
5. Any other matters the general partners choose to include

Amendment to Limited Partnership Certificate

In the event significant information included in the certificate of limited partnership changes, or an error in the certificate is found, the partnership must file an amendment with the corrected information. The amendment must generally be approved and signed by all partners.

Application for Foreign Limited Partnerships

In the event the limited partnership conducts business in a state other than the state in which it organized (the foreign jurisdiction), the partnership must generally notify the secretary of state of the foreign jurisdiction of the intent to conduct business in its state.[9] (See Form 7.2, *Application for Registration of Foreign Limited Partnership.*) The purpose of the filing is to (1) notify the secretary of state of the partnership's intent to do business in the state, (2) allow the state to collect revenue for the privilege of allowing a foreign limited partnership to do business in the state, and (3) put third parties transacting business with the limited partnership on notice of its status.

Failure to file the appropriate application will prevent a limited partnership from bringing suit in the foreign state. However, it will not invalidate business contracts or other transactions of the partnership nor will it affect the limited liability of the limited partners.

LIABILITY

General Partners

A general partner's responsibility for obligations of the partnership is the same in limited partnerships as in general partnerships. (See "Liability" in Chapter 6.) Thus, each general partner is personally liable for all obligations of the partnership arising from contract or tort.

Limited Partners

Unlike general partners, limited partners have no personal liability for obligations of the partnership. As long as limited partners refrain from actively participating in the management of the partnership business, their responsibility for partnership obligations is limited to their capital investment in the partnership. In this sense, limited partners have much the same role as shareholders of a corporation do; they are both merely investors in the business venture.

FORM 7.2.

Application for Registration
of Foreign Limited
Partnership

**Office of the
Secretary of State**

THE STATE OF TEXAS

Corporations Section

P.O. Box 13697
Austin, Texas 78711-3697

APPLICATION FOR REGISTRATION AS A
FOREIGN LIMITED PARTNERSHIP

1. The name of the limited partnership is _____

2. A. If the name does not contain the words "Limited Partnership," "Limited" or the abbreviation "L.P." or "Ltd." as the last words or letters of its name, then the name of the limited partnership with the words or abbreviation which it elects to add for use in Texas is _____

    B. If its name is not available in Texas, then the name which the limited partnership elects to use in Texas is _____

3. It was formed under the laws of _____, on _____
                                     (jurisdiction)   (date)

4. As of the date of this filing, the foreign limited partnership validly exists as a limited partnership under the laws of the jurisdiction of its formation.

5. The nature of the business or purposes to be conducted or promoted in Texas are as follows:

    _____

6. The street address of its proposed registered office in Texas is (a P.O. Box is not sufficient)

    _____

    and the name of its proposed registered agent in Texas at such address is _____

    _____

7. The limited partnership hereby appoints the Secretary of State of Texas as its agent for service of process under the circumstances set forth in section 9.10(b) of the Texas Revised Limited Partnership Act.

TAXATION CONSIDERATIONS

"Pass-through" taxation
Business profits and losses are taxed
as the personal income of partners.

Limited partnerships have the same taxation considerations as general partnerships. (See "Taxation Considerations" in Chapter 6.) As with general partnerships, limited partnerships offer the advantage of **"pass-through" taxation,** with the profits and/or losses of the partnership passing through the partnership, which is not taxed, to the partners who are taxed individually. Although the partnership must file an informational tax return with the Internal Revenue Service (see Form 7.3, *IRS Form 1065, U.S. Partnership Return of Income*) and provide a partner with a schedule of partnership income (see Form 7.4, *IRS Form 1065, Schedule K-1, Partner's Share of Income, Credits, Deductions, etc.*), the partnership does not pay taxes on its profits and losses. Rather, partnership income is apportioned among the partners, who report their pro rata

8.   The name, the mailing address, and the street address of the business or residence of each general partner is as follows:

NAME	MAILING ADDRESS (include city, state, zip code)	STREET ADDRESS (include city, state, zip code)
_____	_____	_____
_____	_____	_____
_____	_____	_____

9.   The date on which the foreign limited partnership first transacted, or intends to transact, business in Texas is _____

_____
                                        General Partner

Form No. 306
Revised 6/96

The Office of the Secretary of State does not discriminate on the basis of race, color, national origin, sex, religion, age or disability in employment or the provision of services.

share of profits or losses as their individual income. (See Form 7.5, *IRS Form 1040, Schedule E, Supplemental Income and Loss.*)

Because of the benefits of pass-through taxation (lower individual tax rates and one-time taxation of partnership profits), many businesses choose to form limited partnerships rather than corporations, which have substantially similar organizational structures (a board of directors, with duties similar to general partners, and shareholders, who are investors similar to limited partners), but suffer double taxation.

Form **1065**	U.S. Partnership Return of Income	OMB No. 1545-0099
Department of the Treasury Internal Revenue Service	For calendar year 1999, or tax year beginning ...., 1999, and ending ...., ... ▶ See separate instructions.	**1999**

A Principal business activity	Use the IRS label. Otherwise, please print or type.	Name of partnership	D Employer identification number
B Principal product or service		Number, street, and room or suite no. If a P.O. box, see page 12 of the instructions.	E Date business started
C Business code number		City or town, state, and ZIP code	F Total assets (see page 12 of the instructions) $

G Check applicable boxes: (1) ☐ Initial return (2) ☐ Final return (3) ☐ Change in address (4) ☐ Amended return
H Check accounting method: (1) ☐ Cash (2) ☐ Accrual (3) ☐ Other (specify) ▶................................
I Number of Schedules K-1. Attach one for each person who was a partner at any time during the tax year ▶................................

Caution: *Include **only** trade or business income and expenses on lines 1a through 22 below. See the instructions for more information.*

Income

1a	Gross receipts or sales	1a		
b	Less returns and allowances	1b	1c	
2	Cost of goods sold (Schedule A, line 8)		2	
3	Gross profit. Subtract line 2 from line 1c		3	
4	Ordinary income (loss) from other partnerships, estates, and trusts *(attach schedule)*		4	
5	Net farm profit (loss) *(attach Schedule F (Form 1040))*		5	
6	Net gain (loss) from Form 4797, Part II, line 18		6	
7	Other income (loss) *(attach schedule)*		7	
8	**Total income (loss).** Combine lines 3 through 7		8	

Deductions (see page 14 of the instructions for limitations)

9	Salaries and wages (other than to partners) (less employment credits)		9	
10	Guaranteed payments to partners		10	
11	Repairs and maintenance		11	
12	Bad debts		12	
13	Rent		13	
14	Taxes and licenses		14	
15	Interest		15	
16a	Depreciation (if required, attach Form 4562)	16a		
b	Less depreciation reported on Schedule A and elsewhere on return	16b	16c	
17	Depletion **(Do not deduct oil and gas depletion.)**		17	
18	Retirement plans, etc.		18	
19	Employee benefit programs		19	
20	Other deductions *(attach schedule)*		20	
21	**Total deductions.** Add the amounts shown in the far right column for lines 9 through 20		21	
22	**Ordinary income (loss)** from trade or business activities. Subtract line 21 from line 8		22	

Please Sign Here Under penalties of perjury, I declare that I have examined this return, including accompanying schedules and statements, and to the best of my knowledge and belief, it is true, correct, and complete. Declaration of preparer (other than general partner or limited liability company member) is based on all information of which preparer has any knowledge.

▶ Signature of general partner or limited liability company member ▶ Date

| Paid Preparer's Use Only | Preparer's signature ▶ | Date | Check if self-employed ▶ ☐ | Preparer's SSN or PTIN |
| | Firm's name (or yours if self-employed) and address ▶ | | EIN ▶ ZIP code ▶ | |

For Paperwork Reduction Act Notice, see separate instructions. Cat. No. 11390Z Form **1065** (1999)

FORM 7.3.

IRS Form 1065, U.S. Partnership Return of Income

SCHEDULE K-1	Partner's Share of Income, Credits, Deductions, etc.	OMB No. 1545-0099
(Form 1065) Department of the Treasury Internal Revenue Service	► See separate instructions. For calendar year 1999 or tax year beginning , 1999, and ending ,	**1999**

Partner's identifying number ►	Partnership's identifying number ►
Partner's name, address, and ZIP code	Partnership's name, address, and ZIP code

A This partner is a ☐ general partner ☐ limited partner
☐ limited liability company member
B What type of entity is this partner? ► ....
C Is this partner a ☐ domestic or a ☐ foreign partner?
D Enter partner's percentage of:

	(i) Before change or termination	(ii) End of year
Profit sharing	.... %	.... %
Loss sharing	.... %	.... %
Ownership of capital	.... %	.... %

E IRS Center where partnership filed return:

F Partner's share of liabilities (see instructions):
Nonrecourse . . . . $ ....
Qualified nonrecourse financing . . $ ....
Other . . . . $ ....
G Tax shelter registration number . . ► ....
H Check here if this partnership is a publicly traded partnership as defined in section 469(k)(2) . . . . . . ☐
I Check applicable boxes: **(1)** ☐ Final K-1 **(2)** ☐ Amended K-1

J **Analysis of partner's capital account:**

(a) Capital account at beginning of year	(b) Capital contributed during year	(c) Partner's share of lines 3, 4, and 7, Form 1065, Schedule M-2	(d) Withdrawals and distributions	(e) Capital account at end of year (combine columns (a) through (d))
			( )	

(a) Distributive share item		(b) Amount	(c) 1040 filers enter the amount in column (b) on:
Income (Loss)	**1** Ordinary income (loss) from trade or business activities . . . **1**		⎫ See page 6 of Partner's Instructions for Schedule K-1 (Form 1065). ⎬
	2 Net income (loss) from rental real estate activities **2**		
	3 Net income (loss) from other rental activities. **3**		⎭
	4 Portfolio income (loss):		
	a Interest **4a**		Sch. B, Part I, line 1
	b Ordinary dividends **4b**		Sch. B, Part II, line 5
	c Royalties **4c**		Sch. E, Part I, line 4
	d Net short-term capital gain (loss) **4d**		Sch. D, line 5, col. (f)
	e Net long-term capital gain (loss):		
	(1) 28% rate gain (loss) . . . . **e(1)**		Sch. D, line 12, col. (g)
	(2) Total for year. . . . . **e(2)**		Sch. D, line 12, col. (f)
	f Other portfolio income (loss) *(attach schedule)* **4f**		Enter on applicable line of your return.
	5 Guaranteed payments to partner **5**		⎫ See page 6 of Partner's Instructions for Schedule K-1 (Form 1065). ⎬
	6 Net section 1231 gain (loss) (other than due to casualty or theft) . **6**		⎭
	7 Other income (loss) *(attach schedule)* **7**		Enter on applicable line of your return.
Deductions	**8** Charitable contributions (see instructions) *(attach schedule)* . . **8**		Sch. A, line 15 or 16
	9 Section 179 expense deduction **9**		⎫ See pages 7 and 8 of Partner's Instructions for Schedule K-1 (Form 1065). ⎬
	10 Deductions related to portfolio income *(attach schedule)* . . . **10**		
	11 Other deductions *(attach schedule)* **11**		⎭
Credits	**12a** Low-income housing credit:		
	(1) From section 42(j)(5) partnerships for property placed in service before 1990 **a(1)**		⎫
	(2) Other than on line 12a(1) for property placed in service before 1990 **a(2)**		
	(3) From section 42(j)(5) partnerships for property placed in service after 1989 **a(3)**		⎬ Form 8586, line 5
	(4) Other than on line 12a(3) for property placed in service after 1989 **a(4)**		⎭
	b Qualified rehabilitation expenditures related to rental real estate activities **12b**		⎫
	c Credits (other than credits shown on lines 12a and 12b) related to rental real estate activities. **12c**		⎬ See page 8 of Partner's Instructions for Schedule K-1 (Form 1065).
	d Credits related to other rental activities **12d**		
	13 Other credits **13**		⎭

For Paperwork Reduction Act Notice, see Instructions for Form 1065.   Cat. No. 11394R   **Schedule K-1 (Form 1065) 1999**

FORM 7.4.

IRS Form 1065, Schedule K-1, Partner's Share of Income, Credits, Deductions, etc.

Schedule K-1 (Form 1065) 1999   Page **2**

	(a) Distributive share item		(b) Amount	(c) 1040 filers enter the amount in column (b) on:
Investment Interest	**14a** Interest expense on investment debts	14a		Form 4952, line 1
	b (1) Investment income included on lines 4a, 4b, 4c, and 4f	b(1)		See page 9 of Partner's Instructions for Schedule K-1 (Form 1065).
	(2) Investment expenses included on line 10	b(2)		
Self-employment	**15a** Net earnings (loss) from self-employment	15a		Sch. SE, Section A or B
	b Gross farming or fishing income	15b		See page 9 of Partner's Instructions for Schedule K-1 (Form 1065).
	c Gross nonfarm income	15c		
Adjustments and Tax Preference Items	**16a** Depreciation adjustment on property placed in service after 1986	16a		
	b Adjusted gain or loss	16b		See page 9 of Partner's Instructions for Schedule K-1 (Form 1065) and Instructions for Form 6251.
	c Depletion (other than oil and gas)	16c		
	d (1) Gross income from oil, gas, and geothermal properties	d(1)		
	(2) Deductions allocable to oil, gas, and geothermal properties	d(2)		
	e Other adjustments and tax preference items (attach schedule)	16e		
Foreign Taxes	**17a** Type of income ▶			Form 1116, check boxes
	b Name of foreign country or possession ▶			
	c Total gross income from sources outside the United States (attach schedule)	17c		Form 1116, Part I
	d Total applicable deductions and losses (attach schedule)	17d		
	e Total foreign taxes (check one): ▶ ☐ Paid ☐ Accrued	17e		Form 1116, Part II
	f Reduction in taxes available for credit (attach schedule)	17f		Form 1116, Part III
	g Other foreign tax information (attach schedule)	17g		See Instructions for Form 1116.
Other	**18** Section 59(e)(2) expenditures: **a** Type ▶			See page 9 of Partner's Instructions for Schedule K-1 (Form 1065).
	b Amount	18b		
	19 Tax-exempt interest income	19		Form 1040, line 8b
	20 Other tax-exempt income	20		See pages 9 and 10 of Partner's Instructions for Schedule K-1 (Form 1065).
	21 Nondeductible expenses	21		
	22 Distributions of money (cash and marketable securities)	22		
	23 Distributions of property other than money	23		
	24 Recapture of low-income housing credit:			
	a From section 42(j)(5) partnerships	24a		Form 8611, line 8
	b Other than on line 24a	24b		

Supplemental Information

25 Supplemental information required to be reported separately to each partner (attach additional schedules if more space is needed):

....

....

....

....

....

....

....

....

....

....

....

....

....

Schedule K-1 (Form 1065) 1999

FORM 7.4. *continued*

SCHEDULE E (Form 1040)	Supplemental Income and Loss	OMB No. 1545-0074

SCHEDULE E
(Form 1040)

Department of the Treasury
Internal Revenue Service (99)

Supplemental Income and Loss

(From rental real estate, royalties, partnerships,
S corporations, estates, trusts, REMICs, etc.)

► **Attach to Form 1040 or Form 1041.** ► **See Instructions for Schedule E (Form 1040).**

OMB No. 1545-0074

1999

Attachment
Sequence No. **13**

Name(s) shown on return

Your social security number

Part I | **Income or Loss From Rental Real Estate and Royalties** Note: *Report income and expenses from your business of renting personal property on* **Schedule C** *or* **C-EZ** *(see page E-1). Report farm rental income or loss from* **Form 4835** *on page 2, line 39.*

1 Show the kind and location of each **rental real estate property:**

A ....

B ....

C ....

2 For each rental real estate property listed on line 1, did you or your family use it during the tax year for personal purposes for more than the greater of:
- 14 days, **or**
- 10% of the total days rented at fair rental value?
(See page E-1.)

	Yes	No
A		
B		
C		

	Income:		Properties			Totals (Add columns A, B, and C.)
			A	B	C	
3	Rents received	3				3
4	Royalties received	4				4
	Expenses:					
5	Advertising	5				
6	Auto and travel (see page E-2)	6				
7	Cleaning and maintenance	7				
8	Commissions	8				
9	Insurance	9				
10	Legal and other professional fees	10				
11	Management fees	11				
12	Mortgage interest paid to banks, etc. (see page E-2)	12				12
13	Other interest	13				
14	Repairs	14				
15	Supplies	15				
16	Taxes	16				
17	Utilities	17				
18	Other (list) ►	18				
19	Add lines 5 through 18	19				19
20	Depreciation expense or depletion (see page E-3)	20				20
21	Total expenses. Add lines 19 and 20	21				
22	Income or (loss) from rental real estate or royalty properties. Subtract line 21 from line 3 (rents) or line 4 (royalties). If the result is a (loss), see page E-3 to find out if you must file **Form 6198**	22				
23	Deductible rental real estate loss. **Caution:** *Your rental real estate loss on line 22 may be limited. See page E-3 to find out if you must file* **Form 8582**. *Real estate professionals must complete line 42 on page 2*	23	( )(	)(	)(	)

24	**Income.** Add positive amounts shown on line 22. **Do not** include any losses	24	
25	**Losses.** Add royalty losses from line 22 and rental real estate losses from line 23. Enter total losses here	25	( )
26	Total rental real estate and royalty income or (loss). Combine lines 24 and 25. Enter the result here. If Parts II, III, IV, and line 39 on page 2 do not apply to you, also enter this amount on Form 1040, line 17. Otherwise, include this amount in the total on line 40 on page 2	26	

For Paperwork Reduction Act Notice, see Form 1040 instructions.   Cat. No. 11344 .   **Schedule E (Form 1040) 1999**

FORM 7.5.

IRS Form 1040, Schedule E, Supplemental Income and Loss

Schedule E (Form 1040) 1999   Attachment Sequence No. **13**   Page **2**

Name(s) shown on return. Do not enter name and social security number if shown on other side.   **Your social security number**

Note: *If you report amounts from farming or fishing on Schedule E, you must enter your gross income from those activities on line 41 below. Real estate professionals must complete line 42 below.*

Part II   **Income or Loss From Partnerships and S Corporations**   **Note:** *If you report a loss from an at-risk activity, you MUST check either column (e) or (f) on line 27 to describe your investment in the activity. See page E-5. If you check column (f), you must attach* **Form 6198.**

27	(a) Name	(b) Enter P for partnership; S for S corporation	(c) Check if foreign partnership	(d) Employer identification number	Investment At Risk? (e) All is at risk	(f) Some is not at risk
A						
B						
C						
D						
E						

	Passive Income and Loss		Nonpassive Income and Loss		
	(g) Passive loss allowed (attach **Form 8582** if required)	(h) Passive income from **Schedule K–1**	(i) Nonpassive loss from **Schedule K–1**	(j) Section 179 expense deduction from **Form 4562**	(k) Nonpassive income from **Schedule K–1**
A					
B					
C					
D					
E					
28a Totals					
b Totals					

29	Add columns (h) and (k) of line 28a	29		
30	Add columns (g), (i), and (j) of line 28b	30	(	)
31	Total partnership and S corporation income or (loss). Combine lines 29 and 30. Enter the result here and include in the total on line 40 below	31		

Part III   **Income or Loss From Estates and Trusts**

32	(a) Name	(b) Employer identification number
A		
B		

	Passive Income and Loss		Nonpassive Income and Loss	
	(c) Passive deduction or loss allowed (attach **Form 8582** if required)	(d) Passive income from **Schedule K–1**	(e) Deduction or loss from **Schedule K–1**	(f) Other income from **Schedule K–1**
A				
B				
33a Totals				
b Totals				

34	Add columns (d) and (f) of line 33a	34		
35	Add columns (c) and (e) of line 33b	35	(	)
36	Total estate and trust income or (loss). Combine lines 34 and 35. Enter the result here and include in the total on line 40 below	36		

Part IV   **Income or Loss From Real Estate Mortgage Investment Conduits (REMICs)—Residual Holder**

37	(a) Name	(b) Employer identification number	(c) Excess inclusion from Schedules Q, line 2c (see page E-6)	(d) Taxable income (net loss) from Schedules Q, line 1b	(e) Income from Schedules Q, line 3b

38	Combine columns (d) and (e) only. Enter the result here and include in the total on line 40 below	38	

Part V   **Summary**

39	Net farm rental income or (loss) from **Form 4835.** Also, complete line 41 below	39	
40	**TOTAL** income or (loss). Combine lines 26, 31, 36, 38, and 39. Enter the result here and on Form 1040, line 17 ▶	40	

41	**Reconciliation of Farming and Fishing Income.** Enter your **gross** farming and fishing income reported on Form 4835, line 7; Schedule K-1 (Form 1065), line 15b; Schedule K-1 (Form 1120S), line 23; and Schedule K-1 (Form 1041), line 14 (see page E-6)	41	
42	**Reconciliation for Real Estate Professionals.** If you were a real estate professional (see page E-4), enter the net income or (loss) you reported anywhere on Form 1040 from all rental real estate activities in which you materially participated under the passive activity loss rules . .	42	

✪   **Schedule E (Form 1040) 1999**

FORM 7.5. *continued*

CHANGES IN PARTNERSHIP ASSOCIATIONS

General partners manage limited partnerships. Therefore, the admission or withdrawal of a general partner can significantly impact the operation of a limited partnership. In order to maintain harmony in the management of limited partnerships, the admission of new general partners is restricted and the withdrawal of a general partner causes the dissolution of the partnerships.

In contrast, a change in the association of limited partners has little effect on the operation of a limited partnership and its business. Limited partners are merely investors in the limited partnership's business. The admission of a new limited partner pads the partnership's coffers and is welcomed by many limited partnerships. However, the withdrawal of investors can have a negative impact on the partnership and the withdrawal of capital may be restricted by the terms of a partnership agreement.

Admission of New Partners

General Partners

General partners may be admitted to a limited partnership by unanimous written consent of all the partners or pursuant to the partnership agreement. It is particularly important for partnerships with a small number of general partners to allow for the admission of new general partners in order to allow continuity in the management of the partnership business. (See "Continuation of a Limited Partnership After Dissolution")

Limited Partners

Additional investors may be admitted into a limited partnership pursuant to the partnership agreement or by amendment of the partnership certificate.[10] This allows partnerships the opportunity to attract and absorb additional investors as their businesses expand and the need for an infusion of additional capital occurs.

Limited partners also have the right to assign their interest(s) in the partnership to third parties. If an assignment/substitution is made, the assignee third party may be admitted into the partnership by the terms of the partnership agreement or by written consent of all the partners.[11]

Withdrawal of Partners

General Partners

The withdrawal or incapacity of a general partner presumptively causes the dissolution of the partnership. The dissolution is governed by the same rights and restrictions applied in a general partnership and should be anticipated and prevented by provisions in the partnership agreement.

Limited Partners

Unlike general partners, limited partners have greater flexibility to withdraw from a limited partnership without causing a dissolution of the partnership because their withdrawal does not affect the operation and management of the partnership business.

TERMINATION OF A LIMITED PARTNERSHIP

Dissolution of a Limited Partnership

A limited partnership dissolves and must generally be wound up under the following circumstances:

♦ All partners agree, in writing, to terminate the partnership.
♦ The partnership agreement specifies the date of termination.
♦ The duration of the partnership is completed.
♦ The court orders dissolution.
♦ A general partner withdraws.

Limited partnerships do not automatically dissolve on the death, retirement, or withdrawal of a limited partner because limited partners are passive investors, not active participants in a partnership business. However, the voluntary or involuntary withdrawal of a general partner, who has participatory rights in the partnership business, can adversely affect the viability of the business; therefore, the withdrawal or incapacity of a general partner dissolves a partnership, absent an agreement to the contrary.

Continuation of a Limited Partnership after Dissolution

The Revised Act recognizes the logistical problems inherent in the automatic dissolution of a partnership and allows a limited partnership to continue upon the withdrawal or incapacity of a general partner if (1) the partnership agreement provides for the continuation of the partnership or (2) the partners agree in writing, within ninety days following the withdrawal, that the partnership will continue. Under either condition, it is, of course, essential that the partnership have one or more general partners, or can elect a general partner, who can manage the business. Similarly, the U.L.P.A. allows the continuation of the limited partnership if (1) there are remaining general partners who continue the partnership business with the consent of all the partners or (2) the right is specifically granted in the certificate of limited partnership.[12]

Winding Up

General partners have the authority to liquidate and distribute the assets of a partnership after its dissolution.[13] If all of the general partners have withdrawn or are incapacitated, limited partners may, by default, direct the winding up of the partnership business.

As with general partnerships, all of the liabilities of the partnership must be paid before the partners are entitled to any reimbursements of capital contributions or distributions. The U.L.P.A. gave limited partners priority over general partners by providing that the claims of limited partners (for reimbursements and distributions) were to be paid in full before general partners were entitled to any distribution of their partnership interests.[14] The distribution of assets to partners could, of course, be altered by the terms of the partnership agreement.

The Revised Act recognizes that both general and limited partners make capital contributions to the partnership, extend credit to the partnership, and should share in the distribution of profits. Therefore, the Revised Act provides that the liquidated assets of the partnership will be paid based upon the following priorities:

1. To creditors, including partners who are creditors
2. To all partners for amounts due, other than for contributions, under the partnership agreement
3. To all partners for return of their contributions to the partnership and then for their proportionate share of the partnership profits[15]

Once the partnership assets are distributed, the limited partnership must notify the secretary of state of the termination of the limited partnership by filing a Notice of Cancellation of Limited Partnership.

Cancellation of Certificate of Limited Partnership

Limited partnerships are creatures of statute. They are created by filing a formal notice of their existence (the certificate of limited partnership) and are terminated by canceling their limited partnership certificate. (See Form 7.6, *Application for Cancellation of Assumed Business Name or Limited Liability Partnership*.) Once this formality is complied with, the limited partnership formally terminates.

LIMITED PARTNERSHIP AGREEMENT

A comprehensive partnership agreement is essential for the successful organization, management, and operation of a limited partnership. The general partnership agreement checklist offered in Chapter 6 should serve as the basis for and be incorporated in a limited partnership agreement. In addition to the guidelines offered for a general partnership

FORM 7.6.

Application for Cancellation
of Assumed Business Name
or Limited Liability
Partnership

STATE OF MONTANA

APPLICATION *for* CANCELLATION *of*
ASSUMED BUSINESS NAME *or*
LIMITED LIABILITY
PARTNERSHIPS
(30-13-213, MCA)

MAIL:

Secretary of State
P.O. Box 202801
Helena, MT 59620-2801
PHONE: ☎(406)444-3665
FAX: (406)444-3976
WEB SITE: *www.state.mt.us/sos*

Prepare, sign and submit an ORIGINAL AND COPY with fee.
This is the minimum information required.
(This space for use by the Secretary of State only)

Form: **ABN-2**
Filing Fee: **$5.00**

☐Priority Filing Fee Add $20.00

PLEASE CHECK ONE BOX:
☐Cancellation of ABN (30-13-213, MCA) $5.00
☐Cancellation of LLP (30-13-213, MCA) $5.00

► **FIRST:** The Assumed Business Name or LLP to be canceled is _____

_____ .

► **SECOND:** The name and address of the original applicant are as follows:

Name _____

Street Address _____

Mailing Address _____

_____

► **I, HEREBY SWEAR AND AFFIRM,** under penalty of law, that the facts contained in this Application
are true.

_____
Signature of Applicant

_____
Title or Ownership Interest in Business Organization

State of _____
County of _____

Signed or attested before me on _____ (date) by [name(s) of person(s)]
_____

_____
(Signature of notarial officer)
Notary Public for the State of _____
Residing at _____
My Commission expires _____

s:\forms\abn-2
Revised: 05/27/99

---

agreement, a limited partnership agreement should contain additional provisions, including but not limited to the following:

1. *Partners' duties.* The rights and duties of general partners and limited partners should be specified.

> **Example:**
> **Management and Authority**
> 1. **General partners.** General partners shall have the sole authority to manage and operate the partnership business. [The specific duties of the general partner(s) should be set forth in detail in this provision.]
> 2. **Limited partners.** Limited partners shall not have authority to manage, operate, or act on behalf of the partnership unless such authority is delegated or granted, in writing, to a limited partner by majority vote of the general partners. However, the limited partner shall not be responsible for accepting and fulfilling any duties that would jeopardize his or her status as a limited partner.

2. *Partners' liability.* The liability of the general and limited partners should be specified.

> **Example:**
>
> **Liability**
> 1. **Priority for satisfaction of partnership obligations.** In the event debts, obligations, or other losses are due from the partnership, they shall be satisfied from the following, in the priority listed:
>   a. The interest, including capital contributions and profits, of general partners in the partnership;
>   b. The interest, including capital contributions and profits, of limited partners in the partnership. No limited partner's interest in the partnership shall be used to satisfy losses of the partnership until such time as the interest(s) of all general partner(s) have been exhausted;
>   c. All remaining liabilities shall be satisfied from the personal assets of the general partners on an equal basis.
> 2. **Personal liability.** No limited partner shall have personal liability for any obligation or loss of the partnership.

3. *Admission or substitution of partners.* The right of the general partners to admit one or more additional limited partners, or allow for the substitution of a limited partner in the event a limited partner assigns his or her interest in the partnership, should be addressed. Additional or substituted partners should be expressly bound to the terms of the limited partnership agreement and any additions or amendments thereto.

> **Example:**
>
> **Admission or Substitution of Partners**
> 1. **Admission of additional partners.** After the formation of the limited partnership pursuant to this agreement, the general partners may admit one or more additional partners if the admission is consented to in writing by a majority of the general partners.
> 2. **Substitution of partners.** In the event a limited partner assigns his or her interest in the partnership to a third party, the general partners may, by majority vote, consent to the substitution of the partner. The substitution, if allowed, would permit the substituted partner to receive the profits and/or compensation for contributions otherwise due to the assignor, including but not limited to reimbursement for capital contributions upon the termination and liquidation of the partnership.
> 3. **Binding effect of partnership agreement.** In the event of the addition or substitution of a limited partner, the limited partner shall be bound to the terms and provisions of this agreement and any additions or amendments hereto, whether or not the agreement and/or amendments were in existence prior to the partner's admission.

4. *Distribution priorities.* The priority for distribution of partnership assets in the course of winding up a limited partnership gives limited partners distribution priority over general partnerships.

> **Example:**
>
> **Distribution of Assets**
> In the event the partnership is terminated and all liabilities of the partnership have been paid to creditors and other third parties, distributions of the remaining proceeds shall be paid in the following order:
> 1. Profits due to limited partners as compensation for their respective contributions
> 2. Reimbursement to limited partners for their capital contributions
> 3. Payment of obligations due to general partners (*e.g.,* for loans to the partnership)
> 4. Profits due to general partners
> 5. Reimbursement to general partners for their capital contributions

These basic considerations should supplement the provisions of general partnerships addressed in Chapter 6. As the discussion of general partnership agreements indicates, additional resources should be consulted in drafting partnership agreements in order to address issues unique to your partnership client.

◆ LIMITED PARTNERSHIPS IN REVIEW

Definition
An association of two or more persons (individuals, corporations, other partnerships, business trusts, estates, government entities, or other associations) carrying on business as co-owners for profit with one or more general partners (managers) and one or more limited partners (investors).

Advantages
♦ Relative simplicity of organization
♦ Limited liability for investors
♦ Continuation upon withdrawal or incapacity of one or more limited partners

Disadvantages
♦ Unlimited personal liability of general (managing) partners
♦ Involuntary termination upon the death, withdrawal, or bankruptcy of one or more general partners, absent agreement for continuation

Key Considerations of the Paralegal:
Formation Procedures
1. Determine partnership name, with designation "limited partnership."
2. File assumed business name/trade name with the secretary of state.
3. File Certificate of Limited Partnership.
4. Contact state and local licensing divisions to determine required licenses and permits.
5. If goods will be sold through the partnership business, apply for a sales tax permit from the state and local revenue agencies.
6. Apply for a tax identification number with the IRS (Form SS-4) and, if required, with the state revenue department.
7. If the partnership intends to hire employees:
   a. contact the IRS to establish employee withholding procedures, and
   b. contact appropriate state agencies to make arrangements for unemployment and workers' compensation coverage.
8. Draft a comprehensive partnership agreement, including provisions addressing the nature of the limited partnership.
9. File a Statement of Partnership Authority with the secretary of state.

◆ KEY TERMS

certificate of limited partnership   "pass-through" taxation

◆ STUDY QUESTIONS IN REVIEW

1. How is a limited partnership different than a general partnership?
2. Explain the distinction between a general partner and a limited partner.
3. What is a limited partner's liability for the debts and obligations of the partnership?
4. How does a partnership notify the public of its status as a limited partnership?
5. Does a limited partnership dissolve automatically if a limited partner leaves?
6. Can a limited partnership continue if a general partner withdraws? Explain your answer.

7. What does it mean for a partnership to "wind up"?
8. Is a limited partnership required to notify the secretary of state of its termination?
9. Can a limited partnership use the same partnership agreement as a general partnership?

10. What types of businesses should consider forming limited partnerships?

◆ CASE STUDIES IN REVIEW

1. Ashley and Rebecca own a small floral shop known as Daisy's Bouquet. The shop was an instant success and a favorite of local businesses. Ashley's parents always knew that their daughter had great artistic talent, so when she asked them for the financial backing for her business, they were happy to provide it. Ashley told her parents that they would not need to be involved in the business; in exchange for their investment, she offered to pay them 25 percent of the business's monthly receipts. Ashley and Rebecca have never made any formal arrangements with Ashley's parents. Are Ashley's parents limited partners in this partnership? Explain your answer.

2. Five years ago, David and Stephen started a children's book publishing company. In order to start up their business, they needed $50,000. Although both David and Stephen had a lot of "publishing know-how," neither one had any money in the bank. David asked his best friend, a Hollywood producer, to invest in his business idea. His friend gave David the entire $50,000 to start the publishing company, on the condition that his name be listed first in the partnership's name. His friend does not have time to be involved in the operations of the business. David asks your firm, which is preparing the partnership agreement, for advice on his friend's request. What would you tell your advising attorney regarding this matter?

◆ PROJECT APPLICATION

Jason Ice and his friend Carsey Cavern want to open an ice skating rink in their hometown. Jason and Carsey own the building worth $25,000 for the ice rink but they need additional financial backing. The friends convince the owner of a local hotel and restaurant located near the ice rink that his business would increase if they opened an ice rink. The owner, Mike, agrees with Jason and Carsey and agrees to contribute the remaining $75,000 needed for the opening of the ice rink. It is to be called the Ice Cavern, located at the hottest mall in town, Southfront Mall, Carson City, (your state) 55555. The owner deposits the money into Jason and Carsey's bank, First Mountain Exchange, 789 Brooks, Missoula, (your state) 55555. They do not have an accountant to handle the books but they think that they are going to hire Carsey's sister, Barbara. In exchange for his investment, the hotel owner

wants the partnership agreement to reflect that he is to receive 35 percent of the net receipts from the rink.

Your supervising attorney has asked you to prepare the limited partnership agreement for Jason and Carsey and their silent partner, Mike. The file contains the following:

Jason Ice
987 Bitterroot Drive
Anywhere, (your state) 55555

Carsey Cavern
789 Seven Mile Road
Anywhere, (your state) 55555

Mike Restaurant
789 Road River
Anywhere, (your state) 55555

◆ ENDNOTES

1. See Revised Uniform Limited Partnership Act § 303.
2. See Uniform Limited Partnership Act § 4.
3. See R.U.L.P.A. § 501.
4. See R.U.L.P.A. § 101(11).

5. See R.U.L.P.A. § 102. Although some states allow the abbreviations L.P. or Ltd., the trend is away from this practice.
6. See U.L.P.A. § 2.

7. See R.U.L.P.A. § 201.
8. See U.L.P.A. § 2.
9. See, e.g., R.U.L.P.A. § 902.
10. See U.L.P.A. § 8 and R.U.L.P.A. § 301(a).
11. See U.L.P.A. § 19 and R.U.L.P.A. § 301(b). Under the U.L.P.A., this was known as substitution of limited partners; however, the Revised Act does not use this designation.
12. See U.L.P.A. at § 20.
13. See R.U.L.P.A. § 803.
14. See U.L.P.A. § 23.
15. See R.U.L.P.A. § 804.

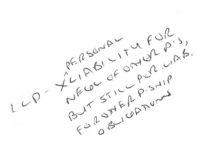

CHAPTER 8

Limited Liability Partnership: Managers without Liability

Limited liability partnerships operate like general partnerships but with the liability protections of limited partnerships. This relatively new partnership form offers all partners the right to participate in the management and the operation of a partnership business without subjecting themselves to unlimited personal liability. As a form of partnership, they offer the benefits of pass-through taxation and simplicity in organization. Because limited liability partnerships offer almost all of the benefits of the available organizational forms without the corresponding disadvantages, scholars predict that they will surface as the dominant form of organization for professionals in the future.[1]

Limited liability partnerships (LLPs) were created in Texas in 1991 and have since been adopted, or are under consideration, in a growing number of jurisdictions, including Louisiana. Because LLPs are a relatively recent form of business organization, they are created and regulated mainly by statute; few courts have had the opportunity to scrutinize their form or operation. Although LLPs are not yet recognized in all states, because of the significant advantages that they offer, more states and business owners will undoubtedly look to this organizational form as a financial haven for their businesses in the future.

LLPs are particularly attractive to professionals (lawyers, accountants, doctors, etc.), who have traditionally been limited to practicing as sole proprietors or in partnerships. Although many states now allow professionals to incorporate, thus shielding them from personal liability, most professionals are opting for the simplicity of the LLP and are attracted to the traditional "partnership" designation.

LIABILITY

The most significant disadvantage of a general partnership is that general partners are subject to personal liability for *all* obligations of their partnerships; thus, if a business cannot pay its debts, its creditors may attach a partner's personal assets (e.g., home or personal bank account). LLPs developed to provide insulation from such unlimited personal liability by providing partners protection from personal liability for the negligence or malfeasance of their partners. All partners remain personally responsible for all other obligations of their partnerships, including contractual debts and any obligations arising from their own wrongdoing. However, their personal assets are protected from attachment for the wrongful actions of their partners that they did not supervise or in which they did not participate.

LLPs were created and authorized on the assumption that the public would be protected from the negligence or malfeasance of partners by liability insurance. In order to conform to this assumption, many states require LLPs to carry liability insurance, in a statutorily prescribed amount, to cover the potential tortious acts of their partners. In lieu of liability insurance, some states allow LLPs to hold funds in trust or have a letter of credit for the statutorily required amounts.

The first statute authorizing LLPs, adopted in Texas, established the liability protections which LLP partners were provided. Texas's statutory entity protects partners from personal liability for the negligence or malfeasance of their partners unless they participated in, supervised, or had knowledge of the acts.

Under the Texas LLP statute:

A partner in a limited liability partnership is not individually liable for debts and obligations of the partnership arising from errors, omissions, negligence, incompetence, or malfeasance committed while the partnership is a registered limited liability partnership and in the course of the partnership business by another partner or representative of the partnership not working under the supervision or direction of the first partner unless the first partner: (A) was directly involved in the specific activity in which the errors, omissions, negligence, incompetence, or malfeasance were committed by the other partner or representative; or (B) had notice or knowledge of the errors, omissions, negligence, incompetence, or malfeasance by the other partner or representative at the time of occurrence and then failed to take reasonable steps to prevent or cure the errors, omissions, negligence, incompetence, or malfeasance.[2]

Some states have expanded on these personal liability protections and offer limited liability partners immunity from liability for *all* debts or other obligations of the partnership, including "tort, contract, or otherwise" unless they participated in, supervised, or had knowledge of the negligence or malfeasance. Such a statutory scheme offers partners of LLPs absolute immunity from any personal liability for the actions of their copartners as well as the contractual obligations of the partnership; however, as with most LLP statutes, it maintains partner liability for their own negligence and malfeasance and that which they supervise or control.

FORMATION

LLPs, like limited partnerships, are formed in much the same way as general partnerships. Therefore, they must do the following:

♦ Register an assumed business name/trade name
♦ File a notice of partnership association, if required by state law
♦ Obtain the required business and/or professional licenses and permits
♦ Draft a comprehensive partnership agreement
♦ Investigate tax considerations
♦ Apply for a sales tax permit, if goods will be sold
♦ Apply for a tax identification number with the Internal Revenue Service (IRS) and/or state
♦ Establish employee withholding as well as unemployment and workers' compensation coverage

Once partners comply with these general partnership provisions, they must apply for LLP status by:

♦ Including the designation "limited liability partnership" or an abbreviated form in its name
♦ Filing an application for registration of a limited liability partnership

Once the LLP is registered with the secretary of state, the LLP is formed and all partners receive the statutory liability protections.

Limited Liability Partnership Name

A limited liability partnership must have the designation "limited liability partnership" or an abbreviated form, "LLP" or "l.l.p.," in its name. If the limited liability partnership is a professional association, its name must reflect this status (e.g., "professional limited liability partnership" or "PLLP").

The classification of a partnership as an LLP notifies third parties dealing with the partnership that partners are not personally liable for the negligence of their copartners, unless they participated in, supervised, or had knowledge of the negligent acts. In states that offer LLPs immunity from *all* obligations of the partnership, the designation will put third-party creditors on notice that no partner will be personally liable for any damages occurring if the partnership breaches any duty (e.g., contractual duties). However, until the general public becomes more informed about LLPs, the designation will generally not deter creditors and other third parties who are deceptively impressed by the formal use of "LLP" in a partnership's name.

Registration of a Limited Liability Partnership

An LLP is a status of partnership. That is, business associates must first form either a general or limited partnership and then apply for registration as an LLP. The LLP is afforded its statutory liability protections only after registering for its status with the secretary of state. (See Form 8.1, *Application for Registration of Limited Liability Partnership.*)

An application for registration of an LLP generally requires the following information:

♦ Name of the LLP
♦ Description of the partnership's business
♦ Designation of the county(ies) in which business will be transacted
♦ Names and addresses of all partners
♦ Address of principal office

The LLP registration will expire after a statutorily prescribed period (e.g., five years) if it is not withdrawn or renewed by the partnership or revoked by the secretary of state (e.g., for partnership misconduct).

TAXATION CONSIDERATIONS

LLPs are taxed in the same manner as general and limited partnerships. Accordingly, the partnership is not taxed on its profits; instead, each partner is assessed his or her pro rata share of the partnership profits or losses and reports this amount as individual income. Although the partnership must file an informational tax return (see Form 8.2, *IRS Form 1065, U.S. Partnership Return of Income*) and report the partner's pro rata share of partnership profits and losses (see Form 8.3, *IRS Form 1065, Schedule K-1, Partner's Share of Income, Credits, Deductions, etc.*), the partnership, as an entity, pays no taxes on its income or losses.

Historically, the IRS ruled that entities with limited liability for all members were corporations for tax purposes; as such, they were taxed twice, once at the corporate level (since the corporation itself is a "person") and then, after the corporate profits were distributed to the shareholders, the shareholders were required to report their dividends as taxable personal income. In an attempt to determine the taxation scheme applicable to unincorporated associations, the IRS ruled that an organization would be taxed as a corporation (suffering double taxation) if it had more corporate characteristics than noncorporate characteristics. To make this assessment, the IRS identified six characteristics of a corporation:

1. Associates for profit
2. An intent to carry on business and divide the profits
3. Continuity of life
4. Centralization of management
5. Limited liability
6. Free transferability of interests

Because the first two characteristics were also shared by partnerships, the IRS determined whether an organization would be taxed as a corporation if it had at least two of the remaining four characteristics: continuity of life, centralization of management, limited liability, and/or free transferability of interests.

LLPs, like general and limited partnerships, have continuity of life (that is, they continue indefinitely) under certain circumstances; however they also offer *all* partners limited liability. Thus, LLPs have four of the six corporate characteristics (associates for profit, intent to carry on business and divide the profits, continuity of life, and limited liability), which ostensibly could make them subject to the double taxation that is imposed on a corporation.

FORM 8.1.
Application for Registration
of Limited Liability
Partnership

**Office of the
Secretary of State**

Corporations Section

P.O. Box 13697
Austin, Texas 78711-3697

APPLICATION FOR
REGISTERED LIMITED LIABILITY PARTNERSHIP

The named partnership hereby applies to become a registered limited liability partnership pursuant to section 3.08(b) of the Texas Revised Partnership Act.

1.   The name of the partnership is_____
_____
(The name must include the words "registered limited liability partnership" or the abbreviation "L.L.P." as the last words or letters of its name.)

2.   The federal tax identification number of the partnership is _____

3.   The street address of its principal office in Texas is _____

_____and the address of its

home state office if located outside of Texas is   _____

4.   The number of partners in the partnership at the date of application is:_____

5.   The partnership engages in the business specified below:
_____
_____
_____

6.   This application has been executed by a majority in interest of the partners or by one or more partners authorized by a majority in interest of the partners.

_____
Name of the partnership

By:_____

_____

_____

_____

_____

However, in 1997, the IRS eliminated the uncertainty surrounding the taxable status of LLPs by adopting what is commonly referred to as the check-the-box regulation. This relatively new approach to the tax classification of LLPs makes the analysis of the four corporate characteristics moot.

The **entity classification election** allows LLPs and other unincorporated entities, such as limited liability companies, to choose whether they will be taxed as a partnership or a corporation literally by checking a box declaring their taxable status. (See Form 8.4, *IRS Form 8832, Entity Classification Election.*) If a business does not formally declare its taxable status, the IRS will, by default, generally classify an unincorporated business as a partnership for tax purposes if it has two or more members.

Entity classification election
Allows unincorporated entities to elect to be taxed as a partnership or a corporation.

Form 1065

Department of the Treasury
Internal Revenue Service

U.S. Partnership Return of Income

For calendar year 1999, or tax year beginning ...., 1999, and ending ...., ...
▶ See separate instructions.

OMB No. 1545-0099

1999

A Principal business activity	Use the IRS label. Otherwise, please print or type.	Name of partnership	D Employer identification number
B Principal product or service		Number, street, and room or suite no. If a P.O. box, see page 12 of the instructions.	E Date business started
C Business code number		City or town, state, and ZIP code	F Total assets (see page 12 of the instructions) $

G   Check applicable boxes: **(1)** ☐ Initial return   **(2)** ☐ Final return   **(3)** ☐ Change in address   **(4)** ☐ Amended return
H   Check accounting method: **(1)** ☐ Cash   **(2)** ☐ Accrual   **(3)** ☐ Other (specify) ▶ _____
I   Number of Schedules K-1. Attach one for each person who was a partner at any time during the tax year ▶ _____

Caution: *Include **only** trade or business income and expenses on lines 1a through 22 below. See the instructions for more information.*

Income

1a	Gross receipts or sales	1a	
b	Less returns and allowances	1b	1c
2	Cost of goods sold (Schedule A, line 8)		2
3	Gross profit. Subtract line 2 from line 1c		3
4	Ordinary income (loss) from other partnerships, estates, and trusts *(attach schedule)*. . .		4
5	Net farm profit (loss) *(attach Schedule F (Form 1040))*		5
6	Net gain (loss) from Form 4797, Part II, line 18.		6
7	Other income (loss) *(attach schedule)*		7
8	**Total income (loss).** Combine lines 3 through 7		8

Deductions (see page 14 of the instructions for limitations)

9	Salaries and wages (other than to partners) (less employment credits) .		9
10	Guaranteed payments to partners		10
11	Repairs and maintenance		11
12	Bad debts		12
13	Rent		13
14	Taxes and licenses		14
15	Interest		15
16a	Depreciation (if required, attach Form 4562) . . .	16a	
b	Less depreciation reported on Schedule A and elsewhere on return	16b	16c
17	Depletion **(Do not deduct oil and gas depletion.)**		17
18	Retirement plans, etc.		18
19	Employee benefit programs		19
20	Other deductions *(attach schedule)*		20
21	**Total deductions.** Add the amounts shown in the far right column for lines 9 through 20 .		21
22	**Ordinary income (loss)** from trade or business activities. Subtract line 21 from line 8 . .		22

Please Sign Here

Under penalties of perjury, I declare that I have examined this return, including accompanying schedules and statements, and to the best of my knowledge and belief, it is true, correct, and complete. Declaration of preparer (other than general partner or limited liability company member) is based on all information of which preparer has any knowledge.

▶ Signature of general partner or limited liability company member   ▶ Date

Paid Preparer's Use Only

Preparer's signature ▶	Date	Check if self-employed ▶ ☐	Preparer's SSN or PTIN
Firm's name (or yours if self-employed) and address ▶		EIN ▶	
		ZIP code ▶	

For Paperwork Reduction Act Notice, see separate instructions.   Cat. No. 11390Z   Form **1065** (1999)

FORM 8.2.

IRS Form 1065, U.S. Partnership Return of Income

SCHEDULE K-1 (Form 1065)	Partner's Share of Income, Credits, Deductions, etc.	OMB No. 1545-0099

Department of the Treasury
Internal Revenue Service

▶ See separate instructions.

For calendar year 1999 or tax year beginning _____, 1999, and ending _____,

1999

Partner's identifying number ▶	Partnership's identifying number ▶
Partner's name, address, and ZIP code	Partnership's name, address, and ZIP code

A This partner is a ☐ general partner ☐ limited partner
☐ limited liability company member

B What type of entity is this partner? ▶ ....

C Is this partner a ☐ domestic or a ☐ foreign partner?

D Enter partner's percentage of:
(i) Before change or termination / (ii) End of year

Profit sharing . . . . % .... %
Loss sharing . . . . % .... %
Ownership of capital . . . . % .... %

E IRS Center where partnership filed return:

F Partner's share of liabilities (see instructions):
Nonrecourse . . . . $ ....
Qualified nonrecourse financing . . $ ....
Other . . . . $ ....

G Tax shelter registration number . . ▶ ....

H Check here if this partnership is a publicly traded partnership as defined in section 469(k)(2) . . . . ☐

I Check applicable boxes: (1) ☐ Final K-1 (2) ☐ Amended K-1

J Analysis of partner's capital account:

(a) Capital account at beginning of year	(b) Capital contributed during year	(c) Partner's share of lines 3, 4, and 7, Form 1065, Schedule M-2	(d) Withdrawals and distributions	(e) Capital account at end of year (combine columns (a) through (d))
			( )	

	(a) Distributive share item		(b) Amount	(c) 1040 filers enter the amount in column (b) on:
Income (Loss)	**1** Ordinary income (loss) from trade or business activities . . .	**1**		See page 6 of Partner's Instructions for Schedule K-1 (Form 1065).
	2 Net income (loss) from rental real estate activities	**2**		
	3 Net income (loss) from other rental activities	**3**		
	4 Portfolio income (loss):			
	a Interest	**4a**		Sch. B, Part I, line 1
	b Ordinary dividends	**4b**		Sch. B, Part II, line 5
	c Royalties	**4c**		Sch. E, Part I, line 4
	d Net short-term capital gain (loss)	**4d**		Sch. D, line 5, col. (f)
	e Net long-term capital gain (loss):			
	(1) 28% rate gain (loss)	**e(1)**		Sch. D, line 12, col. (g)
	(2) Total for year.	**e(2)**		Sch. D, line 12, col. (f)
	f Other portfolio income (loss) *(attach schedule)* . .	**4f**		Enter on applicable line of your return.
	5 Guaranteed payments to partner	**5**		See page 6 of Partner's Instructions for Schedule K-1 (Form 1065).
	6 Net section 1231 gain (loss) (other than due to casualty or theft) ..	**6**		
	7 Other income (loss) *(attach schedule)*	**7**		Enter on applicable line of your return.
Deductions	**8** Charitable contributions (see instructions) *(attach schedule)* . .	**8**		Sch. A, line 15 or 16
	9 Section 179 expense deduction.	**9**		See pages 7 and 8 of Partner's Instructions for Schedule K-1 (Form 1065).
	10 Deductions related to portfolio income *(attach schedule)* . . .	**10**		
	11 Other deductions *(attach schedule)*.	**11**		
Credits	**12a** Low-income housing credit:			
	(1) From section 42(j)(5) partnerships for property placed in service before 1990	**a(1)**		
	(2) Other than on line 12a(1) for property placed in service before 1990	**a(2)**		Form 8586, line 5
	(3) From section 42(j)(5) partnerships for property placed in service after 1989	**a(3)**		
	(4) Other than on line 12a(3) for property placed in service after 1989	**a(4)**		
	b Qualified rehabilitation expenditures related to rental real estate activities	**12b**		
	c Credits (other than credits shown on lines 12a and 12b) related to rental real estate activities.	**12c**		See page 8 of Partner's Instructions for Schedule K-1 (Form 1065).
	d Credits related to other rental activities	**12d**		
	13 Other credits	**13**		

For Paperwork Reduction Act Notice, see Instructions for Form 1065.   Cat. No. 11394R   **Schedule K-1 (Form 1065) 1999**

FORM 8.3.

IRS Form 1065, Schedule K-1, Partner's Share of Income, Credits, Deductions, etc.

Schedule K-1 (Form 1065) 1999   Page **2**

	(a) Distributive share item	(b) Amount	(c) 1040 filers enter the amount in column (b) on:
Investment Interest	**14a** Interest expense on investment debts	14a	Form 4952, line 1
	b (1) Investment income included on lines 4a, 4b, 4c, and 4f	b(1)	See page 9 of Partner's Instructions for Schedule K-1 (Form 1065).
	(2) Investment expenses included on line 10	b(2)	
Self-employment	**15a** Net earnings (loss) from self-employment	15a	Sch. SE, Section A or B
	b Gross farming or fishing income	15b	See page 9 of Partner's Instructions for Schedule K-1 (Form 1065).
	c Gross nonfarm income	15c	
Adjustments and Tax Preference items	**16a** Depreciation adjustment on property placed in service after 1986	16a	See page 9 of Partner's Instructions for Schedule K-1 (Form 1065) and Instructions for Form 6251.
	b Adjusted gain or loss	16b	
	c Depletion (other than oil and gas)	16c	
	d (1) Gross income from oil, gas, and geothermal properties	d(1)	
	(2) Deductions allocable to oil, gas, and geothermal properties	d(2)	
	e Other adjustments and tax preference items *(attach schedule)*	16e	
Foreign Taxes	**17a** Type of income ▶		Form 1116, check boxes
	b Name of foreign country or possession ▶		
	c Total gross income from sources outside the United States *(attach schedule)*	17c	Form 1116, Part I
	d Total applicable deductions and losses *(attach schedule)*	17d	
	e Total foreign taxes (check one): ▶ ☐ Paid ☐ Accrued	17e	Form 1116, Part II
	f Reduction in taxes available for credit *(attach schedule)*	17f	Form 1116, Part III
	g Other foreign tax information *(attach schedule)*	17g	See Instructions for Form 1116.
Other	**18** Section 59(e)(2) expenditures: **a** Type ▶		See page 9 of Partner's Instructions for Schedule K-1 (Form 1065).
	b Amount	18b	
	19 Tax-exempt interest income	19	Form 1040, line 8b
	20 Other tax-exempt income	20	See pages 9 and 10 of Partner's Instructions for Schedule K-1 (Form 1065).
	21 Nondeductible expenses	21	
	22 Distributions of money (cash and marketable securities)	22	
	23 Distributions of property other than money	23	
	24 Recapture of low-income housing credit:		
	a From section 42(j)(5) partnerships	24a	Form 8611, line 8
	b Other than on line 24a	24b	

25 Supplemental information required to be reported separately to each partner *(attach additional schedules if more space is needed)*:

FORM 8.3. *continued*

Form **8832** (December 1996) Department of the Treasury Internal Revenue Service	**Entity Classification Election**	OMB No. 1545-1516

Please Type or Print	Name of entity	Employer identification number (EIN)
	Number, street, and room or suite no. If a P.O. box, see instructions.	
	City or town, state, and ZIP code. If a foreign address, enter city, province or state, postal code and country.	

1   Type of election (see instructions):

a ☐ Initial classification by a newly-formed entity (or change in current classification of an existing entity to take effect on January 1, 1997)

b ☐ Change in current classification (to take effect later than January 1, 1997)

2   Form of entity (see instructions):

a ☐ A domestic eligible entity electing to be classified as an association taxable as a corporation.

b ☐ A domestic eligible entity electing to be classified as a partnership.

c ☐ A domestic eligible entity with a single owner electing to be disregarded as a separate entity.

d ☐ A foreign eligible entity electing to be classified as an association taxable as a corporation.

e ☐ A foreign eligible entity electing to be classified as a partnership.

f ☐ A foreign eligible entity with a single owner electing to be disregarded as a separate entity.

3   Election is to be effective beginning (month, day, year) (see instructions) . . . . ▶ ___ / ___ / ___

4 Name and title of person whom the IRS may call for more information	**5** That person's telephone number

Consent Statement and Signature(s) (see instructions)

Under penalties of perjury, I (we) declare that I (we) consent to the election of the above-named entity to be classified as indicated above, and that I (we) have examined this consent statement, and to the best of my (our) knowledge and belief, it is true, correct, and complete. If I am an officer, manager, or member signing for all members of the entity, I further declare that I am authorized to execute this consent statement on their behalf.

Signature(s)	Date	Title

For Paperwork Reduction Act Notice, see page 2.   Cat. No. 22598R   Form **8832** (12-96)

FORM 8.4.

IRS Form 8832, Entity Classification Election

The check-the-box regulation eliminates the uncertainty of how LLPs will be taxed and allows these business forms to enjoy the pass-through taxation of partnerships. This is just one more reason LLPs are touted as being the dominant organization for professionals in the future.

TERMINATION OF A LIMITED LIABILITY PARTNERSHIP

Dissolution of a Limited Liability Partnership

An LLP may dissolve under the same conditions as a general partnership—that is, generally, when a partner voluntarily dissociates or involuntarily withdraws (by reason of death, incapacity, or bankruptcy) from the partnership. Unlike the limited partner in a limited partnership, all partners of an LLP have management rights and, therefore, their withdrawal will, theoretically, affect the continued viability of the partnership business. Therefore, the withdrawal of one or more partners in an LLP causes an automatic dissolution of the partnership, unless the partnership agreement provides otherwise or there is a deferred dissolution. In addition to these considerations, a partnership's LLP status will also terminate at the expiration of the statutorily prescribed period for registration of an LLP, unless the LLP renews its registration.

Continuation of a Limited Liability Partnership

Because of the difficulties inherent in the automatic and often unexpected termination of an LLP, the partnership agreement may provide for continuation of the partnership. If such a provision is not made, the deferred dissolution provisions of the Revised Uniform Partnership Act will provide a ninety-day grace period during which the partnership business may continue and the withdrawing partner may choose to waive the right to have the partnership business wound up.

Winding Up

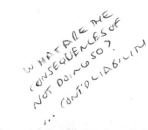

In the absence of a provision for the continuation of the LLP, it will be dissolved and wound up in the same manner as a general partnership; however, the LLP should notify the secretary of state where the LLP is registered of its termination by filing the appropriate notice. (See Form 8.5, *Application for Cancellation of Limited Liability Partnership.*)

◆ LIMITED LIABILITY PARTNERSHIPS IN REVIEW

Definition
A general or limited partnership that registers as a limited liability partnership with the secretary of state, thereby protecting its partners from vicarious liability for the negligence or malfeasance of other partners.

Advantages
♦ Relative simplicity of organization
♦ Limited vicarious liability

Disadvantages
♦ Unlimited personal liability for (1) partnership's breach of its contractual obligations or (2) partner's own negligence or malfeasance
♦ Automatic dissolution upon withdrawal or incapacity of one or more partners, absent agreement to the contrary
♦ Operation in foreign jurisdictions

Key Considerations of the Paralegal:
Formation Procedures
1. Form general or limited partnership.
2. Determine partnership name for limited liability partnership, with designation "limited liability partnership" or abbreviated form.

STATE OF MONTANA

APPLICATION *for* CANCELLATION *of*
ASSUMED BUSINESS NAME *or*
LIMITED LIABILITY
PARTNERSHIPS
(30-13-213, MCA)

MAIL:

Secretary of State
P.O. Box 202801
Helena, MT 59620-2801
PHONE: ☎(406)444-3665
FAX: (406)444-3976
WEB SITE: *www.state.mt.us/sos*

Prepare, sign and submit an ORIGINAL AND COPY with fee.
This is the minimum information required.

(This space for use by the Secretary of State only)

Form: **ABN-2**
Filing Fee: $5.00

☐Priority Filing Fee Add $20.00

PLEASE CHECK ONE BOX:
☐Cancellation of ABN (30-13-213, MCA) $5.00
☐Cancellation of LLP (30-13-213, MCA) $5.00

▸ **FIRST:** The Assumed Business Name or LLP to be canceled is _____

_____ .

▸ **SECOND:** The name and address of the original applicant are as follows:

Name _____

Street Address _____

Mailing Address _____

_____

▸ **I, HEREBY SWEAR AND AFFIRM,** under penalty of law, that the facts contained in this Application are true.

_____
Signature of Applicant

_____
Title or Ownership Interest in Business Organization

State of _____
County of _____

Signed or attested before me on _____ (date) by [name(s) of person(s)]
_____ .

_____
(Signature of notarial officer)
Notary Public for the State of _____
Residing at _____
My Commission expires _____

s:\forms\abn-2
Revised: 05/27/99

FORM 8.5.
Application for Cancellation of Assumed Business Name or Limited Liability Partnership

3. Apply for registration of limited liability partnership.
4. Contact state and local licensing divisions to determine required licenses and permits.
5. If goods will be sold through the partnership business, apply for a sales tax permit from the state and local revenue agencies.
6. Apply for a tax identification number with the IRS (Form SS-4) and, if required, with the state revenue department.
7. File IRS Form 8832 electing partnership or corporate taxation status with the IRS.
8. If the partnership intends to hire employees:
   a. contact the IRS to establish employee withholding procedures, and
   b. contact appropriate state agencies to make arrangements for unemployment and workers' compensation coverage.
9. Draft a comprehensive partnership agreement.
10. File statement of partnership authority with the secretary of state.

◆ KEY TERM

entity classification election

◆ STUDY QUESTIONS IN REVIEW

1. What is the advantage of limited liability partnerships versus general or limited partnerships?
2. Who are the managers of an LLP?
3. Are partners of LLPs liable for the contractual debts and obligations of the partnership?
4. What steps must partners of a general partnership take to receive the statutory liability protections afforded an LLP?
5. What is the purpose of including the LLP designation as part of the partnership's name?
6. How are LLPs taxed?
7. In what way is an LLP like a corporation?
8. Explain the liability protections of an LLP.
9. What are the disadvantages of the LLP?
10. What measures does the Revised Uniform Partnership Act provide to allow an interim continuation of an LLP after the death or withdrawal of a partner?

◆ CASE STUDIES IN REVIEW

1. Renee, Donald, and Van are attorneys in a general practice firm. Last year, they registered as an LLP. Unknown to Renee, Donald has been embezzling funds from several of his clients' trust fund accounts. Van, who oversees the trust fund accounts, has noticed several withdrawals that have not been accounted for. He intended to look into the deductions but he has been involved in a major trial for the past six months and has not had a chance. Four months ago, he mentioned the problems to Renee and Donald and said that he would look into it. Who would be liable for the mismanagement of the client's accounts?

2. Michelle and Kevin own a general accounting firm in western Montana. They have worked as partners for ten years and have never felt the need to file for corporate status. However, last year, Michelle's daughter, Sandy, who was working as a paralegal for a local law firm, told them about LLPs. Sandy told Michelle and Kevin that they could become an LLP, with its attendant liability protections, by simply adding "LLP" at the end of their partnership name. Is this sufficient to allow Michelle and Kevin the liability protections of an LLP?

◆ PROJECT APPLICATIONS

1. Research your state's statutes. Does your state provide for LLPs? Cite the applicable statutory provision.
2. Based upon the results of your research in Project Application 1, what liability protections are afforded partners of an LLP in your state?
3. Contact your state's secretary of state to determine if LLPs are statutorily allowed. If so, prepare the registration forms for the following fictitious partnership:

   Monica and Pam have been practicing general dentistry together for five years. Their state does not allow medical professionals to form corporations; therefore, they have worked together in a general partnership. However, last week, they received a letter from their attorney notifying them that the state has recently adopted a new form of partnership, known as the limited liability partnership. Monica and Pam like the liability protections of the LLP. They ask the firm to draft the registration documents.

   Their file contains the following relevant information:

Monica Tooth	Pam Braces
100 South West	340 Bend Drive #6
Anytown, (your state) 55555	Anyplace, (your state) 55555

Business Address:	Tooth & Braces Dentistry
	400 Brooks Street
	Notown, (your state) 55555
	County: Missoula County

◆ ENDNOTES

1. See Oved, "New York State Limited Liability Partnerships," *New York State Bar Journal* 38 at 73 March/April 1995; but see Murphy, "It's Nothing Personal: The Public Costs of Limited Liability Partnerships," 71 *Indiana Law Journal* 201 (1995).

2. Texas Revised Civil Statute Annotated art. 6132b § 10.03.

SECTION FOUR
Corporations

CHAPTER 9

Corporations: Ownership without Liability

orporations are legal entities which are separate and distinct from their owners; they are, in fact, considered "persons" born of statute. Because the corporation exists independently of its owners (shareholders), it does not automatically terminate upon the withdrawal of a shareholder and is thus said to have a "perpetual life." Corporations offer their shareholders the protection of limited liability and the ability to transfer their ownership interests freely. Unlike partners, shareholders of a corporation do not have the right to participate directly in the management of the company; instead, the corporation is usually operated by its elected board of directors and its appointed **officers.** With its centralization of management (board of directors and officers) and silent investors (shareholders), a corporation resembles a limited partnership with the additional advantage of protecting *both* managers and investors from the liabilities of the corporation.

Corporations are created and governed in accordance with state statute. Most states' statutory regulations are based upon the Model Business Corporation Act, first drafted by the American Bar Association in 1950, and the Revised Model Business Corporation Act, published in 1984. Because these are *model* acts rather than uniform acts, most states have used them as a guideline for drafting their own provisions; no state has adopted the acts verbatim. Therefore, state laws are not uniform as to the formation and operation of corporations.

While state statutes establish the basic parameters for forming and operating a corporation, each corporation adopts its own internal operating procedures in its formation documents, the articles of incorporation and the bylaws. The articles of incorporation set forth the basic information necessary to form the corporation, such as the name of the corporation, the purpose of the corporation, the initial capital structure, the registered agent, and the initial directors. The bylaws establish the corporation's operating procedures, such as dates and places of shareholders' and board of directors' meetings, voting mechanisms, election of directors, duties of directors, and stock issuance and ownership. A corporation's articles of incorporation and bylaws provide shareholders and corporate managers a detailed roadmap to follow to ensure that the corporation complies with the statutory requirements necessary to maintain its corporate status, with its corresponding liability protections.

Officers Individuals appointed by the board of directors to manage the daily operations of a corporation.

CORPORATE CHARACTERISTICS

Corporations are generally characterized by the following:

1. Continuity of life
2. Centralization of management
3. Limited liability
4. Free transferability of interests[1]

Not all corporations possess all four of these traditional corporate attributes, but all four can coexist only in a corporation.

Continuity of Life

Sole proprietorships, partnerships, and limited liability companies all dissolve upon the death or termination of their partners/members. A corporation, however, exists independently of its owners and does not dissolve upon the withdrawal of one or more of its owners. Therefore, it may exist indefinitely and thus, as a "person," may have **"continuity of life."** It is the only business organization that is statutorily given a continuous life.

Centralization of Management

With the exception of limited partnerships, all unincorporated business organizations can allow their partners/members to participate in the management of the business. However, the shareholders of a corporation generally do not have the right to participate in the operation of the corporation or its business. A corporation's management is usually centralized in a board of directors, elected by the shareholders. Such **centralization of management** allows shareholders to serve as "passive investors" in a corporation's business enterprises. Although the board of directors has the authority to manage the business of the corporation, the board may appoint officers (e.g., president, vice president, secretary, treasurer) to manage the day-to-day operations of the corporation and its business.

Limited Liability

Corporations offer their owners (shareholders) and managers protection from personal liability for the contractual debts and other obligations of the corporation. Thus, shareholders risk only their investment in the corporation; generally, their personal assets cannot be attached to satisfy the obligations of the corporation. Managers are liable for their own wrongful acts and not for the corporate liabilities.

Although corporate shareholders are generally not personally responsible for any of the liabilities of the corporation, if the corporation or its shareholders improperly operate the corporation (fail to comply with corporate formalities [fail to file the requisite formation documents and annual reports with the secretary of state, or fail to hold annual shareholders' and/or board of directors' meetings], operate the corporation for a fraudulent purpose, or the corporation itself is underfinanced), the courts may set aside the corporate form and hold the shareholders personally liable for the obligations of the corporation. This is known as "piercing the corporate veil" and is intended to prevent corporations from defrauding the public.

Free Transferability of Interests

Unlike sole proprietorships, partnerships, or limited liability companies, the ownership of a corporation usually may be assigned, sold, or otherwise transferred to a third party outside of the corporation without the consent of the other shareholders. Corporations that are publicly traded on exchanges such as the New York Stock Exchange do not restrict who may own the corporation's stock, because they view their shareholders merely as investors in their business enterprises.

However, small corporations, such as family corporations, may want to restrict their stockholders to family members or other specified individuals or groups of individuals. Small, closely held corporations may limit who may own their corporate stock by putting transfer restrictions on stock certificates (which evidence stock ownership) and by providing restrictions in their articles of incorporation or bylaws.

DISADVANTAGES OF THE CORPORATE FORM

Each of the four unique corporate characteristics offers distinct advantages to a business organization. Liability protections, free transferability of interests, and continuity of life are compelling reasons for adopting a corporate form; however, the disadvantages of the corporate form cannot be overlooked. The two main disadvantages are (1) the requisite formalities in organization, operation, and annual reporting requirements and (2) double taxation. Neither of these considerations is inconsequential.

Corporate Formalities

The **formalities** necessary to form and operate a corporation are substantial. Articles of incorporation, bylaws, and proper meeting documents must be prepared to properly create

Continuity of life Perpetual existence.

Centralization of management Core group of individuals who manage a corporation.

Formalities Statutory requirements for formation of a business entity.

a corporation. Once the corporation is formed, shareholders must convene annual meetings which must be recorded and verified. In addition, annual reports (with fees) must be filed with the secretary of state in order for a corporation to maintain its corporate status.

Failure to comply with the requisite statutory formalities may result in piercing of the corporate veil, thus subjecting the corporate shareholders to personal liability for the debts and obligations of the corporation. Some business owners disfavor the corporate form because of the requisite statutory formalities.

Taxation Considerations

Because corporations are separate legal entities, separate "persons," their profits are taxed at the corporate level based on business tax rates. Once the corporation distributes the profits to the shareholders as dividends, the profits become taxable as personal income of the shareholders. This **double taxation** is seen as the most significant disadvantage of the corporate form.

While large corporations accept double taxation as a cost of the limited liability protections which shareholders receive, the Internal Revenue Service (IRS) provides pass-through taxation to small corporations that can meet specified criteria; these corporations are known as S corporations. If a corporation cannot meet the requirements to become an S corporation (as discussed later in this chapter), the economic returns shareholders receive from corporations are inevitably diminished by the double taxation of corporate profits.

CORPORATE POWERS

State statutes grant corporations broad powers to operate their business enterprises. These enumerated powers provide that the corporation may:

1. Sue and be sued
2. Make and amend its internal operating procedures in its bylaws
3. Buy, hold, and sell real and personal property
4. Make contracts
5. Borrow money
6. Lend money
7. Participate in a partnership or other entity
8. Conduct its business inside and outside its state of origination
9. Elect its managers[2]

A corporation's statutory powers may be defined or restricted in its articles of incorporation. However, even if the articles do not specifically address the corporation's powers, the corporation's **purpose clause,** which describes the intended business purposes of the corporation, implicitly grants the corporation the rights and powers necessary to accomplish its stated purpose. Thus, a purpose clause that provides that a corporation may operate for "any lawful business purpose" grants the corporation all the rights and powers necessary to accomplish all lawful business. Some states statutorily provide that a corporation is organized for all lawful purposes *unless* limited in the corporation's articles. Therefore, artful drafting of a specific purpose clause is important.

A corporation is not permitted to exceed its statutory powers nor those granted it pursuant to its articles of incorporation. If the corporation exceeds its authority, its acts are ***ultra vires.***

Example: The articles of incorporation of A, B, C, Inc. candy corporation provide that its purpose is to "engage in the production and sales of candy." If the directors of A, B, C, Inc. ignore this purpose clause and begin buying and selling cars in its parking lot, the directors' actions are *ultra vires.*

A shareholder may request that a court prevent a corporation from committing an *ultra vires* act, and the directors and/or officers who exceeded their authority may be held personally liable for the losses incurred by the corporation because of their unauthorized actions.

Double taxation   Taxation of corporate income at two levels: (1) the corporate level and (2) the shareholder level.

Purpose clause   Describes the intended purpose(s) of a corporation.

***Ultra vires* acts**   Actions by a corporation that exceed the corporate purpose and/or powers.

CORPORATE FORMS

The term *corporation* often brings to mind images of huge multinational conglomerates whose stocks are publicly traded on the New York Stock Exchange. This glamorous image of the corporation is, in most cases, incorrect. The corporate form is used not only by large companies, but also by small business interests, charitable organizations, and professional associations. Several types of corporations have developed to accommodate the needs of the diverse business interests seeking the liability protections offered by the corporate form. These include the following:

♦ Business corporations
♦ Statutory close corporations
♦ Nonprofit corporations
♦ Professional corporations
♦ *S corporations* (an IRS designation)

The business corporation and the statutory close corporation are the two basic corporate forms. The nonprofit and professional corporations are variations of the basic corporate forms available for specific categories of businesses seeking liability protection for their members. An S corporation is not a separate corporate form. Rather, it is an IRS designation available to all of the preceding corporate forms that meet the requisite criteria (e.g., has fewer than seventy-five shareholders, all of whom are individuals, trusts, or estates [extensions of the individual], and has one class of stock). The S designation allows the profits of qualified corporations to "pass through" the corporation to the shareholders, where the profits are taxed as personal income. This type of "partnership" taxation allows small businesses to avoid the double taxation otherwise imposed on corporations.

Each of these corporate forms offers unique advantages, and corresponding disadvantages, to business owners. The consequences of adopting corporate existence must be carefully analyzed in light of the financial opportunities available to and restrictions imposed upon each form.

Business Corporation

The traditional corporation, known as a **business corporation,** developed to encourage investments in business by protecting investors from personal liability for the debts and obligations of the enterprises in which they invested. The traditional business corporation offers its shareholders the advantages inherent to the corporate form: limited liability, centralization of management, ability to raise capital, free transferability of ownership, and perpetual life; it also is plagued by the disadvantages of corporate existence: corporate formalities and double taxation. Several corporate forms have evolved to meet the needs of small business owners, professional associations, and nonprofit organizations; however, large for-profit companies have little choice but to adopt the traditional corporate form, with its attendant disadvantages.

The business corporation has been modified over time to meet changing needs and concerns of business owners. While the business corporation offers all of the traditional corporate attributes, (including free transferability of interests), small corporations, in which shareholders often participate in the management of the corporation, needed to restrict the ownership of their shares to preserve harmony in their business management. To meet this need, the statutory close corporation, which allows limitations on stock ownership, developed. Special groups, such as charitable organizations and professionals, saw the benefit of corporate existence and also sought its benefits; many states have now developed nonprofit and professional corporate forms that address the special concerns of these groups. In addition, to alleviate the burden of corporate (double) taxation on smaller businesses that wanted the liability protections of a corporation but could not afford the tax consequences of incorporation, the IRS now allows some smaller corporations to qualify as S corporations and receive the pass-through taxation enjoyed by partnerships.

Business corporation A legal entity created to conduct business.

Statutory Close Corporation

A **statutory close corporation** is a corporation owned by closely affiliated shareholders, often friends and family. It has a statutorily limited number of shareholders, most of whom participate in the management of the corporation. Because shareholders have management rights, the shares of statutory close corporations generally cannot be sold or transferred without first giving the corporation or other shareholders the right of first refusal. The organization of a close corporation closely resembles a partnership but with extensive liability protections not available in the partnership form.

Close corporations are generally governed by the same rules that apply to general business corporations. However, many states have adopted the Close Corporation Supplement to the Model Business Corporation Act that sets forth specific provisions for the creation and operation of close corporations; these provisions are intended to simplify the creation of close corporations by imposing minimal formation and operating requirements on these corporate forms.

Close Corporation Election

Shareholders of a qualifying new corporation may elect to become a close corporation simply by providing for this status in their articles of incorporation, which are filed with the secretary of state.[3] Existing corporations may also make this election by amending their existing articles of incorporation if a majority of the shareholders (generally two-thirds) consent to the change in the corporation's status.

The main advantages to electing a close corporation status are to minimize the otherwise cumbersome corporate formalities generally imposed on business corporations and, perhaps more significantly to the corporate owners, restrict the transferability of corporate shares. This election is, therefore, particularly important to family operations and other small businesses.

Ownership Restrictions   Most states restrict the number of shareholders of a close corporation to fifty or fewer shareholders. These types of corporations are intended to be small and are generally adopted by family businesses or close associates. Because most shareholders also participate in the management of the business, shares of close corporations are not publicly traded (e.g., on the New York Stock Exchange) and generally may not be transferred to anyone outside of the corporation without first offering the corporation the right to purchase the shares.

Most stock certificates of a close corporation will contain the following notice to potential purchasers to ensure compliance with transfer restrictions:

> The rights of shareholders in a statutory close corporation may differ materially from the rights of shareholders in other corporations. Copies of the articles of incorporation and bylaws, shareholder agreements, and other documents, any of which may restrict transfers and affect voting and other rights, may be obtained by a shareholder on written request to the corporation.[4]

If an individual purchases shares in violation of the **stock transfer restriction,** the sale may be set aside by the corporation, which may elect to purchase the shares or offer them to other existing shareholders.

Management   Unlike general business corporations, most close corporations are not managed by a board of directors. Rather, the shareholders/owners of the close corporation commonly manage the corporation and its business pursuant to an agreement, known as the shareholders' agreement.[5]

Shareholders' agreements typically eliminate the board of directors and address the operation of the business and the shareholders' authority to participate in the management of the business. They may also delegate authority to corporate officers, specify the amount and frequency of distributions, and create partnership relationships among the shareholders (e.g., by specifying that the corporation will dissolve when a shareholder dies or is incapacitated, or the happening of another event).

Statutory close corporation
A corporation owned by a small number of shareholders whose shares are not freely transferable.

Stock transfer restriction
Restriction on the transfer of ownership (stock) of a corporation.

The shareholders' agreement, which should be comprehensive, can eliminate the need for corporate bylaws, where the provisions for the management and operation of the corporation would normally be found.[6]

Corporate Formalities

Close corporations are not encumbered by many of the formalities statutorily required of business corporations, such as a board of directors, bylaws, and annual meetings.[7] Such corporate formalities are often unnecessary in small corporations that are run by shareholders.

If a general business corporation failed to comply with all of the requisite corporate formalities, the corporate form could be set aside and its shareholders would be subject to personal liability for the obligations of the corporation (piercing the corporate veil). This is not true for a close corporation.

Professional Corporation

Traditionally, professionals practiced as sole proprietors or in partnerships; they were not allowed to incorporate because, theoretically, the corporate liability protections would reduce the individual's accountability for the services provided to the public. More recently, states have allowed professionals to practice as **professional corporations** under restrictive professional corporation acts.

Professional corporation A corporation formed by one or more professionals to conduct business.

Many states follow the Model Professional Corporation Supplement to the Model Business Corporation Act, which allows professionals to incorporate for the "purpose of rendering professional services and services ancillary thereto" within a *single* profession.[8] Some states list the professions that may incorporate, whereas others require that professional corporations, rather than general business corporations, be formed by those engaged in occupations that are required to be licensed by state law. States that enumerate the professions that can incorporate under the state's professional incorporation act generally apply their acts to professions set forth in Table 9.1.

Name Designation

Professional corporations must designate their status in their name. Thus, a professional corporation must include the designation professional corporation, professional association, service corporation, or the associated abbreviations, P.C., P.A., or S.C.[9] In addition, the name of the corporation should be registered as an assumed business name (also known as a trade name), unless the corporation is operated by an individual who uses his or her full name as the corporate name.

Liability Protections

The corporate form is attractive to many professionals because of the limited liability protections it offers. However, the liability protections of a professional corporation are more restrictive than those available in the general business corporation. Unlike the business corporation, which offers its shareholders extensive liability protections, the professional corporation protects professionals from personal liability for the negligence and malfeasance of their associates; it does not protect licensed professionals from personal liability for their own acts or those that they supervise. In this way, states were able to allow professionals incorporation rights while maintaining their personal accountability for the services that they render to the public.

TABLE 9.1.   Professions Permitted Incorporation

Physicians	Insurance agents	Physical therapists
Attorneys	Architects	Accountants
Chiropractors	Pharmacists	Dentists
Engineers	Real estate agents/brokers	Veterinarians

Ownership and Management Restrictions

In addition to the liability restrictions, the ownership and management rights of professional corporations are also restricted in order to maintain the integrity of their participants. Professional corporations may only be owned and managed by licensed professionals or associated professionals; accordingly, the corporation's shares may only be transferred to qualified individuals. This limitation on the category of potential investors and managers will, theoretically, curb the influences on the professionals participating in the corporation. Thus, professionals will not be motivated to produce profits for investor-shareholders; rather, they will be influenced by their professional peers who will encourage and monitor compliance with professional standards, thereby preserving the integrity of the corporation and its participants.

Nonprofit Corporation

States encourage nonprofit organizations to incorporate, thus protecting benefactors from personal liability for the debts and obligations of their organizations. Nonprofit corporations are generally formed for charitable, educational, cultural, religious, and other benevolent purposes.

In addition to the limited liability protections provided by nonprofit corporations, these entities may qualify for a state and federal tax exemption on the profits they generate. This qualification is not automatic and must be applied for pursuant to Internal Revenue Code 501(c).

Nonprofit corporation
Corporation formed for charitable purposes.

Unlike a business corporation, the profits of a **nonprofit corporation** may not be distributed to its shareholders, directors, or officers. This limitation is intended to preserve the charitable purposes for which the corporation was formed by avoiding the profit motivation that fuels most business corporations.

S Corporation

Some small corporations may qualify to be taxed as partnerships, thus avoiding the double taxation characteristic of the corporate form. Corporations that qualify for this special tax status are referred to as S corporations. An S election is merely a tax designation available to small corporations that have, *inter alia,* fewer than seventy-five shareholders, all of whom are individuals, trusts, or estates. The S corporation is not a separate corporate form; it merely refers to the manner in which a business corporation, statutory close corporation, or professional corporation will be taxed.

An Overview of Corporate Forms

The various corporate forms available to businesses demonstrate that the "evolution" of the corporation has made it more accessible and viable for smaller business organizations. (See Table 9.2.) With more states allowing limited liability partnerships and limited liabil-

TABLE 9.2   An Overview of Corporate Forms

	Advantages				Disadvantages	
	Perpetual Life	**Centralization of Mgmt.**	**Limited Liability**	**Free Transferability of Interests**	**Formalities**	**Double Taxation**
Business	X	X	X	X	X	X*
Close	X	X	X			X*
Nonprofit	X	X	X	X	X	Exempt
Professional		X	X**		X	X*

* Unless S election is made.
** All professionals remain personally liable for their own negligence or malfeasance and that which they supervise or have knowledge of.

ity companies, the corporate form should still be considered by business owners because of its increasing flexibility and broad liability protections.

CORPORATIONS IN REVIEW

Corporation

A legal entity existing independently of its owners and traditionally characterized by (1) continuity of life, (2) centralized management, (3) limited liability, and (4) free transferability of interests.

Advantages

♦ Continuity of life
♦ Centralization of management
♦ Limited liability
♦ Free transferability of interests

Disadvantages

♦ Formalities
♦ Double taxation

Key Considerations of the Paralegal: Consideration of Corporate Form

♦ Business Corporation
♦ Statutory Close Corporation
♦ Nonprofit Corporation
♦ Professional Corporation
♦ S Corporation election (IRS designation)

KEY TERMS

officers	double taxation	statutory close corporation
continuity of life	purpose clause	stock transfer restriction
centralization of management	ultra vires acts	professional corporation
formalities	business corporation	nonprofit corporation

STUDY QUESTIONS IN REVIEW

1. Who owns a corporation?
2. What document must be filed with the secretary of state before a corporation can begin its existence?
3. What is the purpose of corporate bylaws?
4. What is "continuity of life" for a corporation?
5. Who manages a corporation?
6. What are the responsibilities of a corporate shareholder?
7. What does "free transferability of interests" mean, as it applies to corporations?
8. What are the main disadvantages to incorporating a business?
9. What is double taxation of a corporation?
10. What is the difference between a business corporation and a statutory close corporation?

◆ CASE STUDIES IN REVIEW

1. Toybox, Inc., a California-based toy manufacturer, has been losing money for the last five years. It is now $500,000 in debt. It has considered bankruptcy but its new chief executive officer believes that he can turn the company around within the next two years. However, the corporation's creditors are getting impatient. Can the creditors sue the shareholders to cover the corporation's debts?

2. The Davis family owns a large ranch in western Wyoming. All ten members of the family live and work on the ranch, raising cattle. The family wants to incorporate. Based on your review of the available corporate forms, what corporate form would you recommend and why?

◆ PROJECT APPLICATIONS

1. Research your state's statutes applicable to corporate business organizations. Provide the statutory cites for each type of corporate form (business, close, nonprofit, and professional).

2. Refer to the statutory provisions applicable to professional corporations. What types of professions may incorporate in your state?

◆ ENDNOTES

1. See Treasury Regulation § 301.7701–2.
2. See Model Business Corporation Act § 3.02.
3. See also Model Statutory Close Corporation Supplement (MSCCS) § 3.
4. MSCCS § 10(a).
5. See MSCCS § 20.
6. See MSCCS § 22 providing that "A statutory close corporation need not adopt bylaws if provisions required by law to be contained in bylaws are contained in either the articles of incorporation or a shareholder agreement [ ]."
7. See MSCCS §§ 21, 22, and 23.
8. See Model Professional Corporation Act (hereafter referred to as M.P.C.A) § 3.
9. See M.P.C.A. § 15(a).

CHAPTER 10

Formation of a Corporation

A corporation is a "person" that exists as an entity independent of its owners. As such, it must be "created," or formed. Although the process of forming a corporation may intimidate some business owners, the decisions made during the incorporation phase are crucial to the operation and existence of the corporation. Therefore, the issues addressed in this section must be carefully discussed with and considered by each client prior to and during incorporation.

PREINCORPORATION CONSIDERATIONS

Before a corporation is formed, consideration must be given to the organization of the corporation, the place of incorporation, the financing of the corporation, and the preparation of the documents necessary to create the corporation. A corporation does not exist until these preincorporation matters are completed.

Promoters/Organizers

A corporation is formed by promoters, who organize the corporation and solicit investors, and the incorporators, who sign and file the corporation's articles of incorporation. The promoters and the incorporators are often attorneys or their support staff personnel.

The promoters often enter into agreements on behalf of the corporation during the formation process (e.g., for the sale of corporate stock, for the lease of property for the business operations, for the purchase of business equipment, and for the hiring of corporate employees). Promoters are solely liable for all of the contractual obligations that they create on behalf of the corporation until the corporation approves and accepts (ratifies) the contracts. Even when the corporation ratifies and adopts a preincorporation contract, the promoter is still jointly liable on the contract unless the corporation enters into a new contract (a novation) with the other party to the contract. If a corporation does not ratify a preincorporation transaction, the promoter can be held personally liable for the transaction.

The role of the promoter is generally significant only for large corporations that require considerable preincorporation organization (e.g., investment backing, stock issuance, and property acquisition). Smaller corporations that do not require substantial investment capital generally do not require promoters; therefore, their role is minimal in many, if not most, corporations.

Selection of Jurisdiction

The selection of the jurisdiction in which to incorporate a business has, in the past, been an important consideration for many incorporators. "**Forum shopping**" occurred because the corporate laws of some states were more flexible and permissive than others with regard to such matters as formation requirements, filing fees, and meetings requirements. However, the practical distinctions between state laws have significantly decreased in the last few years as states have brought their corporate laws into conformity with "modernized" statutory provisions such as the American Bar Association's Model Business Corporation Act (M.B.C.A.) or the Revised Model Business Corporation Act (R.M.B.C.A.).

In addition, some jurisdictions impose local law on out-of-state corporations, known as **foreign corporations,** thus removing the incentive to forum "shop." As a result, corporate forum shopping is no longer as profitable as it once was and businesses can and do often incorporate in the state in which they intend to do most of their business. These corporations that transact business "at home" (in the state in which they are incorporated) are known as **domestic corporations.**

Promoter The individual who organizes and forms a corporation.

Incorporater The individual who signs and files the corporation's articles of incorporation.

Forum shopping Selection of a jurisdiction in which to do business.

Foreign corporation A corporation operating in a state other than the state in which it was incorporated.

Domestic corporation A corporation operating in the state in which it was incorporated.

Corporate Financing

Capital must be raised to finance the corporation and its business ventures. This is usually done through offers by potential investors to purchase shares in the corporation once it is formed; these offers are known as **preincorporation share subscriptions** and serve as the basis for the capital of a corporation.

Corporate Name

The name of a corporation must indicate its corporate status. Most states as well as the R.M.B.C.A. therefore require that a corporation's name contain the word *corporation, incorporated, company, limited,* or a corresponding abbreviation.[1] In addition, the secretary of state will not allow a corporation to use a name that is the same as or deceptively similar to a name used by another corporation authorized to transact business in the state. This preclusion is intended to prevent consumer confusion and unfair competition between businesses.

> **Example:** Old Town Café, Inc. operates a small coffee shop in West Yellowstone. Harry wants to open a restaurant in Missoula. He intends to incorporate his business and wants to call his restaurant Old Town Coffee, Inc. He files his articles of incorporation with the secretary of state with the name Old Town Coffee, Inc. The secretary rejects his choice of name as being deceptively similar to another name in use, Old Town Café, Inc.

Assumed Business Name/Trade Name

Some corporations may choose to operate under a name other than their corporate names. For example, "The Taco Company, Inc." may find that the name "Taco Bell" is more appealing to consumers and therefore register the latter as an assumed business name (also known as a trade name). Most states allow the use of an assumed business name by a corporation as long as the name is not in use or deceptively similar to another corporation's name in use in the state.

Reservation of Corporate Name

If a corporation wants to reserve the use of a name before it begins business in a state, it may generally reserve the name for a specified period of time before it intends to actually use the name. (See, e.g., Form 10.1, *Application for Reservation of Assumed Business Name* and R.M.B.C.A. at §4.02 [allowing reservation of a corporate name for a nonrenewable 120-day period] and §4.03.) This procedure is often invoked by large businesses that intend to initially begin business in one or more states but anticipate expanding their markets into other states.

PREINCORPORATION DOCUMENT PREPARATION

Articles of Incorporation

A corporation's life begins when its formation document, the articles of incorporation or its equivalent (e.g., Delaware requires a certificate of incorporation), is filed and accepted by the secretary of state. The corporation statutes of each state set forth the provisions that must, at a minimum, be contained in a corporation's articles of incorporation. The laws of the state in which the business is incorporated must be complied with; failure to do so will result in improper incorporation and the attendant consequences. (See "Defective Incorporation Doctrines.")

In accordance with the M.B.C.A., most states require that, at a minimum, the following information be set forth in the articles of incorporation:

1. Corporate name, including the designation "corporation" or "incorporated" or an identifying abbreviation
2. Corporate address and agent for service of process
3. Purpose(s) of the corporation

Form **BCA-4.15/ 4.20**
(Rev. Jan. 1999)

APPLICATION TO ADOPT, CHANGE OR CANCEL, AN ASSUMED CORPORATE NAME

File #

Secretary of State
Department of Business Services
Springfield, I. 62756
Telephone (217) 782-9520
http://www.sos.state.il.us

Remit payment in check or money order, payable to "Secretary of State".

SUBMIT IN DUPLICATE

This space for use by Secretary of State

Date

Filing Fee

Approved:

1. CORPORATE NAME: _____

2. State or Country of Incorporation:_____

3. Date incorporated *(if an Illinois corporation)* or date authorized to transact business in Illinois *(if a foreign corporation)*: _____ , _____ .
   (Month & Day)   *(Year)*

   (Complete No. 4 and No. 5 if adopting or changing an assumed corporate name.)

4. The corporation intends to adopt and to transact business under the assumed corporate name of:
   _____

5. The right to use the assumed corporate name shall be effective from the date this application is filed by the Secretary of State until_____ , _____ , the first day of the corporation's anniversary
   (Month & Day)   *(Year)*
   month in the next year which is evenly divisible by five.

   (Complete No. 6 if changing or cancelling an assumed corporate name.)

6. The corporation intends to cease transacting business under the assumed corporate name of:
   _____

7. The undersigned corporation has caused this statement to be signed by its duly authorized officers, each of whom affirms, under penalties of perjury, that the facts stated herein are true.

   Dated _____ , _____
         (Month & Day)   *(Year)*

   _____ *(Exact Name of Corporation)*

   attested by _____   by _____
   (Signature of Secretary or Assistant Secretary)   *(Signature of President or Vice President)*

   _____   _____
   (Type or Print Name and Title)   *(Type or Print Name and Title)*

NOTE: The filing fee to adopt an assumed corporate name is $20 plus $2.50 for each month or part thereof between the date of filing this application and the date upon which the corporation may renew its use.

The fee for cancelling an assumed corporate name is $5.00.

C-148.11 The fee to change an assumed name is $25.

4. Description of capital structure, including the number of shares authorized for issuance
5. Name(s) and signatures of the incorporators[2]

Form 10.2, *Articles of Incorporation,* provides a sample of the information required to register a corporation. In addition to these general provisions, most states require corporations that elect close corporation status to set forth the election in their articles. It is important that you become familiar with the information necessary to conform to a state's incorporation requirements; clients can and do seek recourse for improperly prepared articles.

Although you should be sure to properly conform to incorporation requirements, articles may be difficult to amend and are readily available for public inspection; therefore, it is generally advisable to provide only the minimal information required by state statute for the articles. Additional information regarding corporate organization and operation can and should be set forth in the corporate bylaws, which are easier to amend than the articles and are not a matter of public record.

FORM 10.2.
Articles of Incorporation for
Domestic Profit Corporation

STATE *of* DELAWARE
CERTIFICATE *of* INCORPORATION
A STOCK CORPORATION

- **First:** The name of this Corporation is _____

  _____

- **Second:** Its registered office in the State of Delaware is to be located at _____

  _____ Street, in the City of _____

  County of _____ Zip Code _____. The registered agent in

  charge thereof is _____

  _____

  _____

- **Third:** The purpose of the corporation is to engage in any lawful act or activity for

  which corporations may be organized under the General Corporation Law of

  Delaware.

- **Fourth:** The amount of the total authorized capital stock of this corporation is

  _____Dollars ($_____) divided into _____ shares of _____

  _____Dollars ($_____) each.

- **Fifth:** The name and mailing address of the incorporator are as follows:

  Name _____

  Mailing Address_____

  _____Zip Code_____

- **I, The Undersigned,** for the purpose of forming a corporation under the laws of the
  State of Delaware, do make, file and record this Certificate, and do certify that the
  facts herein stated are true, and I have accordingly hereunto set my hand this
  _____day of _____, A.D. 19_____.

  BY:_____
  (Incorporator)

  NAME:_____
  (Type or Print)

Filing Requirements for the Articles of Incorporation

Once the articles of incorporation are prepared, they must be filed with the secretary of state of the jurisdiction of incorporation. If the articles comply with the state's statutory requirements and the requisite filing fees are paid, the secretary will issue a filing receipt indicating that the corporation formally exists. Until the corporation receives acknowledgment that its articles have been approved and accepted by the secretary of state, the corporation will not be afforded the liability protections of a corporation and should not begin transacting business as a corporation.

Licensing Requirements

Corporations, as other businesses, must conform to all state and local licensing requirements for their business enterprises. All states and counties in which a corporation intends to transact business should be contacted to determine the applicable licensing requirements for the corporate business.

POSTINCORPORATION PROCEDURES

Once the articles of incorporation are accepted by the secretary of state, the corporation must be organized. This is done by drafting bylaws and holding an organizational meeting of the incorporators and the initial directors.

Bylaws

Bylaws are written guidelines and procedures for the operation and management of a corporation. The bylaws establish the rights and obligations of the officers, directors, and shareholders of a corporation. They are generally more comprehensive than a corporation's articles of incorporation and, unlike the articles, are not available for public inspection. In addition, the bylaws may be amended by a vote of the directors, as opposed to the articles, which generally require the consent of the shareholders to amend.

Although most law firms have sample form bylaws on file, all bylaws should be drafted with the needs of your particular corporate client in mind. Bylaws may be as simple or complex as the client requires, but it is generally advisable to include, at a minimum, information about directors and officers, including the election procedures and the duties of the officers; information about directors' and shareholders' meetings, including the time, place, and notice required for meetings; and information about the corporate finances, including the name and location of corporate accounts and the officers authorized to conduct banking on behalf of the corporation. Form bylaws cannot address all of the needs of a particular client. However, the following checklist illustrates the basic provisions that corporate bylaws may contain:

1. *Name* of corporation.
2. *Address* of the corporation's principal office and other office locations.
3. Designation of the corporation's *registered agent.*
4. *Purpose* of the corporation.
5. *Shareholders.* The bylaws should contain specific information regarding the rights and obligations of shareholders of the corporation, particularly with respect to the meeting provisions for shareholders.
   a. Date and time of *shareholders' annual meeting.*
   b. Procedures for calling *special meetings* of shareholders.
   c. *Notice* provisions for all regular and special meetings, including provisions for identifying the shareholders entitled to notice and the right of identified shareholders to waive notice of meetings.
   d. *Quorum and proxy requirements*, e.g., the number of shareholders required to be actually present or present by proxy at a shareholder meeting for issues to be submitted to shareholder voting.
   e. *Voting rights* of classes of stock.
   f. Right of shareholders to *inspect corporate records.*
6. *Management.* The bylaws should contain specific provisions regarding the directors and officers of the corporation, including the authorization for directors and the duties of officers.
   a. *Authorization for board of directors* and *delegation of authority to officers* to manage the business. This section may also include provisions for indemnification (reimbursement) to directors for costs incurred in defending a lawsuit brought against a director in the normal course of his or her duties as director of the corporation.
   b. Constitution of board of directors, including the *number and election procedures for directors.*
   c. *Appointment procedures* for officers.
   d. Specification of the *date and time for directors' and officers' meetings.*
   e. Procedures for calling *special directors' and officers' meetings,* including notice requirements and provisions for directors waiving notice of special meetings.

f. *Quorum requirements* for directors' and officers' meetings, e.g., the minimum number of directors required to be present at a directors'/officers' meeting in order to submit issues to a valid vote by the board.

g. Procedures for *electing and removing directors/officers.*

h. *Compensation* of directors and/or officers.

7. *Share issuance and transfer.*

8. *Dividend distributions.* The right of the directors to distribute corporate profits to shareholders.

9. *Financial considerations:*

a. Designation of corporate fiscal year.

b. Name and location of corporate banks and/or lenders.

c. Name of directors and/or officers entitled to authorize payment or withdrawal of corporate funds.

10. *Election of S designation.* See "Taxation Considerations."

11. Provisions for *amending the corporate bylaws.*

12. *Signatures* of the officers approving the bylaws.

Form bylaws for a business corporation can be found at Appendix E. As with all forms, the bylaws must be tailored to meet the needs of your firm's clients and must comply with your state's specific statutory provisions for corporate bylaws, including but not limited to organizational and operational requirements.

Organizational Meeting

Once the bylaws have been drafted, the incorporators and/or the initial directors should hold the first corporate meeting, known as the organizational meeting. At the organizational meeting, directors are elected (if none were appointed in the corporation's articles of incorporation), corporate officers are appointed, the corporation's articles of incorporation are approved, the corporate bylaws are adopted, all preincorporation transactions of the organizers/promoters are ratified, and all other organizational matters are addressed. (See Form 10.3, *Minutes of the Organizational Meetings of the Incorporator and the Board of Directors.*)

The organizational meeting is a necessary postincorporation activity for a corporation. Although the corporate existence begins with the filing and acceptance of the articles of incorporation, statutory formalities, such as meeting requirements, must continually be observed in order for the corporation to maintain its corporate status and the attendant liability protections for the shareholders.

DEFECTIVE INCORPORATION DOCTRINES

De jure corporation A corporation properly formed in accordance with state law.

A corporation that substantially complies with the statutory organizational requirements of the state of incorporation is a valid *de jure* **corporation** (that is, a corporation "of law"). The corporate status (which offers shareholders personal liability protection) of a *de jure* corporation cannot be challenged, unless the requisite statutory formalities are not followed by the corporation subsequent to its formation (e.g., meeting and reporting requirements). This means that a creditor cannot try to circumvent the corporation and sue the shareholders directly for any debts that the corporation may not be able to pay.

Example: The driver of a delivery van for Harry's Floral Shop, Inc. hits a pedestrian during a routine delivery to downtown New York. The pedestrian sues Harry's Floral Shop for personal injury damages. The jury finds that the driver was indeed negligent and awards the pedestrian $1,000,000. The assets of Harry's Floral Shop are only $500,000. The pedestrian tries to sue the shareholders of the corporation personally to recover the remaining $500,000 by arguing that Harry's Floral Shop did not substantially comply with the statutory incorporation requirements of the state of New York because a director's name is misspelled in the corporation's articles of incorporation. The court finds that Harry's Floral Shop substantially complied with all the statutory requirements for incorporation and therefore the corporate status protects the shareholders from personal liability for any obligations of the corporation.

Minutes of the Organizational Meetings of the Incorporator
and the Board of Directors of _____

The organizational meetings of the incorporator and the board of directors of _____ was held at _____, (city), (state), at _____.m. on (date), pursuant to call and waiver of the notice of the time, place and purpose of the meeting signed by the incorporator and each director consenting to holding the meeting to transact business that came before the meeting, said written consent and waiver to be incorporated into the records of the corporation.

_____ called the meeting to order and stated its object.

Present at the meeting were the incorporator and the following directors:

_____

_____

_____

_____ presided as chairperson and _____ was secretary of the meeting.

Call and Waiver of Notice.

The chairperson announced the meeting was held pursuant to the written call and waiver of notice of first meeting of the incorporator and members of the board of directors. The secretary was directed to make the call and waiver a part of the records of the corporation.

Articles of Incorporation.

The chairperson stated the original articles of incorporation were filed with the Secretary of State of the State of ( ) and the certificate of incorporation issued on _____, (year.) The secretary was directed to file the certificate and articles in the corporate file.

By-laws.

The secretary presented a proposed form of by-laws for the regulation of the affairs of the corporation. After consideration, on motion duly made and seconded, the following resolution was adopted:

RESOLVED, that the by-laws submitted to this meeting are adopted as the by-laws of this corporation, and the secretary is instructed to insert the by-laws in the corporate files with the articles of incorporation;

FURTHER RESOLVED, that the board of directors is authorized and empowered to amend the by-laws as provided in the by-laws.

Board of Directors.

On motion duly made, seconded and carried, the incorporator and board of directors ratified the election of those directors as listed in the articles of incorporation. The following were declared duly elected directors to serve a term of one year or until their successors are duly elected and qualified:

_____

_____

_____

Each director so elected being present accepted office.

Officers.

The following officers were elected:

President	_____
Vice-President	_____
Secretary/Treasurer	_____

Each officer so elected being present accepted the office.

FORM 10.3.

Minutes of the Organizational Meetings of the Incorporator and the Board of Directors

On motion duly made, seconded and carried, it was ordered that the secretary/treasurer act without bond.

Principal Office.
On motion duly made, seconded and carried, it was:
RESOLVED, that the principal office of the corporation for the transaction of its business is _____, (city), (state)

Books.
The secretary was authorized and directed to procure the proper corporate books, including stationery and office supplies, necessary for the administration of the affairs of the corporation.

Depository.
On motion duly made, seconded and carried, it was:

RESOLVED, that _____ (bank), (city), (county), (state), is selected as a depository for the moneys, funds and credits of the corporation; and that the following officers, president and secretary/treasurer, are authorized and shall sign for the transfer or withdrawal of funds on deposit in the bank and are authorized and empowered to draw checks (including checks payable to their own order or to bearer) on the above depository, against the account of the corporation with the depository, and to endorse in the name of the corporation and receive payment of all checks, drafts and commercial papers payable to the corporation, either as payee or endorsee;

FURTHER RESOLVED, that the authority conferred shall remain in full force and effect until revoked and until a formal written notice of the revocation shall have been given to and received by _____ (bank);

FURTHER RESOLVED that the certification of the secretary of the corporation as to the election and appointment of persons so authorized to sign checks and as to the signatures of the persons shall be binding on the corporation;

FURTHER RESOLVED, that the president of the corporation is authorized to deliver to _____ (bank) a copy of these resolutions properly certified by the corporation, if so requested.

Execution of Contracts.
On motion duly made, seconded and carried, it was:

RESOLVED, that all contracts of the corporation shall be signed by the president and attested by the secretary.

Officers' Salaries.
Upon recommendation of the chairperson and on motion duly made, seconded and carried, it was:

RESOLVED, that the officers of the corporation shall receive no salary.

Reports.
On motion duly made, seconded and carried, it was:

RESOLVED, that the president, or any officer chosen, has the power to file necessary reports required by state or federal law.

There being no further business to come before the meeting, on motion duly made, seconded and carried, the meeting was adjourned.

_____
Secretary of the Meeting

FORM 10.3. *continued*

If a corporation fails to substantially comply with the requirements for formation of a corporation, the corporation does not exist in the eyes of the law, leaving the shareholders personally liable for debts and obligations of the defective corporation. Lawmakers recognize that the statutory formalities required for the creation of a corporation are cumbersome and can be a trap for the unwary. Therefore, it is possible for a business that does not strictly comply with a state's incorporation procedures to receive some of the liability protections afforded shareholders of a properly formed corporation based upon the theory that the business is either a de facto corporation or a corporation by estoppel.

De Facto Corporations

A business owner who, in good faith, attempts to satisfy the state's statutory incorporation procedures, but fails to strictly comply, may have his or her business classified as a ***de facto corporation*** if the business is conducted in good faith as though it were in fact a corporation (e.g., under its corporate name). As a *de facto* corporation, a creditor of the corporation cannot hold the shareholders personally liable for the corporate debts and obligations. However, it must be noted that the shareholders of a *de facto* corporation are not protected from personal liability in actions brought by the state to declare the corporation invalid.

> **Example:** The shareholders of ABC T-shirts, Inc. contract with the local high school to provide marching band shirts for a school fundraiser. Prior to delivery of the shirts, the school pays ABC an advance of $5,000. ABC has an equipment failure and does not provide the shirts. The high school tries to sue the corporation for recovery of the money, however, the corporation has assets of only $500. The high school then attempts to sue the individual shareholders on the theory that the corporation was not validly incorporated because it did not identify a registered agent in its articles of incorporation. The court finds that ABC is a *de facto* corporation and dismisses the high school's suit against the shareholders.

The R.M.B.C.A. recognizes that it is not uncommon for business owners to fail to strictly comply with a state's intricate incorporation requirements. To protect these owners, it provides that acceptance of a corporation's articles of incorporation by the secretary of state is conclusive proof that the business has complied with all statutory requirements for formation of a corporation. This provision does not, however, grant de jure status to these corporations. As with the *de facto* incorporation doctrine, the R.M.B.C.A. prevents creditors of these corporations from holding shareholders personally liable for the debts and obligations of the corporation; it does not prevent the state from challenging its corporate status.[3]

Despite the protections that a defective corporation may be afforded, attorneys and paralegals are employed to ensure that business owners properly comply with statutory incorporation procedures. Therefore, it is imperative that you become familiar with the statutory incorporation provisions for your state.

Corporation by Estoppel

Generally, if a business is not properly incorporated and has not made a good faith effort to comply with the state's statutory requirements for incorporation, the shareholders will be held personally liable for the debts and obligations of the corporation. However, in limited cases involving contract disputes with corporations, courts have found that creditors of a corporation are estopped from denying the corporate status of a business and suing the shareholders personally.

The theory of **incorporation by estoppel** is intended to reflect the parties' expectations in a contract situation. That is, if a party to a contract believes that it is dealing with a corporation, it does not expect that the shareholders of the corporation will be personally liable in the event the corporation breaches its contract. Therefore, if the contracting party later learns that the business is not in fact incorporated, the party cannot seek to set aside the corporate status and hold the shareholders personally liable. To do so would not fulfill

De facto corporation A business that has not strictly complied with the state's statutory incorporation process but conducts business in good faith as though it were a corporation.

Incorporation by estoppel A business that is not properly incorporated but may be extended the liability protections of a corporation in a contract dispute.

> **Example:** American Books, Inc., a local bookstore, contracts with Pen Publishers to purchase 2,000 book titles for its store. While Pen Publishers provides the books in accordance with its contract with American Books, Inc., American fails to pay the amounts due for the books. As Pen Publishers is preparing to bring suit against American Books, Inc., it finds that American is not, in fact, a corporation. Therefore, Pen Publishers brings suit against the owner of American for the full amount of the contract price. The court finds that the owner of American did not intentionally deceive Pen Publishers, he simply did not understand that any paperwork needed to be filed with the state in order to form a corporation. Furthermore, the court finds that because Pen Publishers believed it was contracting with a corporation, it did not expect that the owner would have any personal liability for a breach of the contract. Therefore, the court holds that Pen Publishers is *estopped* from trying to circumvent the liability protections which it believed, at the time of contracting with American, that American would be afforded in the event of a breach.

the expectations of the parties to the contract; at the time of entering into the contract, both parties believed that they were dealing with a corporate entity, with its accompanying liability protections.

TAXATION CONSIDERATIONS

Federal Income Taxation

The corporation is a separate legal entity from its shareholders and is, therefore, taxed as a "person" on its business income. Accordingly, the corporation must file its own income tax return, with its own tax identification number. (See Form 10.4, *IRS Form 1120, U.S. Corporation Income Tax Return.*) Once the corporate profits are distributed as dividends to the shareholders, each shareholder must pay taxes on the distribution as personal income. (See Form 10.5, *IRS Form 1040, Schedule B, Interest and Dividend Income.*)

This taxation structure is the most significant disadvantage of the corporation and discourages many business owners from choosing this form of business organization.

The corporation is the only business organization that suffers double taxation. Although corporate taxation is a distinct disadvantage of corporations and businesses acting like a corporation, corporations can structure their business organization and finances to minimize the impact of double taxation. For example, they can hire shareholders as officers or employees of the corporation and pay them salaries, which are a deductible expense to the corporation. Corporations can also hold profits and not make dividend distributions to shareholders, as long as they do not do so unreasonably.[4]

Although good tax advice can reduce the effect of the double taxation suffered by the corporation and its shareholders, most large publicly held corporations accept it as the cost of doing business. Smaller corporations may, however, be able to alleviate the disadvantages of double taxation if they can qualify as an S corporation.[5]

S Corporations

Most corporations are referred to as C corporations and suffer the disadvantage of double taxation on their business income.[6] However, many small businesses may qualify for special tax treatment as an S corporation and effectively eliminate the significant burden of double taxation of their corporate profits.

If an S election is made, the corporation is taxed as a partnership. Thus, the corporate profits "pass through" the corporation tax-free and the shareholders are taxed personally on their percentage of the corporate profits, whether or not the corporation has actually distributed all of the profits to its shareholders. This taxation scheme is particularly beneficial to small, closely held corporations that expect a net loss during the first years of business. The losses of the corporation during this time can be passed through to the shareholders who may use the losses to offset other sources of income.

Form **1120**	U.S. Corporation Income Tax Return	OMB No. 1545-0123
Department of the Treasury Internal Revenue Service	For calendar year 1999 or tax year beginning ...., 1999, ending ...., ... ▶ Instructions are separate. See page 1 for Paperwork Reduction Act Notice.	**1999**

A Check if a:	**Use IRS label. Otherwise, print or type.**	Name	**B** Employer identification number
1 Consolidated return (attach Form 851) ☐			
2 Personal holding co. (attach Sch. PH) ☐		Number, street, and room or suite no. (If a P.O. box, see page 5 of instructions.)	**C** Date incorporated
3 Personal service corp. (as defined in Temporary Regs. sec. 1.441-4T—see instructions) ☐		City or town, state, and ZIP code	**D** Total assets (see page 6 of instructions)

E Check applicable boxes: (1) ☐ Initial return (2) ☐ Final return (3) ☐ Change of address $

	1a	Gross receipts or sales _____ **b** .ess returns and allowances _____ **c** Bal ▶	**1c**	
	2	Cost of goods sold (Schedule A, line 8)	**2**	
	3	Gross profit. Subtract line 2 from line 1c	**3**	
	4	Dividends (Schedule C, line 19)	**4**	
Income	**5**	Interest	**5**	
	6	Gross rents	**6**	
	7	Gross royalties	**7**	
	8	Capital gain net income (attach Schedule D (Form 1120))	**8**	
	9	Net gain or (loss) from Form 4797, Part II, line 18 (attach Form 4797) . .	**9**	
	10	Other income (see page 7 of instructions—attach schedule)	**10**	
	11	**Total income.** Add lines 3 through 10 . . . . ▶	**11**	

Deductions (See instructions for limitations on deductions.)	**12**	Compensation of officers (Schedule E, line 4)	**12**	
	13	Salaries and wages (less employment credits)	**13**	
	14	Repairs and maintenance	**14**	
	15	Bad debts	**15**	
	16	Rents	**16**	
	17	Taxes and licenses	**17**	
	18	Interest	**18**	
	19	Charitable contributions (see page 9 of instructions for 10% limitation)	**19**	
	20	Depreciation (attach Form 4562) **20**		
	21	Less depreciation claimed on Schedule A and elsewhere on return . . . **21a**	**21b**	
	22	Depletion	**22**	
	23	Advertising	**23**	
	24	Pension, profit-sharing, etc., plans	**24**	
	25	Employee benefit programs	**25**	
	26	Other deductions (attach schedule)	**26**	
	27	**Total deductions.** Add lines 12 through 26 . . . . . ▶	**27**	
	28	Taxable income before net operating loss deduction and special deductions. Subtract line 27 from line 11	**28**	
	29	**Less:** **a** Net operating loss (NO.) deduction (see page 11 of instructions) **29a**		
		b Special deductions (Schedule C, line 20) **29b**	**29c**	

Tax and Payments	**30**	**Taxable income.** Subtract line 29c from line 28	**30**	
	31	**Total tax** (Schedule J, line 12)	**31**	
	32	**Payments: a** 1998 overpayment credited to 1999 **32a**		
	b	1999 estimated tax payments . . . **32b**		
	c	Less 1999 refund applied for on Form 4466 **32c** ( ) **d** Bal ▶ **32d**		
	e	Tax deposited with Form 7004 . . . . **32e**		
	f	Credit for tax paid on undistributed capital gains (attach Form 2439) . . . **32f**		
	g	Credit for Federal tax on fuels (attach Form 4136). See instructions . . . **32g**	**32h**	
	33	Estimated tax penalty (see page 12 of instructions). Check if Form 2220 is attached . . . . ▶ ☐	**33**	
	34	**Tax due.** If line 32h is smaller than the total of lines 31 and 33, enter amount owed	**34**	
	35	**Overpayment.** If line 32h is larger than the total of lines 31 and 33, enter amount overpaid . . .	**35**	
	36	Enter amount of line 35 you want: **Credited to 2000 estimated tax** ▶ **Refunded** ▶	**36**	

Sign Here

Under penalties of perjury, I declare that I have examined this return, including accompanying schedules and statements, and to the best of my knowledge and belief, it is true, correct, and complete. Declaration of preparer (other than taxpayer) is based on all information of which preparer has any knowledge.

▶ _____ _____ ▶ _____
Signature of officer   Date   Title

Paid Preparer's Use Only	Preparer's signature ▶	Date	Check if self-employed ☐	Preparer's SSN or PTIN
	Firm's name (or yours if self-employed) and address ▶		EIN ▶	
			ZIP code ▶	

Cat. No. 11450Q   Form **1120** (1999)

FORM 10.4.

IRS Form 1120, U.S. Corporation Income Tax Return

Schedules A&B (Form 1040) 1999   OMB No. 1545-0074   Page **2**

Name(s) shown on Form 1040. Do not enter name and social security number if shown on other side.   **Your social security number**

Schedule B—Interest and Ordinary Dividends
Attachment Sequence No. **08**

Note. If you had over $400 in taxable interest, you must also complete Part III.

Part I Interest

(See page B-1 and the instructions for Form 1040, line 8a.)

1 List name of payer. If any interest is from a seller-financed mortgage and the buyer used the property as a personal residence, see page B-1 and list this interest first. Also, show that buyer's social security number and address ▶

Amount

Note. If you received a Form 1099-INT, Form 1099-OID, or substitute statement from a brokerage firm, list the firm's name as the payer and enter the total interest shown on that form.

2 Add the amounts on line 1	2
3 Excludable interest on series EE and I U.S. savings bonds issued after 1989 from Form 8815, line 14. You **MUST** attach Form 8815	3
4 Subtract line 3 from line 2. Enter the result here and on Form 1040, line 8a ▶	4

Note. If you had over $400 in ordinary dividends, you must also complete Part III.

Part II Ordinary Dividends

(See page B-1 and the instructions for Form 1040, line 9.)

5 List name of payer. Include only ordinary dividends. If you received any capital gain distributions, see the instructions for Form 1040, line 13 ▶

Amount

Note. If you received a Form 1099-DIV or substitute statement from a brokerage firm, list the firm's name as the payer and enter the ordinary dividends shown on that form.

6 Add the amounts on line 5. Enter the total here and on Form 1040, line 9 ▶	6

Part III Foreign Accounts and Trusts

(See page B-2.)

You must complete this part if you **(a)** had over $400 of interest or ordinary dividends; **(b)** had a foreign account; or **(c)** received a distribution from, or were a grantor of, or a transferor to, a foreign trust.   Yes No

7a At any time during 1999, did you have an interest in or a signature or other authority over a financial account in a foreign country, such as a bank account, securities account, or other financial account? See page B-2 for exceptions and filing requirements for Form TD F 90-22.1 . . . .

b If "Yes," enter the name of the foreign country ▶

8 During 1999, did you receive a distribution from, or were you the grantor of, or transferor to, a foreign trust? If "Yes," you may have to file Form 3520. See page B-2 . . . .

For Paperwork Reduction Act Notice, see Form 1040 instructions.   Schedule B (Form 1040) 1999

FORM 10.5.
IRS Form 1040, Schedule B, Interest and Dividend Income

In order to qualify as an S corporation, an existing corporation must:

♦ be a domestic corporation (incorporated under one of the fifty states);
♦ not have more than seventy-five shareholders;
♦ have only natural persons or their estates as shareholders (i.e., it cannot have corporations or partnerships as shareholders);
♦ have only shareholders who are United States citizens or resident aliens; and
♦ have only one class of stock.

In order for a corporation to receive the pass-through taxation benefits of a partnership, it must maintain compliance with these requirements. If at any time it fails to do so, it will lose its status as an S corporation and will be taxed as a C corporation.

The election to become an S corporation is made by the corporation's board of directors with the consent of its shareholders. (See Form 10.6, *IRS Form 2553, Election by a Small Business Corporation.*) The S election must be made before the fifteenth day of the third month of the corporation's calendar year in order for the corporation to receive pass-through taxation for that year. Thus, a corporation with a calendar year January 1 to December 31 must make the election before March 15 in order to be taxed as an S corporation for the year. Once the election is made, the corporation must report its income and losses as well as each shareholder's percentage of the income and losses to the IRS. (See Form 10.7, *IRS Form 1120S, U.S. Income Tax Return for an S Corporation.*) The individual shareholders then report their respective portion of the corporate profits or losses as their personal income. (See Form 10.8, *IRS Form 1040, Schedule E, Supplemental Income and Loss.*)

Example: ABC Cleaning, Inc., an S corporation, has two shareholders, each owning 50 percent of the corporation. ABC's profits for the year 1997 were $40,000. ABC properly reports its income to the IRS and each shareholder's respective percentage of the profits ($20,000 each). Each shareholder then reports $20,000 (50 percent) of the profits of ABC Cleaning, Inc. as personal income.

S corporations have been popular in the past because of their unique tax advantage combined with the liability protections of the corporation. However, as more states adopt the limited liability company, which offers the corporate liability protections, member management, and few operational formalities, the popularity of the S corporation will likely decrease in the future.

State Income Taxation

In addition to the federal taxation imposed upon corporations, all corporations must also consider their state income tax liability. Corporations are subject to state income tax, as any person is. However, because corporations typically conduct business in more than one state, each state in which the corporation does business may tax the corporation only on the business activity that the corporation transacts in its state.

PRO-RATA

Example: Toys 'N Kids, Inc. is incorporated in the state of California, where it conducts 48 percent of its business. It conducts 30 percent of its business in Nevada, 4 percent of its business in Utah, and 18 percent of its business in Washington State. In 1997, Toys 'N Kids reports a profit of $100,000. Theoretically, it should pay California taxes on $48,000, Nevada taxes on $30,000, Utah taxes on $4,000, and Washington State taxes on $18,000.

However, each state has its own method for determining what business a corporation conducts within its borders. A state in which many corporations reside (corporate headquarters, factories, etc.) may tax businesses based upon the corporate assets within the state. In contrast, states in which few corporations are located but in which corporations transact business, may tax a corporation on its sales profits earned within the state. Although each state will attempt to maximize the taxes it collects from business activity

Form **2553**	**Election by a Small Business Corporation**	
(Rev. July 1999)	(Under section 1362 of the Internal Revenue Code)	OMB No. 1545-0146
Department of the Treasury Internal Revenue Service	▶ See Parts II and III on back and the separate instructions. ▶ The corporation may either send or fax this form to the IRS. See page 1 of the instructions.	

Notes:
1. *This election to be an S corporation can be accepted only if all the tests are met under **Who may elect** on page 1 of the instructions; all signatures in Parts I and III are originals (no photocopies); and the exact name and address of the corporation and other required form information are provided.*
2. *Do not file **Form 1120S**, U.S. Income Tax Return for an S Corporation, for any tax year before the year the election takes effect.*
3. *If the corporation was in existence before the effective date of this election, see **Taxes an S corporation may owe** on page 1 of the instructions.*

Part I   Election Information

Please Type or Print	Name of corporation (see instructions)	A Employer identification number
	Number, street, and room or suite no. (If a P.O. box, see instructions.)	B Date incorporated
	City or town, state, and ZIP code	C State of incorporation

D Election is to be effective for tax year beginning (month, day, year) . . . . ▶   /   /

E Name and title of officer or legal representative who the IRS may call for more information

F Telephone number of officer or legal representative   (   )

G If the corporation changed its name or address after applying for the EIN shown in **A** above, check this box . . . . ▶ ☐

H If this election takes effect for the first tax year the corporation exists, enter month, day, and year of the **earliest** of the following: (1) date the corporation first had shareholders, (2) date the corporation first had assets, or (3) date the corporation began doing business . . . . ▶   /   /

I Selected tax year: Annual return will be filed for tax year ending (month and day) ▶----------

If the tax year ends on any date other than December 31, except for an automatic 52-53-week tax year ending with reference to the month of December, you **must** complete Part II on the back. If the date you enter is the ending date of an automatic 52-53-week tax year, write "52-53-week year" to the right of the date. See Temporary Regulations section 1.441-2T(e)(3).

J Name and address of each shareholder; shareholder's spouse having a community property interest in the corporation's stock; and each tenant in common, joint tenant, and tenant by the entirety. (A husband and wife (and their estates) are counted as one shareholder in determining the number of shareholders without regard to the manner in which the stock is owned.)	K Shareholders' Consent Statement. Under penalties of perjury, we declare that we consent to the election of the above-named corporation to be an S corporation under section 1362(a) and that we have examined this consent statement, including accompanying schedules and statements, and to the best of our knowledge and belief, it is true, correct, and complete. We understand our consent is binding and may not be withdrawn after the corporation has made a valid election. (Shareholders sign and date below.)		L Stock owned		M Social security number or employer identification number (see instructions)	N Share-holder's tax year ends (month and day)
	Signature	Date	Number of shares	Dates acquired		

Under penalties of perjury, I declare that I have examined this election, including accompanying schedules and statements, and to the best of my knowledge and belief, it is true, correct, and complete.

Signature of officer ▶   Title ▶   Date ▶

For Paperwork Reduction Act Notice, see page 2 of the instructions.   Cat. No. 18629R   Form **2553** (Rev. 7-99)

FORM 10.6.

IRS Form 2553, Election by a Small Business Corporation

Form **1120S**	**U.S. Income Tax Return for an S Corporation**	OMB No. 1545-0130
Department of the Treasury Internal Revenue Service	▶ **Do not file this form unless the corporation has timely filed Form 2553 to elect to be an S corporation.** ▶ See separate instructions.	**1999**

For calendar year 1999, or tax year beginning _____ , 1999, and ending _____ ,

A Effective date of election as an S corporation	Use IRS label. Other- wise, please print or type.	Name	C Employer identification number
B Business code no. (see pages 26–28)		Number, street, and room or suite no. (If a P.O. box, see page 10 of the instructions.)	D Date incorporated
		City or town, state, and ZIP code	E Total assets (see page 10) $

F Check applicable boxes: (1) ☐ Initial return   (2) ☐ Final return   (3) ☐ Change in address   (4) ☐ Amended return

G Enter number of shareholders in the corporation at end of the tax year . . . . ▶

Caution: *Include **only** trade or business income and expenses on lines 1a through 21. See page 10 of the instructions for more information.*

Income

1a Gross receipts or sales _____ **b** Less returns and allowances _____ **c** Bal ▶		**1c**	
2 Cost of goods sold (Schedule A, line 8)		**2**	
3 Gross profit. Subtract line 2 from line 1c		**3**	
4 Net gain (loss) from Form 4797, Part II, line 18 *(attach Form 4797)*		**4**	
5 Other income (loss) *(attach schedule)*		**5**	
6 **Total income (loss).** Combine lines 3 through 5 . . . . ▶		**6**	

Deductions *(see page 11 of the instructions for limitations)*

7 Compensation of officers		**7**	
8 Salaries and wages (less employment credits)		**8**	
9 Repairs and maintenance.		**9**	
10 Bad debts		**10**	
11 Rents		**11**	
12 Taxes and licenses.		**12**	
13 Interest		**13**	
14a Depreciation *(if required, attach Form 4562)* **14a**			
b Depreciation claimed on Schedule A and elsewhere on return . **14b**			
c Subtract line 14b from line 14a		**14c**	
15 Depletion **(Do not deduct oil and gas depletion.)**		**15**	
16 Advertising		**16**	
17 Pension, profit-sharing, etc., plans		**17**	
18 Employee benefit programs		**18**	
19 Other deductions *(attach schedule)*		**19**	
20 **Total deductions.** Add the amounts shown in the far right column for lines 7 through 19 ▶		**20**	
21 Ordinary income (loss) from trade or business activities. Subtract line 20 from line 6		**21**	

Tax and Payments

22 **Tax: a** Excess net passive income tax *(attach schedule)*. . . **22a**			
b Tax from Schedule D (Form 1120S) **22b**			
c Add lines 22a and 22b (see page 14 of the instructions for additional taxes)		**22c**	
23 **Payments: a** 1999 estimated tax payments and amount applied from 1998 return **23a**			
b Tax deposited with Form 7004 . . . . . **23b**			
c Credit for Federal tax paid on fuels *(attach Form 4136)* . . . **23c**			
d Add lines 23a through 23c		**23d**	
24 Estimated tax penalty. Check if Form 2220 is attached . . . . . . ▶ ☐		**24**	
25 **Tax due.** If the total of lines 22c and 24 is larger than line 23d, enter amount owed. See page 4 of the instructions for depository method of payment . . . . ▶		**25**	
26 **Overpayment.** If line 23d is larger than the total of lines 22c and 24, enter amount overpaid ▶		**26**	
27 Enter amount of line 26 you want: **Credited to 2000 estimated tax** ▶ _____ **Refunded** ▶		**27**	

Please Sign Here

Under penalties of perjury, I declare that I have examined this return, including accompanying schedules and statements, and to the best of my knowledge and belief, it is true, correct, and complete. Declaration of preparer (other than taxpayer) is based on all information of which preparer has any knowledge.

▶ _____ _____ ▶ _____
Signature of officer   Date   Title

Paid Preparer's Use Only

Preparer's signature ▶		Date	Check if self- employed ▶ ☐	Preparer's SSN or PTIN
Firm's name (or yours if self-employed) and address	▶		EIN ▶	
			ZIP code ▶	

For Paperwork Reduction Act Notice, see the separate instructions.   Cat. No. 11510H   Form **1120S** (1999)

FORM 10.7.
IRS Form 1120S, U.S. Income Tax Return for an S Corporation

SCHEDULE E
(Form 1040)

Department of the Treasury
Internal Revenue Service   (99)

Supplemental Income and Loss

(From rental real estate, royalties, partnerships,
S corporations, estates, trusts, REMICs, etc.)

▶ Attach to Form 1040 or Form 1041.   ▶ See Instructions for Schedule E (Form 1040).

OMB No. 1545-0074

1999

Attachment
Sequence No. **13**

Name(s) shown on return

Your social security number

| Part I | Income or Loss From Rental Real Estate and Royalties | Note: *Report income and expenses from your business of renting personal property on* **Schedule C** *or* **C-EZ** *(see page E-1). Report farm rental income or loss from* **Form 4835** *on page 2, line 39.* |

1 Show the kind and location of each **rental real estate property:**	2 For each rental real estate property listed on line 1, did you or your family use it during the tax year for personal purposes for more than the greater of:		Yes	No
A			A	
B	● 14 days, **or**		B	
C	● 10% of the total days rented at fair rental value? (See page E-1.)		C	

Income:			Properties			Totals (Add columns A, B, and C.)
			A	B	C	
3 Rents received	3					3
4 Royalties received	4					4
Expenses:						
5 Advertising	5					
6 Auto and travel (see page E-2) .	6					
7 Cleaning and maintenance . . .	7					
8 Commissions	8					
9 Insurance	9					
10 Legal and other professional fees	10					
11 Management fees	11					
12 Mortgage interest paid to banks, etc. (see page E-2)	12					12
13 Other interest	13					
14 Repairs	14					
15 Supplies	15					
16 Taxes	16					
17 Utilities	17					
18 Other (list) ▶...................	18					
19 Add lines 5 through 18	19					19
20 Depreciation expense or depletion (see page E-3)	20					20
21 Total expenses. Add lines 19 and 20	21					
22 Income or (loss) from rental real estate or royalty properties. Subtract line 21 from line 3 (rents) or line 4 (royalties). If the result is a (loss), see page E-3 to find out if you must file **Form 6198** . . .	22					
23 Deductible rental real estate loss. **Caution:** *Your rental real estate loss on line 22 may be limited. See page E-3 to find out if you must file* **Form 8582**. *Real estate professionals must complete line 42 on page 2* . .	23	(	)(	)(	)	
24 **Income.** Add positive amounts shown on line 22. **Do not** include any losses					24	
25 **Losses.** Add royalty losses from line 22 and rental real estate losses from line 23. Enter total losses here					25	( )
26 Total rental real estate and royalty income or (loss). Combine lines 24 and 25. Enter the result here. If Parts II, III, IV, and line 39 on page 2 do not apply to you, also enter this amount on Form 1040, line 17. Otherwise, include this amount in the total on line 40 on page 2					26	

For Paperwork Reduction Act Notice, see Form 1040 instructions.   Cat. No. 11344 .   **Schedule E (Form 1040) 1999**

FORM 10.8.

IRS Form 1040, Schedule E, Supplemental Income and Loss.

Schedule E (Form 1040) 1999

Attachment Sequence No. **13**

Page **2**

Name(s) shown on return. Do not enter name and social security number if shown on other side.

Your social security number

Note: *If you report amounts from farming or fishing on Schedule E, you must enter your gross income from those activities on line 41 below. Real estate professionals must complete line 42 below.*

| Part II | Income or Loss From Partnerships and S Corporations |

Note: *If you report a loss from an at-risk activity, you MUST check either column (e) or (f) on line 27 to describe your investment in the activity. See page E-5. If you check column (f), you must attach Form 6198.*

27	(a) Name	(b) Enter P for partnership; S for S corporation	(c) Check if foreign partnership	(d) Employer identification number	Investment At Risk? (e) All is at risk	(f) Some is not at risk
A						
B						
C						
D						
E						

	Passive Income and Loss		Nonpassive Income and Loss		
	(g) Passive loss allowed (attach Form 8582 if required)	(h) Passive income from Schedule K–1	(i) Nonpassive loss from Schedule K–1	(j) Section 179 expense deduction from Form 4562	(k) Nonpassive income from Schedule K–1
A					
B					
C					
D					
E					
28a Totals					
b Totals					

29	Add columns (h) and (k) of line 28a	29	
30	Add columns (g), (i), and (j) of line 28b	30	( )
31	Total partnership and S corporation income or (loss). Combine lines 29 and 30. Enter the result here and include in the total on line 40 below	31	

| Part III | Income or Loss From Estates and Trusts |

32	(a) Name	(b) Employer identification number
A		
B		

	Passive Income and Loss		Nonpassive Income and Loss	
	(c) Passive deduction or loss allowed (attach Form 8582 if required)	(d) Passive income from Schedule K–1	(e) Deduction or loss from Schedule K–1	(f) Other income from Schedule K–1
A				
B				
33a Totals				
b Totals				

34	Add columns (d) and (f) of line 33a	34	
35	Add columns (c) and (e) of line 33b	35	( )
36	Total estate and trust income or (loss). Combine lines 34 and 35. Enter the result here and include in the total on line 40 below	36	

| Part IV | Income or Loss From Real Estate Mortgage Investment Conduits (REMICs)—Residual Holder |

37	(a) Name	(b) Employer identification number	(c) Excess inclusion from Schedules Q, line 2c (see page E-6)	(d) Taxable income (net loss) from Schedules Q, line 1b	(e) Income from Schedules Q, line 3b

38	Combine columns (d) and (e) only. Enter the result here and include in the total on line 40 below	38	

| Part V | Summary |

39	Net farm rental income or (loss) from Form 4835. Also, complete line 41 below . . . . . . ▶	39	
40	TOTAL income or (loss). Combine lines 26, 31, 36, 38, and 39. Enter the result here and on Form 1040, line 17 ▶	40	

41	**Reconciliation of Farming and Fishing Income.** Enter your gross farming and fishing income reported on Form 4835, line 7; Schedule K-1 (Form 1065), line 15b; Schedule K-1 (Form 1120S), line 23; and Schedule K-1 (Form 1041), line 14 (see page E-6)	41	
42	**Reconciliation for Real Estate Professionals.** If you were a real estate professional (see page E-4), enter the net income or (loss) you reported anywhere on Form 1040 from all rental real estate activities in which you materially participated under the passive activity loss rules . .	42	

Schedule E (Form 1040) 1999

FORM 10.8. *continued*

within its borders, prorated state taxing is intended to prevent corporations from paying multiple states income tax on the same business profits.

FURTHER CONSIDERATIONS

The creation of a corporation requires strict compliance with statutory requirements of the state of incorporation. The benefits of incorporation, particularly shareholder liability protections, must be weighed against the disadvantages of the corporate form, notably the extensive formalities required before and during incorporation as well as the double taxation suffered by larger corporations.

Most clients who choose to incorporate their businesses do so in order to gain the extensive liability protections of this form of business organization. However, with the emergence of the limited liability company and the limited liability partnership, which also offer liability protections to their owners, clients now have more options for organizing their businesses.

◆ FORMATION OF A CORPORATION IN REVIEW

Preincorporation Considerations
◆ Selection of jurisdiction
◆ Corporate financing through preincorporation share subscriptions

Key Considerations of the Paralegal
◆ Preincorporation document preparation
  1. Reserve corporate name with the secretary of state prior to doing business in a state.
  2. Register assumed business name with the secretary of state.
  3. Prepare and file corporate articles of incorporation with the secretary of state.
  4. Obtain required business and/or professional licenses and permits.
◆ Postincorporation transactions
  1. Prepare corporate bylaws.
  2. Hold organizational meeting.
◆ Taxation considerations
  1. Apply for a sales tax permit if goods will be sold.
  2. Apply for a tax identification number with the IRS and state.
  3. If employees will be hired:
     a. establish employee withholding accounts, and
     b. establish unemployment and workers' compensation coverage.
  4. Elect and file S election on IRS Form 2553, if applicable.

◆ KEY TERMS

promoter	foreign corporation	*de jure* corporation
incorporater	domestic corporation	*de facto* corporation
forum shopping	preincorporation share subscription	incorporation by estoppel

◆ STUDY QUESTIONS IN REVIEW

1. How does a corporation notify the public of its corporate status?
2. Once a business files its articles of incorporation with the secretary of state, does its corporate existence begin?
3. What is the purpose of the corporation's organizational meeting?
4. Distinguish between a *de jure* corporation and a *de facto* corporation.

5. Will the owners (shareholders) of a corporation be held personally liable for the debts and obligations of the corporation if the business has not properly complied with the state's statutory requirements for formation of a corporation?

6. What unincorporated business entity most closely resembles a corporation?

7. What is an S corporation?

8. What are the qualifications necessary for a corporation to seek an S election?

9. Distinguish between the manner in which a partnership is taxed and the manner in which a corporation is taxed.

10. Flint, Inc. conducts 75 percent of its business in California, 15 percent in Idaho, and 10 percent in Washington. Which state can tax the company on its profits?

◆ CASE STUDIES IN REVIEW

1. Larry, Joe, and Curly own an excavating business together. Because of their potential liability for errors (hitting a gas line) or omissions (failing to locate electrical or other service lines before a dig), they want to incorporate to protect their personal assets. They ask Joe's girlfriend, a paralegal student, how they go about forming a corporation. She tells them that all they have to do is add the designation "Inc." after their name. Larry, Joe, and Curly therefore call their company Big Hole, Inc. No documents are prepared for the corporation or filed with the secretary of state.

   Big Hole, Inc. contracts with a local homebuilder to excavate the foundation for a new home in downtown Dallas. The parties' contract recites that the excavators will have all service lines located prior to beginning excavation work. Curly is responsible for scheduling the location; however, his wife has a baby the week before the work is to begin and he forgets to have the lines located. During the excavation, Larry hits a main power line that supplies power to over 1 million Dallas residents. The cost for the repairs is $500,000; Big Hole, Inc. does not have the insurance or funds to pay for the repairs. The power company's attorney learns that Big Hole, Inc. is not even a registered corporation with the secretary of state. Therefore, the attorney files suit against Larry, Curly, and Joe personally. Can the power company sue Larry, Joe, and Curly personally to cover the repairs?

2. Beehive Honey, Inc., a California corporation, is owned by the Arthur brothers of Sacramento. Each of the three brothers has an equal interest in the business (e.g., the same class of stock). The brothers have asked your supervising attorney to help them find a way to reduce the tax liability. What ideas would you offer your supervising attorney?

3. Explain the tax structure that would result from your ideas in Case Study #2. (Hint: You need to know the answer to #2 to answer this question.)

◆ PROJECT APPLICATIONS

1. Your supervising attorney has given you the following task:

   TO: File
   FROM: MEB
   DATE: June 9, 1999
   RE: Incorporation of Book Club 2000

   Book Club 2000 is a publisher of children's books, headquartered in Dallas, Texas. The company is owned by a husband and wife team, Jan and Hal Steven; the business is run out of their garage. They want to incorporate their business, but they are very concerned about the tax consequences of incorporating. They intend to be the only shareholders of the corporation and hold equal interests. Hal will be the president of the corporation (and the agent for service of process) and Jan will be the vice president. Their daughter Tracy Steven, who lives with them, will be the secretary. Their accountant and banker will be Ron Bill of Texas Security Bank, 111 NW Blvd., Dallas, Texas, 78626.

   I have explained to them the benefits of a sub-S election. Prepare the documents necessary to incorporate their business and complete the necessary tax forms for the sub-S election.

   Cc: Hal and Jan Steven
         459 Forkline Rd.
         Dallas, Texas 78626

2. After you have prepared the documents requested in Project Application #1, your supervising attorney tells you that the Stevens want their company to be a Delaware corporation because a friend told them that Delaware is "corporate friendly." Prepare the documents necessary for Book Club 2000 to be a Delaware corporation. (Hint: Obtain the filing requirements/forms from the Delaware Secretary of State.)

3. Prepare corporate bylaws for Book Club 2000, as a Delaware corporation.

◆ ENDNOTES

1. See R.M.B.C.A. at §4.01.
2. See M.B.C.A. § 2.02.
3. See R.M.B.C.A. §2.03(b).
4. See Internal Revenue Code (hereafter I.R.C.) 26 U.S.C.A. § 531.
5. See I.R.C. 26 U.S.C.A. § 1361(a)(1).
6. See I.R.C. 26 U.S.C.A. § 1361(3).

Corporate Organizational Structure

A corporation is owned by its shareholders, governed by its board of directors, and managed by its officers. Many people think of the corporate structure as a pyramid, with thousands of shareholders at the bottom, a large ominous-looking board of directors making corporate decisions, and a small group of corporate officers managing the daily operations of the corporation. However, most corporations do not fit this stereotype. In fact, a large percentage of corporations are owned and operated by a handful of people, sometimes just family members or friends investing in a business venture. In such small corporations, the shareholders are often also the directors and officers. (See "Statutory Close Corporations" in Chapter 9.) With the exception of such close corporations, the organizational structure of corporations is generally three-tiered, although the tiers may be overlapping (i.e., one or more shareholders can also be managers and/or directors), as demonstrated in Table 11.1.

SHAREHOLDERS: CORPORATE OWNERS

The owners of a corporation are called *shareholders* or *stockholders*. Shareholders contribute investment capital to a corporation and receive an ownership interest, represented by a stock certificate, in return. The shareholders do not own the assets of the corporation (buildings, cars, etc.). Rather, a shareholder "owns" the right to receive distributions of corporate profits (if the board of directors declares a dividend), elect or remove directors, vote on extraordinary corporate matters, and receive a proportionate share of corporate assets, if any, in a dissolution.

Because shareholders do not manage the corporation, they generally are not personally liable for the debts and obligations of the corporation. Their liability is limited to the amount of their investment in the corporation (their shares).

SHAREHOLDERS' RIGHTS

Distribution Rights

The main reason that most individuals invest in a business is that they hope to receive a return on their investment. Although shareholders are owners of their corporation, they

---

TABLE 11.1. Corporate Organizational Structure

Shareholders	Corporate Owners
	Elect/limit directors
	Vote on extraordinary corporate actions
Directors	Policy Makers
	Make corporate policy
	Determine management of corporation
Officers	Daily Managers
	Implement corporate policies
	Manage daily operations of corporation

Distribution of
profits to shareholders.

are not automatically entitled to receive a distribution of the corporation's profits, known as corporate **dividends.** Shareholders only receive a share of the corporate profits if either:

1. the board of directors declares a corporate dividend, or
2. the corporation is dissolved and liquidated and there are still assets (money or corporate property) to distribute to the shareholders.

The board of directors may declare a dividend at any time, as long as the corporation would remain solvent after the distribution is made.[1] If the corporation can still pay its debts after it pays the dividend to the shareholders, the board of directors may distribute corporate profits to its shareholders. However, a board of directors is under no obligation to pay dividends on a regular basis or at all. In fact, it is common for new corporations to reinvest corporate profits back into the corporation in the hopes of increasing future profits rather than declaring a dividend.

Example: Films, Inc., earned a $100,000 profit on the release of its first feature film, *Hyperspace.* Rather than distributing any of the profit to its shareholders, the board of directors of Films, Inc. voted to use the profits to fund the company's next film, *Green Men.*

Dividends may be in the form of either cash or corporate property (including stock dividends). Although the dividends of most large publicly held corporations are cash distributions, shareholders may also receive corporate property as their share of the corporation's profits.

Example: Flyers, Inc., a locally owned airline specializing in backcountry pack trips, recently replaced one of its outdated six-seat airplanes with a new twelve-seat airplane. Because they no longer needed the airplane and could not find a buyer for the plane, the board of directors declared the airplane as a dividend to its sole shareholder, an avid pilot.

Such property distributions are not limited to small corporations; even Disney could distribute a video to its shareholders in lieu of cash.

Regardless of the form that a corporate dividend may take, corporate ownership does not guarantee a regular cash return on a shareholder's investment. Although many large corporations try to declare dividends on a consistent basis to encourage investment in their companies, short of selling stock, a shareholder cannot anticipate a monthly or even yearly dividend check.

Inspection Rights

Although shareholders do not have the right to participate in the ordinary management of the corporation, they do have the right to oversee the management of the corporation by inspecting the corporate books, including minutes of directors' meetings, bylaws, shareholder lists, and financial records. As long as the shareholder's purpose in inspecting corporate records is in good faith (e.g., reasonably related to the shareholder's interest in the corporation), a shareholder may inspect the corporate books after providing advance written notice to the corporation.[2]

Voting Rights

Shareholders have the right to elect and remove directors of the corporation and to vote on extraordinary corporate matters; the corporation's articles of incorporation can expand or restrict these rights. Shareholders' voting rights allow them to indirectly participate in management of the corporation. By electing directors who share the stockholders' views regarding operation of the corporation and by voting on fundamental corporate changes (e.g., amendment of the articles of incorporation, mergers), shareholders can and do have a say in how their corporation is run.

Election of Board of Directors

Shareholders have the right to elect the directors of the corporation. Although initial directors are often appointed in the corporation's articles of incorporation, shareholders generally hold the right to elect new directors at the first annual shareholders' meeting.

Because shareholders have the right to elect corporate policy makers, they indirectly control operation of the corporation. Many states recognize that it is important for all shareholders, even minority shareholders, to have representation on the board of directors. These states provide an opportunity for minority shareholders to combine their votes for directors in order to secure a director who will represent their interests. This procedure, known as **cumulative voting,** allows each shareholder to cast as many votes as there are vacancies on the board. Thus, if shareholder A owns 100 shares and there are four directors to elect, shareholder A would have 400 votes, which may be divided in any manner shareholder A wishes, including casting all 400 votes for one candidate. Although corporations can reduce the effectiveness of cumulative voting by, for example, reducing the number of directors elected at any one time (thereby reducing the overall number of votes a minority shareholder may cast), cumulative voting is an effective mechanism for providing minority shareholders the ability to secure representation of their interests on the board of directors. Without cumulative voting, majority shareholders could elect all of the corporation's directors without providing minority shareholders the power to elect any directors to represent their interests.

Extraordinary Corporate Matters

If an action by the board of directors will materially affect the ownership interests of the shareholders, the shareholders have the right to vote on the issues. Such **extraordinary corporate matters** include but are not limited to amendment of the articles of incorporation, mergers, sale of corporate assets not in the ordinary course of business, and corporate dissolution. Because such actions may have an adverse effect on the value of corporate shares, shareholders hold the right to review and reject a board of directors' actions with regard to such matters. Shareholders who object to a fundamental change in the corporate structure (e.g., merger, sale of business assets not in the ordinary course of business, and dissolution) have the right to have their stock appraised and purchased by the corporation.[3]

Voting Mechanisms

Quorum

A minimum number of shares issued by the corporation (represented by shareholders) must be present at the meeting in order for matters to be submitted to the shareholders for a valid vote. The minimum number of shares needed for a binding vote by shareholders is called a **quorum.**

Most corporations' articles of incorporation or bylaws provide the number of shares that must be represented in order to have a quorum; in the absence of such a provision, the Revised Model Business Corporation Act (R.M.B.C.A.) provides that a majority of the votes entitled to be cast constitute a quorum.[4] Once a quorum is present, a vote of the majority of shares of the quorum will constitute a valid and binding decision by the shareholders;[5] however, the corporation's articles of incorporation can require a larger number of voting by shareholders for a binding decision.

If a quorum is not present at a shareholders' meeting, the meeting must be adjourned and rescheduled until a quorum is present.

> **Example:** At the annual shareholders' meeting for Home Helpers, Inc., new directors will be elected. One thousand shares may vote for the directors. In order to have a quorum pursuant to the R.M.B.C.A., 501 shares must be present before matters may be submitted to the shareholders for a vote.

Proxies

Ideally, all shareholders will be present at a shareholders' meeting. Unfortunately this is impractical, especially for larger corporations with numerous shareholders living in

Cumulative voting A voting mechanism that allows each shareholder to cast as many votes as there are vacancies on a board of directors.

Extraordinary corporate matter An action that will affect the organization of the corporation.

Quorum The minimum number of shares or directors that must be present at a meeting for an action by shareholders or directors.

different states. In order to maximize the representation of shareholders at a meeting, and ensure that quorum requirements are met, shareholders may vote by proxy if they are unable to attend a meeting. A **proxy** is a written authorization for another person to vote on behalf of a shareholder. The shareholder may direct the proxy holder how to vote on particular issues (creating a **limited proxy**) or may allow the proxy holder to vote at his or her discretion (creating a **general proxy**). Proxies are often sent to shareholders with a notice of a shareholders' meeting, and corporations encourage shareholders who cannot attend the meeting to vote by proxy.

> **Example:** *General Proxy*
> I, Shareholder, appoint Cathy Kipp as my agent to vote on my behalf at the annual shareholders' meeting of Cat & Mouse, Inc., to be held on April 4, 1999, at 10:00 A.M. at the Holiday Inn Conference Room, 656 South Avenue West, Fremont, California, 59806. I hereby grant my agent the authority to act at her discretion on any matters presented at the meeting. Dated this _____ day of December, 2000.
>
> _____
> Shareholder

Preemptive Rights

Corporations occasionally issue new shares of stock to increase their capital and thus their investment potential. In order for existing shareholders to maintain their proportionate ownership interest of the corporation, and thus their proportionate voting power, the corporation may allow them to purchase the new shares of stock in the same proportion as they owned prior to the new issuance.[6] This right to preempt ownership and control of the corporation by outsiders is known as a shareholder's **preemptive right.**

Many states automatically grant shareholders preemptive rights, unless the corporation's articles of incorporation specifically prohibit them. However, the R.M.B.C.A. and other states provide that a shareholder has preemptive rights only if the corporation's articles of incorporation specifically provide such rights.[7] A statement as simple as "the corporation elects to have preemptive rights" is sufficient to ensure that existing shareholders will maintain their proportionate ownership interests in a corporation in the event the corporation issues new stock.

Meeting Rights of Shareholders

Meeting Prerequisites

Shareholders elect directors and vote on extraordinary corporate matters at annual or special shareholders' meetings. However, before a shareholders' meeting can be held, the shareholders entitled to vote at the meeting must be identified and given proper notice of the date, time, and place of the meeting.

Shareholders Eligible to Vote
Only shareholders who own corporate stock (with voting rights) according to the corporation's records on the date the board of directors issues notice of annual or special shareholder meetings, are entitled to vote at the noticed meeting. This date, known as the **record date,** is generally specified in the corporation's bylaws and is often thirty days before the meeting. Only shareholders who appear on the corporate books as stock owners on this date are entitled to notice of the meeting, even if they actually sell their respective shares prior to the actual meeting date.

Proxy Written authorization for another person to vote on behalf of a shareholder.

Limited proxy A proxy directing a proxy holder how to vote on a particular issue.

General proxy A proxy allowing a proxy holder to vote at his or her discretion.

Preemptive right The right of a shareholder to purchase newly issued shares of stock in order to maintain the shareholder's proportionate ownership interest of corporation.

Record date The date set for determining shareholders entitled to notice of a shareholders' meeting.

> **Example:** Hughlite Pickard, Inc. will hold its annual shareholders' meeting on May 1, 2000. Pursuant to the corporate bylaws, the board of directors will give notice to the shareholders of record on April 1, 2000 (the record date). Jamie owns 500 shares of Hughlite Pickard, Inc. stock on April 1, 2000. She sells all of her shares to her brother-in-law on April 15, 2000. However, because Jamie was the owner of record on the record date (April 1, 2000) when the board of directors sent notice of the meeting to shareholders, Jamie will receive notice of the annual shareholders' meeting and be entitled to vote at the meeting, even though she is no longer a shareholder of the corporation.

Notice of Meetings   Shareholders entitled to vote must be given reasonable notice of annual or special shareholder meetings. Generally, the notice of the meeting must include the date, place, and time of the meeting and must be given no fewer than ten and no more than sixty days before the meeting.[8] In addition, if a special shareholders' meeting is called, the notice for the meeting must specify the purpose for which it is called. If notice of a shareholder meeting is improper, the actions taken by the shareholders at the meeting will be invalid and can be set aside by any shareholder who did not receive notice.

Example: *Notice of Annual Meeting of Shareholders of ABC Computers, Inc.*
The board of directors of ABC Computers, Inc. hereby gives notice to all holders of record of ABC Computers, Inc. stock as of April 1, 2000, that the Annual Meeting of Shareholders of ABC Computers, Inc. will be held on May 1, 2000, at 10:00 A.M. at the Florence Hotel, 5th Floor, 555 Main Street, Missoula, Montana, 59801 for the purposes of: (1) electing two directors for the term of two years; (2) ratifying the board of directors' recommendation to sell corporate warehouses in Kansas; and (3) transacting all other business as may properly come before the shareholders at that time.

DATED this 1st day of April 2000   By the Board of Directors of ABC Computers, Inc.
                                                                    Margaret Jones, Secretary

---

To avoid the cumbersome requirements for notifying shareholders of annual and special meetings, shareholders may waive the notice of meetings required by statute, the corporate bylaws, or the articles of incorporation.[9] Shareholders who attend a meeting that was not properly noticed waive their right to object to the improper notice unless they do so at the beginning of the meeting.

Example: *Waiver of Notice of Annual Shareholder's Meeting of ABC Computers, Inc.*
The undersigned shareholder of ABC Computers, Inc. hereby waives notice of the annual meeting of the shareholders of ABC Computers, Inc. and consents and agrees that a meeting of the shareholders may be held as provided pursuant to the corporate bylaws on May 1, 2000, at 10:00 A.M. at the Florence Hotel, 5th Floor, 555 Main Street, Missoula, Montana, 59801 for the purpose of transacting all business properly presented and voted on at the meeting.

Dated this ___ day of March, 2000

                                                        _____
                                                        Peggy Flint, Shareholder

---

Place of Meetings   The corporation's bylaws generally specify where shareholders' meetings will be held; in the absence of such a provision, the directors may designate the place of the meeting in advance of the meeting date. Many states allow the meetings to be held in the state of incorporation or another state.[10] This allows multistate corporations with shareholders in several states to rotate their shareholders' meetings to maximize shareholder participation on corporate matters.

Shareholder Meetings

Shareholders elect new directors and vote on fundamental corporate changes at their annual shareholder meetings or special meetings of shareholders. These meetings are the shareholders' opportunity to participate in management of the corporation. (See Form 11.1, *Minutes of Annual Shareholders' Meeting.*)

Annual Meetings   Corporations must hold an annual shareholders' meeting, the primary purpose of which is election of the board of directors. However, other matters that require shareholder approval (*e.g.,* amendment of the articles of incorporation, mergers, and management reports) will also be addressed at the meeting.

Special Meetings   Special shareholder meetings may be called at any time between annual shareholder meetings to address any matters that require shareholder approval or

Minutes of Annual Shareholders' Meeting

_____ meeting of the shareholders of _____, a corporation organized and existing under the laws of the state of _____, was held at the principal office of the corporation, at _____, _____, _____ County, *(state)*, on _____, *(year)*, pursuant to the provisions of the bylaws and due notice having been given by the secretary.

_____ presided over the meeting, and _____ acted as secretary_____.

The following shareholders were present, in person or by proxy, and represented the number of shares of stock set opposite their names:

NAME   PERSON OR PROXY   NUMBER OF SHARES

_____   _____   _____

A majority of the stock being represented, a quorum was declared present.

The minutes of the last shareholders' meeting, held on _____, were read and approved.

The treasurer presented a full financial report, which report was read, approved and accepted subject to audit.

The president presented a verbal report of the business of the corporation subsequent to the last annual meeting, and a motion was duly made, seconded and carried that such report be approved.

Upon motion duly made, seconded and carried, the following resolutions were adopted:

WHEREAS, the directors and officers of this corporation, in the conduct of the corporation's business since _____, have spent large sums of money, made contracts, entered into agreements, bought and sold property, borrowed money and performed many other acts;

NOW, THEREFORE, BE IT RESOLVED, that the actions of the board of directors and officers of this corporation so taken in all of the above matters be and they are in all respects approved, ratified and confirmed as of the date so done or taken respectively.

The next business to come before the meeting was the election of the board of directors for the ensuing year. Upon motion duly made, seconded and carried, the following directors were elected to serve for the ensuing year or until the election and qualification of their successors:

_____

_____

_____

_____

There being no further business to come before the meeting, the meeting was adjourned.

DATED: _____,

(Corporate Seal)

_____

_____, Secretary

FORM 11.1.
Minutes of Annual Shareholders' Meeting

consideration (e.g., amendment of the articles of incorporation, approval of merger, or fraud by director). They are typically called when the annual shareholders' meeting is not scheduled for a significant period of time and shareholder approval is needed more promptly.

Shareholder Action by Unanimous Written Consent   In lieu of annual or special shareholders' meetings, shareholders may vote on corporate matters by written consent. This procedure allows corporations to circumvent the cumbersome notice and meeting requirements of most states. However, unlike annual or special shareholder meetings, actions taken by written consent of shareholders generally require that *all* shareholders unanimously agree on corporate matters submitted for shareholder approval; obviously, this limits the effectiveness of this type of action to small corporations in which shareholders are few and agreement is more likely. Because of the impracticability of unanimous consent, some states, such as Delaware, no longer require that written consent be unanimous. Instead, only the votes necessary to approve or disapprove of an action at a regular meeting are required.

Minutes of Shareholder Meetings   Because of the importance of maintaining corporate formalities, including holding annual and special shareholder meetings, **minutes** of all shareholder meetings should be taken by the corporation's secretary. The minutes should reflect, at a minimum, that the meeting was properly noticed, that a quorum was present, what matters were submitted for shareholder vote, and the outcome of the voting.

Enforcement Rights of Shareholders

As the owner of a corporation, a shareholder may protect the interests of the corporation by filing a lawsuit against a third party who has wronged the corporation if the corporation does not act to protect its own interests.

Example: The top scientist of Medicine, Inc. recently developed the cure for cancer while working as a researcher for the corporation. The scientist, however, refuses to allow Medicine, Inc. to market the new drug, despite the fact that his employment agreement requires that all discoveries made by employees while working for the company become the property of the corporation. The scientist also happens to be the chairman of the board of directors of Medicine, Inc. and he knows that his colleagues will not sue him. However, Mrs. Simpson, a North Dakota physician who owns stock in the corporation, learns of the discovery and after a few calls finds out that another company will be marketing the drug. Furious about the prospect of not being able to get a share of the profits the drug will certainly generate, Mrs. Simpson files a lawsuit on behalf of Medicine, Inc. against the scientist to force him to market the drug through Medicine, Inc.

Derivative lawsuits offer shareholders the opportunity to oversee the actions of the corporation. However, a shareholder cannot initiate a legal proceeding on behalf of the corporation unless the corporation first refuses to act for itself. The R.M.B.C.A. requires that before shareholders file a derivative suit, they must first demand, in writing, that the board of directors act on behalf of the corporation.[11] Only after the board refuses to act, can a shareholder then file the suit. Even then, the shareholder risks having to pay the legal fees for such action out of his or her own pocket.[12] Because of this financial disincentive, derivative suits are relatively uncommon.

SHAREHOLDERS' LIABILITY

One of the most significant advantages to incorporation is that it generally provides its owners, the shareholders, protection from personal liability for the debts and obligations of the corporation. Thus, shareholders generally risk only the amount of their investment in the corporation; if the corporation is not able to pay its debts and obligations, the personal assets of its shareholders cannot be taken to satisfy corporate creditors. Therefore, it is said that there is a "veil" between the corporation and its shareholders. Creditors generally cannot pierce the corporate veil to reach the personal assets of shareholders to pay corporate debts.

Minutes   Written summary of proceedings of shareholders' or directors' meeting.

Derivative lawsuit   Lawsuit filed by shareholders on behalf of the corporation to protect corporate interests.

> **Example:**   Sally purchases 400 shares of Toys "R" You, Inc. stock in 1995. In 1996 the corporation declares bankruptcy because it cannot pay all of its creditors. Because Toys "R" You, Inc. is a corporation, its creditors cannot seize Sally's personal assets (house, car, etc.) to pay the debts of Toys "R" You, Inc.

There are two exceptions to the general rule that a shareholder will not be held personally liable for the debts and obligations of the corporation. A shareholder may be held personally liable (1) to prevent fraud and injustice or (2) if the shareholder personally guarantees loans made to the corporation, thereby voluntarily waiving the liability protections.

Piercing the Corporate Veil

Although the corporate status generally provides shareholders broad liability protection, a shareholder's limited liability may be set aside to prevent fraud or injustice by a corporation. This is known as **piercing the corporate veil.** The three most common reasons that the corporate veil may be pierced are (1) failure to comply with necessary corporate formalities, (2) commingling of personal and corporate assets, and (3) inadequate capitalization. In each of these instances, the shareholders have failed to recognize and treat the corporation as a separate entity and, therefore, the courts will not make this distinction either. However, it is generally only those shareholders who actively participate in the management of the business who will be held personally liable for the obligations of the corporation.

Lack of Corporate Formalities

Even if a business complies with all of the requisite incorporation procedures, it must thereafter continue to observe all of the statutory formalities necessary to maintain its corporate status. For example, a corporation must hold annual shareholders' meetings, and regular board of directors' meetings, and must maintain corporate records (e.g., minutes of corporate meetings). A corporation that does not maintain such formalities may be set aside by a creditor who seeks to hold the shareholders personally liable for corporate obligations.

Commingling of Assets

A corporation legally exists as an entity separate from its shareholders/owners. As such, it must maintain financial independence from its shareholders; at the very least, this means that it must maintain its own bank accounts and books and pay its own bills. There can be no **commingling of assets;** therefore, a shareholder cannot use corporate accounts to pay personal debts or consistently use corporate assets (e.g., cars) for personal pleasure; such transactions indicate that the corporation is merely an **alter ego** of its shareholders. Because the shareholder does not treat the corporation as a separate entity, the court will not recognize the separateness of the corporation and may hold the shareholders personally liable for the debts and obligations of the corporation.

Piercing the corporate veil
When individual shareholders are held personally liable for corporate debts to prevent fraud or injustice.

Commingling of assets
Combining personal assets with business assets.

Alter ego   Literally "the other self"; when shareholders do not treat a corporation as a separate entity and use it to conduct private business, they may be held personally liable for the obligations of the corporation under the *alter ego* doctrine.

Inadequate capitalization
Insufficient funding for corporate ventures.

> **Example:**   Sam and Joe own Tires, Inc. Sam is having personal financial difficulties and, on a regular basis, does not have the money to make his mortgage payment. Therefore, he writes a check from the business account to pay his mortgage when he cannot pay it from his personal funds; he always repays the loan when he gets his next paycheck. Sam has commingled funds and his business may lose its corporate status.

Inadequate Capitalization

Corporations must maintain enough money in their corporate accounts to be able to pay their potential debts and obligations as they become due. The directors of the corporation must determine what the corporation's outstanding debts are and what other liabilities may become due; sufficient funds should be held in the corporate accounts to pay these amounts and/or the corporation should insure against its potential liabilities. **Inadequate capitalization,** or the failure to maintain these funds, suggests that the corporation is a shell for its owners and the court will not allow it to perpetrate fraud on the public.

> **Example:** A and Z Taxi Cab, Inc. owns more than 100 taxi cars and employs 150 drivers. The company does not carry insurance for any of its cars or drivers. Late one night one of its drivers hits a pedestrian, who sues for personal injury damages. The court allows the pedestrian to join the shareholders in the lawsuit (i.e., sue the shareholders personally) based upon its finding that personal injury damages are a foreseeable liability of a company with 100 cabs and 150 drivers.

Personal Guarantee by Shareholder

Even if the corporation maintains all of the necessary statutory formalities, a shareholder may agree to be personally liable for certain debts and obligations of the corporation. The shareholder's obligation in such cases is a voluntary agreement by the shareholder to accept personal responsibility to corporate creditors, thereby waiving the statutory limited liability for such obligations.

A shareholder may agree to become personally liable for corporate obligations in order to induce third parties (e.g., creditors) to invest in a corporation and its business ventures. This is not a waiver of the corporate veil. The shareholder has voluntarily become a guarantor of one or more corporate debts. The shareholder still retains liability protections for corporate debts that the shareholder did not guarantee.

It is often necessary for shareholders of new businesses to personally guarantee loans to their businesses in order to obtain the financing necessary to fund their corporation's business ventures.

> **Example:** Cary and Melissa own C & M Contractors, Inc., which builds luxury homes. Although Cary and Melissa have both worked as architects for several years, neither has any contracting experience and they have yet to build their first home as contractors. However, a friend of theirs enters into a contract to have C & M build a luxury home for him. C & M applies to the Bank of USA for a construction loan; the bank turns the company down, based on its lack of assets (it only has $2,000 in its business accounts), Cary and Melissa's lack of experience as contractors, and the company's lack of a track record. To get their business started, Cary and Melissa therefore each agree to give the Bank of USA a second mortgage on their family homes in order to finance the loan. The Bank of USA agrees to give C & M the loan based on Cary and Melissa's personal guarantees.

DIRECTORS: CORPORATE POLICY MAKERS

The directors of a corporation are often referred to as the managers of the corporation. Directors do, in fact, manage the corporation; however, they are more like general managers than team managers. Although directors are responsible for making corporate policy (e.g., deciding what products a corporation may sell), it is the corporate officers who are generally responsible for implementing the policy and managing the daily business operations of the corporation (e.g., deciding how many products to make to sell to the consumer). Thus, directors may be seen as general managers while the officers of the corporation are the team managers, overseeing the day-to-day business of the corporation. Although directors must use good judgment in performing their duties, they are not expected to nor do they guarantee the success of the corporation's business. As long as they act in good faith and with due care, the court will uphold the actions they take on behalf of the corporation.

A corporation's directors can and should be advisors for its business ventures, and the corporate organizers may be wise to consider enlisting attorneys, accountants, or other related professionals to serve on a corporation's board, whether or not they are corporate shareholders. Many corporations need the advice of experts in making corporate decisions and, therefore, may appoint experts who do not own shares of the corporation to their boards. These individuals are generally compensated for their services as directors but do not own shares in the corporation.

Example: The board of directors for Oil, Inc., a national gas company, includes an attorney, a geologist, a trade relations specialist, and two scientists. The organizer of the company invited these professionals to serve on the board (and offered big stock options to each of them) in the hope that they would be able to advise the company on proposed business ventures. Mr. Nelson, the geologist, has offered invaluable information about the advisability of purchasing property to use as oil fields. His knowledge of geology has helped the company to locate fields that might serve as an abundant source of oil for the company.

All corporations must have a board of directors, unless the shareholders agree to eliminate the board and otherwise manage the corporation.[13] However, most states allow a corporation to have as few as one person on its board; the number of directors is generally specified in the corporation's articles of incorporation or its bylaws.[14] The number of directors needed by a corporation depends in large part upon the size of the corporation and the type of its business ventures (i.e., a local hot tub manufacturer selling its products locally needs fewer advisors than would a large international company such as Disney). However, whether the corporation has one director or fifteen, the board should consist of an odd number of directors to avoid a deadlock in voting.

Example: Airplanes, Inc. has four directors on its board. The company is considering expanding its markets into several new areas. The vote is put before the board of directors; two directors vote for the expansion and two vote against it. The board is deadlocked and therefore a decision cannot be made by the board. Had there been an odd number of directors, a deadlock would have been less likely.

Of course, it is important to be aware that an odd number of directors does not guarantee that a deadlock will not occur. Even if a corporation has an odd number of directors, a director may abstain from a vote, leaving the board with an even number of voting directors.

ELECTION OF DIRECTORS

The initial directors of a corporation are generally named in the corporation's organizing document, the articles of incorporation. Thereafter, directors are elected by the corporate shareholders at their annual meetings. However, not all directors must run for re-election every year. The corporation's bylaws may provide for staggered terms, to ensure continuity in management of the corporation.

Example: Toys, Inc. has nine directors on its board. Directors A, B, and C must run for re-election in 1999; directors C, D, and E will run in 2000; and directors F, G, and H will run in 2001. Staggering the election of the directors, ensures that the board always has directors who have experience with the corporation's business.

Elections are an opportunity for shareholders to oversee management of the corporation by holding directors accountable to the corporate owners for their actions. Through electing directors, shareholders can play a minimal management role by voting for directors who share their business philosophy.

Example: Directors A and B are up for re-election in 1999. Director A has voted in favor of several business projects that have caused the corporation to lose money. Many of the shareholders are upset by director A's voting record and intend to vote against him in the re-election.

Voting Mechanisms

Directors are elected by a plurality of the corporate shares outstanding, unless the articles of incorporation specify otherwise.[15] Therefore, if a corporation has three directors' positions slated for election and 900 shares of stock are voting in the election, a candidate who receives less than a majority of the outstanding shares of stock could win the election.

> **Example:** Navy, Inc. has one director's position open for election in 1999. The corporation has issued 900 shares of stock; however, only the shareholders of 500 shares show up at the annual shareholders' meeting to elect directors. If 299 votes are cast for candidate A, 302 for candidate B, and 299 for candidate C, candidate B will win the election.

In order to understand the voting mechanisms used for the election of directors, it is important to distinguish between the number of shares issued by the corporation and the number of shareholders who may vote in an election. Only the holders of issued and outstanding shares have voting rights. Because a shareholder will inevitably own more than one share of stock, the number of shares voted is counted, rather than the number of shareholders voting.

> **Example:** At the annual shareholders' meeting of Yo-Yo, Inc., three shareholders were present to elect one director. Shareholder A owned 400 shares of stock, shareholder B owned 200 shares, and shareholder C owned 100 shares. If shareholder A voted all of his shares for candidate Nelson while shareholders B and C voted for candidate O'Brien, then candidate Nelson would win, even though the majority of *shareholders* voted for candidate O'Brien.

Minority shareholders may be able to successfully elect a candidate if the corporation's articles of incorporation allow shareholders to cumulate their votes. Such cumulative voting allows shareholders to pool all of their votes to elect a candidate who would otherwise not be elected if the corporation allowed only straight voting (one vote per share for each candidate). The preceding example demonstrates straight voting. Cumulative voting, however, maximizes a shareholder's voting power by assigning each shareholder votes according to the number of vacancies to be filled on the board (e.g., a shareholder owning 100 shares would, in an election to fill three directors' positions, have 300 votes). Straight voting minimizes the minorities' votes because directors are elected one at a time (thus the shareholder would only have 100 shares to vote for a single candidate). In contrast, cumulative voting allows all directors' vacancies to be voted on at the same time. This allows minority shareholders to pool all of the votes to be cast in an election for one candidate (thus, instead of having only 100 votes to cast for one candidate, the director would have 300).

> **Example:** Forest, Inc., a timber company, has nine shareholders, with 900 outstanding shares (each shareholder owns 100 shares of stock). The board of directors has three members. Three of the shareholders support clear cutting tactics for logging because they believe it is economical. However, six shareholders support selective harvesting of timber to preserve the forests. The clear cutters want to elect a board member who will vote for slashing and burning because they believe it will increase the company's profit margin. However, the remaining shareholders want all of the directors to use selective harvesting methods. If the corporation elected directors by straight voting, each shareholder would have only 100 shares to vote for each candidate. However, if the shareholders could cumulate their votes, each shareholder would have 300 votes to cast (representing the number of shares times the number of directors' positions available); all of these votes could be cast for one candidate of their choosing. If the shareholders who supported clear cutting pooled their votes, they would have 900 votes to elect their candidate (100 shares × 3 candidates = 300 × 3 shareholders = 900 votes). Depending on how the other shareholders split their votes, the minority could elect at least one director to represent their interests.

Removal of Directors

Once elected, directors maintain their position unless they resign, die, or are removed by special action of the shareholders. Although directors historically could only be removed for such reasons as fraud or dishonesty, directors today may be removed with or without cause.[16] In order to remove a sitting director, however, shareholders owning at least 10 percent of the corporation must request that a special shareholder meeting be called for the purpose of removing a director. If the appropriate number of votes are cast against the director, the director may be removed and the remaining directors may elect a new director to serve for the remainder of the deposed director's term.

DIRECTORS' DUTIES

Directors are elected to oversee the business operations of the corporation. They are, in a very practical sense, the collective head of any corporation, and their decisions can and do affect the ability of the corporation to maintain itself and its business. Their management decisions have far more impact on the internal procedures of the corporation than do any of the actions of the corporation's officers. Although their management responsibilities are primarily policy making, they are responsible for the financial condition, and thus the viability, of the corporation.

Directors act collectively as a unit by majority vote. As long as directors use good judgment and are loyal to the interests of the corporation in exercising their duties, they will not be liable for the actions they take as directors, whether their decisions are right or wrong. Courts presume that directors use reasonable judgment in serving on the board and afford them protection from liability for all but acts of gross negligence.

Management Responsibilities

The primary management duties of the board of directors are as follows:

♦ Make corporate policy
♦ Declare corporate dividends
♦ Elect and remove officers of the corporation
♦ Initiate extraordinary corporate matters (e.g., dissolution)

In carrying out their management responsibilities, directors do not act as individuals. They only have authority to act as a team that makes decisions by majority vote. Therefore, directors hold regular meetings to determine corporate policy. Directors must attend the meetings in person or by telephone.[17] If it is impractical for the directors to meet, the R.M.B.C.A. allows directors to make decisions by unanimous written consent. The increased flexibility the R.M.B.C.A. allows reflects the need for corporations to make accommodations for their directors and by doing so allows corporations to retain directors who are from a variety of educational, professional, and geographic backgrounds.

Directors' Meetings

The frequency and manner of conducting directors' meetings is generally set forth in a corporation's bylaws. Directors hold regularly scheduled meetings (weekly, monthly) where they review and conduct business arising in the ordinary course of the corporation's life. (See Form 11.2, *Minutes of Annual Board of Directors' Meeting.*) In addition, they hold special meetings to address issues that must be determined before the next regularly scheduled meeting.

Voting Requirements and Restrictions   Unlike shareholders, directors are not permitted to act by proxy. Directors are expected to vote responsibly and may only vote on matters when they are present at the board's meeting and are fully aware of the issues relating to the matters under the board's consideration. Even though directors may not vote on issues presented at a meeting they do not attend, directors are not required to be at every meeting of the board. The presence of all of the directors is not required for the board to have a valid vote; as long as the majority of directors is present at a meeting, the directors can vote on any matter before them. Some corporation bylaws even allow less than a majority of directors to be present at a board meeting in order for the board to vote on corporate matters. The R.M.B.C.A. requires that at least one-third of the directors must be present at the board's meeting in order for the board to make a decision for the corporation.[18] The minimum number of directors who can be present at a meeting in order to have a valid vote is known as a quorum.

Minutes of Annual Board of Directors' Meeting

The annual meeting of the board of directors of _____, a corporation duly organized and existing under the laws of the state of Montana, was held at the principal office of the corporation at (city), (state), (County), Montana, on (date) at _____ _____.m. immediately following the adjournment of the annual meeting of shareholders.

The secretary presented the notice of the meeting pursuant to which the meeting was held. The same was ordered to be entered in the corporation records.

The following directors, being all of the directors of the corporation, were present:

_____

_____

_____

The minutes of the meeting of the board of directors held on (date) were read and approved.

The treasurer's report was presented and accepted.

On motion duly made, seconded and unanimously carried, the following officers were elected:

President   _____

Vice President   _____

Secretary   _____

Treasurer   _____

On motion duly made and seconded, the following resolution was adopted:

RESOLVED, _____

There being no further business to come before the meeting, the meeting was adjourned.

DATED: _____ _____

(Corporate Seal)   _____

                                    _____, Secretary

FORM 11.2.
Minutes of Annual Board of Directors' Meeting

Directors should vote either for or against matters presented to the board. A director who is present at a board meeting but does not vote on a matter submitted for the board's vote is presumed to have agreed with the majority's decision.[19] This type of presumption requires that directors be aware of and involved in corporate matters.

In order to protect both themselves and the corporation from potential liability, directors must be meticulous about maintaining minutes of their corporate meetings. The minutes of a directors' meeting should specify all of the matters addressed by and voted on by the board, including how each member voted on a particular issue. In this way, the members of the board can protect themselves against shareholder action by verifying their position on corporate issues and, if necessary, demonstrate the information that was provided to the board on a particular matter.

Action by Unanimous Written Consent   Although board members have traditionally decided corporate matters through regular and special directors' meetings, the R.M.B.C.A. recognizes that directors do not always have the time or opportunity to attend meetings.[20] In lieu of a formal directors' meeting, the R.M.B.C.A. allows directors to make decisions on corporate matters by unanimous written consent. As long as all the directors agree on a matter in writing, the board's written vote is a valid decision of the board. While this option would appear to simplify the formal meeting requirements for directors, unless the decision is one that all directors would definitely agree on (e.g., a decision that the corporation will comply with federal wage regulations) or a board has only a few members, it is very difficult to have all directors agree on a particular issue. Therefore, voting by written consent should only be used by a board in limited circumstances.

Directors' Fiduciary Duties

Shareholders trust that the directors of a corporation will act for the benefit of the corporation in all matters. Because of this position of trust, directors are considered to be fiduciaries of the corporation and its owners. As fiduciaries, directors must act in good faith and with care in making decisions for the corporation. Implicit in the responsibilities of directors is that they always act in the best interests of the corporation and its shareholders.[21] It is not appropriate for directors to consider their own interests in making decisions for the corporation. To do so could subject them to liability for their actions.

> **Example:**   Jerry is a director of Oil, Inc., a multinational oil company. During a board meeting, he learns about several pieces of property that have excellent potential for producing oil. Using this information, Jerry contacts his real estate agent and asks her to buy several of the properties under the name of a phony corporation he has set up. He intends to resell the properties to the corporation at a substantial profit to himself. This type of action is a breach of Jerry's duty of loyalty to the corporation.

As long as directors act with due care and are loyal to the corporation, they cannot be held responsible for the actions they take as directors, even if those actions may cause the corporation to lose money. A shareholder cannot, therefore, sue a director because the shareholder disagrees with the way a director voted on a matter at a board meeting. As long as the director had sufficient information about the issue being voted on and voted in the belief that the decision was good for the corporation, a court will not later scrutinize the director's decisions at the request of an unhappy shareholder. Without this type of expansive protection afforded to directors, few individuals would be willing to serve as corporate directors.

Duty of Care

Directors must act reasonably in the decisions they make for the corporation. That is, they must do what any other ordinary persons would do in the same situation.[22] The general standard that the courts use for determining if a director acted with due care is whether the director, acting as a reasonable person, would have used the same degree of care in his or her own personal business affairs.

Example: Tom is on the board of directors of Banana Computers. The board is asked to decide whether the company should produce its hard drives in America or open a plant in Taiwan, in order to take advantage of its cheap labor force. The board votes against producing the drives in Taiwan because of their concern for the labor practices of the foreign companies. Several of the shareholders are unhappy about the board's decision because they believe it will reduce the company's profit margin. However, even if the shareholders are unhappy about the board's vote, they cannot sue the directors for the decision because the directors acted reasonably in making their decision, which they based on their personal philosophies.

A director who does not agree with an action proposed by the board must be sure to vote against the matter. By doing so, the director is protected from liability for the board's action. However, if the director fails to vote either for or against a matter before the board, then it will be presumed that the director supported the final position of the board.

Example: Shelter North, Inc., a housing development company, has never complied with county building codes requiring them to install smoke detectors in all new home construction. Several years ago, the corporation's board of directors voted against installing the detectors because they wanted to cut corners and make their homes more affordable for the large market of first-time home buyers. Tom was on the board of directors when the vote was taken. Although he was present during the board's vote on installation of smoke detectors, he was not paying attention to the meeting and he did not vote or abstain from voting on the matter. Tom could therefore be held liable to a homebuyer because it would be presumed that he agreed with the decision of the board to violate the county ordinance.

If the shareholders disagree with the actions of the board of directors, they can remove the directors from office. However, short of this type of extreme action, shareholders cannot control the decisions of a corporation's board of directors, as long as the board acts reasonably. Therefore, it is incumbent on shareholders to choose their directors wisely.

Business Judgment Rule   Courts presume that directors use good judgment in making decisions for the corporation and generally will not subject the directors' decisions to judicial scrutiny. The **business judgment rule,** adopted by most jurisdictions, recognizes that directors are not infallible and they may make mistakes. However, as long as directors have a reasonable basis for their decisions and appear to have used care in their actions, the court will not hold them liable for their errors, even errors that might cause the corporation financial losses.

In making decisions for the corporation, it is important for directors to be informed about the issues before them. Directors should consider all potential sources of information before they vote on corporate matters. It is reasonable and advisable for directors to rely on information, reports, opinions, and statements of officers of the corporation as well as professional advisors, such as accountants, attorneys, or other specialists. In addition, many boards appoint smaller committees, made up of board members, officers, or other professionals, to research issues the board is asked to consider. The committee then reports its findings to the board, thereby providing the board with specific information about the advisability of proposals under its consideration.

Business judgment rule
General rule adopted by courts immunizing directors from liability for their actions if due care is used (e.g., seeking the opinion of an expert, etc.).

Example: The board of directors of Home Improvement, Inc. is considering expanding its markets into the Connecticut area. The board appoints a committee to research the need for large home improvement stores in the major cities of Connecticut. The committee reports to the board that most of the cities do not have large home improvement centers. Based on the committee's report, the board votes to build two stores in Connecticut.

As long as directors have attempted to avail themselves of a reasonable amount of information about an issue, the court, who has the benefit of hindsight, will not hold the directors responsible for losses that the corporation might suffer as a result of the directors' actions.

Duty of Loyalty

Directors act on behalf of the corporation and its owners and are, therefore, expected to be loyal to the interests of the corporation and its shareholders. Although most directors recognize their responsibility to act for the corporation, problems arise when (1) a director has a conflict of interest with the corporation, (2) a director usurps a corporate opportunity, or (3) a director uses information about the corporation that is not available to the general public in order to profit from the purchase and sale of the corporation's stock.

Conflict of Interest

A director who has a personal interest in a corporate transaction has a conflict between his or her own interests and those of the corporation. An **interested director** who has such a conflict risks violating the duty of loyalty to the corporation and must take special precautions to safeguard his or her interests as well as those of the corporation.

> **Example:**   ABC, Inc. wants to purchase land that is owned by one of its directors, Mrs. Miller. Mrs. Miller's personal interest in maximizing her profit on the sale of the property to the corporation will conflict with her duty to be loyal to the interests of the corporation and obtain the land for the best price.

A director does not violate the duty of loyalty to the corporation merely because he or she may gain a personal benefit from the corporation's business. An interested director is protected from liability for the transaction as long as (1) the director fully discloses information about his or her interest to either the board of directors or the shareholders and they approve of the transaction (without the interested director's participation) and (2) the transaction is fair to the corporation. If there is full disclosure and the director does not unfairly take advantage of the corporation, the transaction cannot be set aside on the basis that the interested director has breached the duty of loyalty.

Usurpation of Corporate Opportunity

A director is obligated to be loyal to the corporation and to act solely for its benefit. Therefore, directors must give the corporation the chance to act on business opportunities in which it might be interested before taking advantage of the opportunity for themselves. Failure of a director to fully disclose his or her intent to take advantage of an opportunity constitutes **usurpation of corporate opportunity,** and would clearly violate the duty of loyalty. Compare the following examples.

> **Examples:**
> 1. Dan, a director of Helate Pickard, Inc., a computer hardware manufacturer, learns about a new and cheaper method of packaging computers for shipping. Dan knows that the new method could save the company millions of dollars each year but he does not inform the board about the opportunity. Instead, he asks the developer for the exclusive rights to market the process himself. He intends to sell the method, which he expects to patent, to Helate Pickard, Inc. as well as other hardware companies for a substantial profit. Clearly, Dan has usurped an opportunity that Helate Pickard would have been interested in considering.
> 2. Dan learns about a new and cheaper method for making baseball bats developed by a local inventor. He buys the exclusive rights to make the bats from the developer of the technology. Dan has not usurped a corporate opportunity from Helate Pickard because the corporation is a computer hardware corporation, not a sports equipment manufacturer.

Interested director   A director who has a personal interest in a corporate transaction.

Usurpation of corporate opportunity   When a director takes advantage of a corporate opportunity for him/herself without first allowing the corporation the opportunity.

Insider trading   Transaction by a corporate insider who has information that is not available to the general public; prohibited by SEC Rule 10b-5.

Securities and Exchange Commission   Federal agency that regulates securities.

Insider Trading

Directors are *insiders* of their corporations because they have information about the corporation that may not be available to the general public. Directors have a fiduciary obligation to the corporation and its shareholders not to use the inside information to make a personal profit by buying and selling the corporation's stock based on information that other investors do not have.

Directors who use inside information to trade the corporation's stock for their personal benefit are guilty of **insider trading** and violate their relationship of trust with the corporation and its shareholders. In order to curb insider trading, the federal agency responsible for regulating the purchase and sale of corporate securities, the **Securities and Exchange Commission** (SEC), has adopted regulations that severely restrict and penalize individuals who trade stock of publicly held corporations with inside information.

Example: Cathy is a director of McRonald's Happy Land, Inc. She knows that the company is losing money and will officially announce the closing of all restaurants in January. Cathy decides to sell her stock in the company and reinvest in the corporation's rival, Burger Queen. Because the closing of McRonald's Happy Land, Inc. has not been announced to the general public, several investors, who believe that the company is experiencing a temporary slump, are eager to buy Cathy's stock. Cathy has inappropriately traded on inside information.

The SEC's dagger is the **Securities Exchange Act of 1934** (hereafter the 1934 Act). The 1934 Act prohibits, *inter alia,* corporate insiders from buying or selling stock of the corporation unless they disclose the inside information to the potential buyer or seller. A director cannot, of course, disclose inside information to the public without violating the duty of loyalty; therefore, the rule to *disclose or abstain* forces directors to refrain from trading stock of the corporation based on inside information.

The SEC recognizes that it is difficult to prove that an insider purchased or sold stock based on inside information, rather than some more innocuous reason (e.g., the director needed to sell stock to fund a child's education). Therefore, the 1934 Act automatically imposes liability for insider trading on directors, officers, and shareholders owning 10 percent or more of the corporation if they make a profit from buying and selling stock of the corporation within a six-month period. Such short-term profits, known as **short swing profits,** are presumptively the result of inside information, because most investors would hold stock in their own companies for longer periods of time. The SEC can and will take away the short swing profits of qualified insiders, whether or not they had inside information. The intent, and the result, of such stringent provisions is to regulate insiders and protect outside investors from potential misrepresentations and omissions.

Directors' Liability

Significant measures have been taken to protect directors from potential liability in order to encourage individuals to serve as directors. As long as directors act in good faith and in the interests of the corporation, they generally will not be held liable for any losses that the corporation might suffer as a result of their actions. However, even if directors were to be found liable for their actions, director and officer liability insurance is available to pay the attorneys' fees, costs, and judgments that could be incurred in defending legal actions brought against directors who have acted in good faith for the corporation. These types of expansive protections are necessary as incentives for individuals to serve as directors.

Although directors generally escape liability for the performance of their duties, if they exceed their authority or breach their fiduciary duties, they can and will be held accountable for their misfeasance and/or malfeasance. The penalties for these types of actions generally require the director to pay losses that the corporation suffered as a result of the director's action or, as in the case of insider trading, require them to forfeit profits that they made at the expense of the corporation or its shareholders.

Ultra Vires Acts

When directors exceed the authority granted to them by the corporation, their actions are ultra vires acts. For example, if a board declares a cash dividend that leaves the corporation unable to pay its debts, the directors have exceeded their authority, since dividends may only be declared if the corporation has the money to pay the dividends and still pay its creditors. In such a case, the directors may be personally responsible to the shareholders or creditors for the error.

Because of the potential liability, directors tend to be cautious about distributing corporate profits without first receiving assurances from corporate accountants that the corporation is financially sound. By relying on the advice of such experts they can demonstrate that they acted with due care in performing their duties.

Securities Exchange Act of 1934 Federal law regulating the disclosure of information in the sale or exchange of securities.

Short swing profits Profits made by directors, officers, or 10 percent shareholders from the purchase and sale of a corporation's shares within a six month period.

Breach of Fiduciary Duties

Duty of Care   Directors breach their fiduciary duty of care when they do not act reasonably in carrying out their duties. If their actions are not reasonable (i.e., they do use sound business judgment), they may be held liable for their negligent acts and/or omissions.

> **Example:**   The directors of ABC Cleaning, Inc. vote against hiring women. Vivian, a shareholder who has applied for employment with ABC Cleaning, Inc., sues the company for discrimination. Clearly, the action of the board was a breach of their fiduciary duty; the directors may be responsible to the corporation for any damages it may have to pay because of the directors' action.

Duty of Loyalty   *Conflict of interest.* A director who has a conflict of interest in a corporate transaction, must disclose this interest and take special precautions to ensure that the transaction is fair. If the director has not made full disclosure and/or the transaction is not fair to the corporation, the transaction may be set aside and the director may be required to pay any profits made on the transaction to the corporation.

    Usurpation of corporate opportunity. It is incumbent on directors to be loyal to the corporation and avoid taking as their own a financial opportunity available to the corporation. If a director misappropriates a corporate opportunity, the court may impose a constructive trust on the property acquired by the director, thus constructively making the director's property the corporation's.

> **Example:**   A shareholder of Jet Set, Inc., an international airline company, learns that one of the corporation's directors has been buying new planes from a German manufacturer and reselling them to Jet Set at a substantial profit. The director did not disclose his "business" to the board or the shareholders. Therefore, the court imposes a constructive trust on all of the profits that he has earned since the first resale.

    Insider trading. A director of a publicly held corporation who trades his or her corporation's stock based on information that is not generally available to the public, can be held liable for any and all profits made from the improper trading. In addition, the SEC may impose substantial penalties on the director and/or bring criminal charges against the director for malfeasance.

    These types of penalties, as well as those discussed previously, are imposed on directors who ignore the trust that shareholders place in them to manage the corporation and all of its business affairs. Although expansive protections are afforded directors for the performance of their duties, directors who breach their duties to the corporation can and will be held accountable for their actions.

OFFICERS: CORPORATE MANAGERS

The officers of a corporation implement the policies adopted by the board of directors and manage the daily business operations of the company. They are, in a very real sense, the working arms of the board of directors. If a corporation is analogized to the human body, the board of directors would be the brain and the heart, making decisions for the company and pumping life into the business by ensuring its financial stability; however, the board needs its working arms—the officers—to do the tasks that the brain tells it to. Although this analogy is simplistic, it demonstrates the interrelationship of the board and the officers; a corporation could not function efficiently without both.

    The R.M.B.C.A. does not specify the minimum number of officers that a corporation must have. It simply requires that a corporation have an officer who prepares minutes of directors' and shareholders' meetings and an officer who can authenticate records of the corporation; these positions may be held by the same person. (See R.M.B.C.A. § 8.40(d).) Typically, a corporation's bylaws provide for the following officers:

♦ President
♦ Vice president
♦ Secretary
♦ Treasurer

A corporation may have fewer officers or it may have more. Large corporations often expand the ranks of their officers by providing for numerous vice presidential positions (e.g., vice president in charge of production, vice president in charge of west coast distribution, vice president in charge of east coast distribution).

APPOINTMENT AND REMOVAL OF OFFICERS

Corporate officers serve at the pleasure of the board of directors. The directors are responsible for appointing, supervising, and removing corporate officers. Generally, the initial officers of a corporation are selected at the first meeting of the board of directors.

Officers may be removed by the board of directors at any time, with or without cause. However, if the officer has an employment contract with the corporation (i.e., an agreement that the employee will work for a specified period of time), the directors must comply with the terms of the contract and cannot remove the officer in violation of the provisions of the employee's contract.

Example: KPBC, Inc. requires all of its employees, including its officers, to sign a one-year employment contract. The contract provides that the corporation's secretary may only be removed for "failure to perform his record keeping duties." Six months after KPBC signs the employment contract with the secretary, the board votes to remove him from office because he recently dyed his hair purple. The secretary threatens to sue, arguing that his employment contract does not specify that he maintain a "mainstream" hair color or a conservative appearance, therefore, he argues, to remove him on the basis of his hair color would be a violation of his employment contract.

Directors must use care and good judgment in appointing, supervising, and removing officers. If they are negligent in these responsibilities, they breach their fiduciary duty of care to the corporation and its shareholders and may be held personally liable for any errors or omissions of the officers.

OFFICERS' DUTIES

The only duties that officers of a corporation are *required* to perform are (1) preparation of the minutes of the meetings of the shareholders and board of directors and (2) authentication of corporate records.[23] Most corporations, however, impose additional duties on their officers so that the business will run efficiently. The specific duties of corporate officers are set forth in the corporation's bylaws or determined by its board of directors.

Traditionally, most corporations appoint a president, vice president, secretary, and treasurer, assigning each officer specific duties required of the respective offices.

President

The president of the corporation oversees the general management of the corporation. The president is "the boss," although the board of directors is, admittedly, "the boss's boss."

Vice President

The job of a vice president can and does vary significantly depending on the size and type of corporation. Every corporation should have at least one vice president who is designated to act in the place of the president in his or her absence. In addition, many larger corporations have several vice presidents, each of whom has different duties (e.g., vice president of distribution, vice president of marketing, vice president of manufacturing).

Secretary

The primary duty of a secretary is to keep the records of the corporation. In particular, the secretary is required to take and maintain notes of the meetings of shareholders and directors. In addition, secretaries generally prepare correspondence and reports (e.g., investment prospectus) for the corporation.

Treasurer

The treasurer is responsible for the financial affairs of the corporation and generally pays the bills of the corporation as they become due.

AGENCY

Officers are agents of the corporation, with the authority to act on behalf of the corporation in its business matters. As an agent, everything an officer does is binding on the corporation; it is as though the corporation itself acted. This general rule of agency is intended to provide protection to third parties who reasonably assume that an officer participates in the management and operation of the corporation, including entering into contractual or other business arrangements on its behalf.

> **Example:** The president of ABC Movies, Inc. hires a new designer to create costumes for an upcoming film production. The president promises the designer that after the movie is completed, he will be able to continue as a designer on all films for the next two years. With the expectation of this job offer, the designer quits his other job. Because the president of a corporation appears to have the authority to hire employees, his promises of future and continued employment to the designer create an employment contract with the designer.

The authority granted to an officer of a corporation may be express, implied, or apparent. Officers are granted express authority to act on corporate matters by statute or in the corporation's articles of incorporation and/or bylaws. An officer also has the implied authority to perform acts necessary to exercise the express authority granted by the corporation (e.g., a corporate treasurer, who is responsible for paying corporate debts, has the implied authority to respond to correspondence from a corporation's creditors). Sometimes an officer does not have actual express or implied authority to act for a corporation; however, the corporation may make it appear that the officer has the right to act on behalf of the corporation. Officers who act with such apparent authority may still bind the corporation.

> **Example:** *Apparent Authority.*
> David is the vice-president of pond development for Trees, Inc. David creates pond designs for the company's clients. However, before he may make any purchases of materials for a client's project, he must first submit the proposal and an itemized price list of materials to the company. Although David is aware of this limitation on his authority, he consistently orders materials for pond developments without first receiving approval. The treasurer always pays for the materials, even though the board has not reviewed David's proposal or costs; the board is aware that the treasurer pays these bills. Because the corporation consistently pays for the materials ordered by David, vendors may reasonably assume that David has the apparent authority to purchase these same types of materials on behalf of the company.

Express Authority

Corporations generally grant their officers specific rights and duties through their articles of incorporation, their bylaws, or in some cases, by a decision of the board of directors. In addition, many state statutes impose specific duties on corporate officers in order to establish and assign responsibility for corporate management. This type of authority to act on behalf of the corporation is known as express authority.

Example: David is the vice president of pond development for Trees, Inc., a landscaping company. A friend of David's offers to sell Trees, Inc. a bulldozer to use in large pond projects. The corporation's bylaws authorize the vice president of pond development to purchase the equipment necessary to fulfill the corporation's objectives, in particular, developing ponds. Because David has the authority to agree to the purchase, he signs a contract with his friend to purchase the bulldozer for the benefit of Trees, Inc. By signing the contract as the vice president of pond development, it was just as though the corporation had itself signed the contract.

All articles of incorporation and/or corporate bylaws should contain sections that specify the duties and the limitations imposed on the corporation's officers. An officer who exceeds his or her express authority may be personally liable to the corporation and its shareholders for any losses that the corporation suffers as a result of the unauthorized action. Unfortunately, however, such provisions may not protect the corporation from a lawsuit by a corporate outsider who has been wronged by the unauthorized actions of an officer.

Example: John is the president of Toys "R" You, Inc., a national retail toy store chain. A young entrepreneur sends John a model for a new Batman action figure called "FarmMan Batman," a Batman who rides on a toy horse and herds sheep. John, a farm boy during his early years, loves the idea and orders 2 million copies. Batman Figures, Inc. starts production of the new toys; however, four weeks later the vice president of Toys "R" You cancels the order, claiming that John never received approval to order the new doll, as required by the corporate bylaws. The president of Batman Figures, Inc. calls Toys "R" You, Inc. and informs them that it is too late to cancel the order since the company has already spent $1.5 million on production costs. If Toys "R" You cancels the contract, Batman Figures, Inc. could sue the company for its production costs and lost profits because it was reasonable to assume that John could enter into the contractual agreement. In turn, however, the corporation could sue John for any damages that it has to pay Batman Figures, Inc. because of John's unauthorized act.

Implied Authority

The public generally assumes that an officer of a corporation has the authority to act for the corporation in matters normally associated with the officer's position. For example, most people would assume that the treasurer of a corporation has the authority to sign a corporate check. The authority that officers must have to carry out their express duties is known as implied authority.

Example: Jason is the treasurer of Hidden Valley Homeowners, Inc. As the treasurer, Jason has the authority to "handle the financial matters of H.V.H., Inc." In order to carry out this duty, Jason has the implied authority to deposit the homeowners' annual membership dues into H.V.H.'s accounts and pay the creditors of H.V.H., Inc.

Apparent Authority

If an officer of a corporation acts beyond the actual authority granted by the corporation, the corporation may still be bound by the officer's actions if the corporation gave the impression that the actions were authorized. The extension of apparent authority is intended to protect the public from unauthorized acts of corporate officers that appear to be condoned by the corporation.

Example: Jeremy is the vice president of marketing for ABC, Inc. The local high school newspaper contacts Jeremy and asks him to buy an advertisement for ABC, Inc. in its graduation edition. Jeremy agrees. Unknown to the local high schoolers, Jeremy is really a glorified errand boy. His father, who is the president of the corporation, wanted Jeremy to have a title that would look respectable on his resume. However, because ABC, Inc. gave Jeremy the title of vice president of *marketing,* it is reasonable for the paper to assume that he has the right to market the company and its products; therefore, the company will be bound to pay for the advertisement.

The corporation is bound to obligations undertaken by an officer acting with apparent authority only if the person dealing with the officer believed that he or she acted with the approval of the corporation. If the third party knows that an officer does not have the authority to act on behalf of the corporation, the officer's authority is not "apparent" and the corporation will not be required to fulfill the obligation created by the unauthorized act.

> **Example:** The president of Burger Queen, Inc. agrees to buy a local bookstore. Neither the corporation's articles of incorporation nor its bylaws authorizes this type of a purchase, which is unrelated to Burger Queen's business interests. The corporation's articles specifically provide that the corporation was formed only for the purpose of providing fast food to the public. In addition to the limited purpose clause, the board of directors did not approve of the purchase, and the seller of the bookstore knew that the president's agreement to purchase the bookstore was outside of the scope of his regular duties as a director. Therefore, Burger Queen should not be bound to the purchase contract.

FIDUCIARY DUTIES

As managers of the corporation's business, officers are considered fiduciaries of the corporation. Therefore, the same duties of care and loyalty that are imposed on directors of a corporation are also required of corporate officers. Officers must act with due care, using their best business judgment in managing the business of the corporation. (See "Directors' Fiduciary Duties.") In addition, the interests of the corporation must always be paramount in the minds of its officers; they have a duty to be loyal to the corporation and its business interests. (See "Directors' Duty of Loyalty.")

Officers' Liability

The duties required of corporate officers are substantially the same as those imposed on the directors; therefore, their potential liabilities are almost identical. (See Directors' Liability.) If officers breach their fiduciary duties of care or loyalty, they may be held personally liable for the losses suffered by the corporation because of their improper actions. However, because courts presume that officers, like directors, use their best business judgment in managing the affairs of the corporation, officers generally are not found liable unless they are guilty of gross negligence in the management of corporate affairs.

Even if officers are found liable for a breach of their fiduciary duties, however, significant measures have been taken to insulate them from personal financial responsibility for their actions. (See, e.g., R.M.B.C.A. § 8.42.) Officers, like directors, are not guarantors of the success of the corporate business. As long as they act reasonably in performing their duties, they should not be forced to defend themselves when the corporation suffers losses or when a shareholder does not think the officers are adequately performing their duties. Officers simply could not afford the costs and expenses of such lawsuits.

To protect their officers, many corporations purchase director and officer liability insurance to pay attorneys' fees, costs, and judgments that could be incurred in defending legal actions brought against directors or officers for alleged breaches of their fiduciary duties. Such liability insurance is intended only to protect directors and/or officers who acted in good faith; therefore, the board or the corporation may also want to insure itself for losses due to bad faith misconduct by its directors or officers (e.g., embezzlement by the corporate treasurer).

Corporations that do not carry liability insurance for their directors and/or officers, generally provide that officers will be reimbursed for any costs incurred in defending lawsuits brought against them in their official capacity, as long as they acted reasonably in carrying out their duties. These types of expansive protections are necessary to protect officers from the financial disasters that unfounded lawsuits could bring.

◆ CORPORATE ORGANIZATIONAL STRUCTURE IN REVIEW

Organization

Shareholders: Corporate owners
Directors: Policy makers
Officers: Daily managers

Shareholders

Contribute investment capital and receive ownership interest.

Shareholders' Rights

1. Distribution rights
2. Inspection rights
3. Voting rights (on election of directors and extraordinary matters)
4. Preemptive rights
5. Meeting rights
6. Enforcement rights

Shareholders' Liability

Limited liability for shareholders unless corporate veil is pierced.

Directors

Responsible for making corporate policy.

Directors' Duties

1. *Management responsibilities:* making corporate policy, declaring corporate dividends, elect and remove officers, initiate extraordinary corporate matters
2. *Fiduciary duties:* require directors to act in good faith with due care and be loyal to the corporation and its business interests

Directors' Liability

No personal liability if acted in good faith and with due care for the benefit of the corporation

Officers

Implement corporate policy and manage daily business operations of company.

Corporate Officers

President
Vice President
Secretary
Treasurer

Officers' Liability

No personal liability if acted in good faith and with due care for the benefit of the corporation

◆ KEY TERMS

dividends
cumulative voting
extraordinary corporate matter
quorum
proxy
limited proxy
general proxy
preemptive right

record date
minutes
derivative lawsuit
piercing the corporate veil
commingling assets
alter ego
inadequate capitalization

business judgment rule
interested director
usurpation of corporate opportunity
insider trading
Securities and Exchange Commission
Securities Exchange Act of 1934
short swing profits

◆ STUDY QUESTIONS IN REVIEW

1. Identify the structure of a corporation by answering the following questions:
   a. Who owns a corporation?
   b. Who determines the policy for a corporation?
   c. Who manages the daily business of the corporation?
2. What does a shareholder of a corporation actually own?
3. Are shareholders automatically entitled to receive dividends if the corporation earns profits?
4. Under what circumstances are shareholders entitled to vote on the business matters of a corporation?
5. What is a quorum?
6. What is the purpose of granting preemptive rights to shareholders?
7. Are directors of a corporation required to be shareholders of the corporation?
8. Why is it advisable for a board of directors to consist of an odd number of directors?
9. Is a director a fiduciary of a corporation?
10. Does a director's obligation to use due care with regard to corporate matters make him or her a guarantor of the corporation's business?
11. What should directors do if they have a conflict of interest with the corporation?
12. What is an *ultra vires* act?
13. What is insider trading?
14. Are officers agents of their corporations?

◆ CASE STUDIES IN REVIEW

1. Sam and Ted convinced their doctor friend Shauna to invest in their new production company. They assured Shauna that the company would be able to generate revenues of more than $250,000 annually. In fact, the first year, the company's revenues exceeded $250,000. However, Sam and Ted, the directors of the corporation, decided to reinvest all of the company's profits into new projects. Shauna is very upset and contacts your law firm to represent her in demanding the corporation declare a substantial dividend. Your advising attorney asks you to look into this to determine Shauna's rights. What are Shauna's rights? Can she force the corporation to declare a dividend?

2. Jeremy is a director of Toys 'N Tots, a national toy manufacturer. An employee of the corporation submits a proposal to the board of directors suggesting that the company manufacture interactive dolls. The marketing director of the company recommends against the proposal on the basis that the public is not interested in buying interactive toys. The board votes against manufacturing the doll. Six months later, Playskool starts distributing an interactive doll, very similar to the one proposed to Toys 'N Tots' board of directors. Playskool earns over $10 million in profits the first year the doll is on the market; *Newsweek* calls it the "Success Toy of the Year." The shareholders of Toys 'N Tots are furious that its board passed up on the doll. Can the shareholders sue the directors for their decision?

◆ PROJECT APPLICATION

Your firm represents Toys 'N Tots against a lawsuit brought by its shareholders for the profits lost by the company in failing to manufacture an interactive doll. Prepare a research memorandum to your supervising attorney explaining your response to Case Study #2. In preparing your memo, research your state's statute addressing the duties of corporate directors.

◆ ENDNOTES

1. See R.M.B.C.A. §6.40 (c).
2. See R.M.C.A. § 16.02.
3. See R.M.B.C.A. § 13.02.
4. See id. at § 7.25.
5. See id. at § 7.25 (c).
6. See ibid.
7. See R.M.C.A. § 6.30 (b).
8. See R.M.B.C.A. §7.05(a).
9. See id. at §7.06.
10. See also id. at §7.01(b) and §7.02(c).
11. See R.M.B.C.A. §7.42.
12. See id. at §7.46.
13. See R.M.B.C.A. §§8.01 and 7.32(a).
14. See R.M.B.C.A. §8.03.
15. See R.M.B.C.A. § 7.28.
16. R.M.B.C.A. § 8.08(a).
17. See R.M.B.C.A. § 8.20.
18. See R.M.C.A. § 8.24(b).
19. See R.M.C.A. § 8.24(d).
20. See R.M.B.C.A. § 8.21.
21. See R.M.B.C.A. § 8.30.
22. See R.M.B.C.A. at § 8.30(a)(2).
23. See R.M.B.C.A. § 8.40.

CHAPTER 12

Fundamental Changes in Corporate Structure

Throughout the life of a corporation, **fundamental corporate changes** will inevitably need to be made to accommodate the evolving needs of the corporation and its business ventures. For example, a corporation may take over another company in order to expand the products it sells, two corporations may merge to increase their manufacturing facilities, or an unsuccessful corporation may dissolve because it is no longer profitable. Changes that significantly affect the basic foundation of the corporation are considered "fundamental" to its existence and require special approval by both the corporate managers and owners.

The following are considered fundamental changes to corporate structure that require special approval:

♦ Merger
♦ Consolidation
♦ Sale, lease, or exchange of corporate assets not in the ordinary course of business
♦ Amendment to articles of incorporation
♦ Dissolution

STANDARD APPROVAL PROCEDURE

Fundamental changes in corporate structure must be approved by the corporation's board of directors *and* shareholders before they can occur. The two-step **standard approval procedure** ensures that both the corporate managers as well as the corporate owners agree on proposed changes that will affect how and/or if the corporation functions or continues to exist.

Once a fundamental change is approved, the corporation must notify the secretary of state of the intended change by filing **articles of amendment.** This filing is a crucial final step of "approval" of a fundamental corporate change; until the secretary of state receives and approves the articles of amendment, the fundamental change is not legally effective.

Board of Director's Approval and Recommendation

If a fundamental change to the structure of a corporation is presented to the board of directors, the board must vote on the proposal. The board's main consideration in determining whether to approve of fundamental changes is whether the change is in the best interests of the shareholders. Generally, this boils down to whether or not the change will enable the corporation to maintain or increase its current or future financial condition.

Fundamental corporate change Change that significantly affects the basic foundation of a corporation.

Standard approval procedure Two-step process for approval of fundamental corporate change requiring (1) board of directors approval and recommendation and (2) shareholder approval.

Articles of amendment Document notifying the secretary of state of a fundamental corporate change.

> **Example:** The board of directors of United Pacific Railroad, Inc. is presented with the opportunity to merge with United Atlantic Railroad, Inc., a smaller railroad company with railroad lines along the Atlantic Coast. Although the merger will cost United Pacific Railroad $1 billion, the board anticipates that it will increase the company's future revenues $10 billion over the next seven years. Therefore, the board votes to present the merger to its shareholders for their approval.

If the board of directors approves of a fundamental change to the corporation's structure, it must present its recommendation to the shareholders for their approval. Like the board, the shareholders are concerned with the financial effect of a proposed change, although shareholders may be more interested in the short-term effects of the change than in the long-term picture envisioned by the board.

Example: The shareholders of United Pacific Railroad, Inc. are asked to consider whether the company should merge with United Atlantic Railroad, Inc. The shareholders' main concern in approving the merger is the short-term costs: if the companies merge, the shareholders will probably receive no dividends for five years. The board's recommendation states that if the merger is approved, any profits of United Pacific for the next five years will be used to pay off the $1 billion loan taken to purchase United Atlantic Railroad, Inc. In addition, United Pacific will have to invest any other profits to rebuild and improve the decrepit lines of Atlantic Railroad. However, after these initial costs are paid, the board anticipates in the sixth and seventh year, the company will increase its earnings $10 billion. The question for the shareholders then becomes whether they are long- or short-term investors (i.e., short-term investors may be current retirees interested in immediate returns on their investments versus long-term investors who may be young people just out of college).

Shareholder Approval

A fundamental change must be approved by a majority of the corporate shareholders; some states require a two-thirds vote of approval. Although shareholders do not generally participate in the management of the corporation, when the board of directors is considering a fundamental change in the corporation, the shareholders have the right to approve or disapprove of proposed changes. Shareholders are entitled to vote on such extraordinary matters because the changes will, in all likelihood, affect their interest in the corporation (i.e., their investment).

Dissenters' Rights

Shareholders who object to fundamental changes to the corporation and who have voted against the change can force the corporation to buy their shares at a fair market price; such buyout rights are known as **dissenters' rights.**[1] This right of dissenting shareholders to force a purchase of their shares is intended to protect shareholders from holding shares in a corporation fundamentally different from that in which they invested.

Dissenters' rights Rights of shareholders who object to a fundamental corporate change to force the corporation to buy their shares at a fair market price.

FUNDAMENTAL CHANGES

The fundamental changes that may occur during the life of a corporation, or at its termination, are varied. It is important to understand the potential changes as well as the ramifications of each.

Amendment to Articles of Incorporation

The articles of incorporation create the corporation and organize its initial management. In many respects, the articles define the corporation by identifying the corporation's name, the purpose of the corporation, the ownership of the corporation, and even the duration of the corporation. Therefore, any addition, change, or deletion to the articles is considered a fundamental change in the corporate structure and requires approval by the corporation's shareholders.

The Revised Model Business Corporation Act (R.M.B.C.A.) recognizes that a corporation may need to make amendments to its articles at some point during its lifetime. A corporation's articles should be drafted with its future in mind. However, it is difficult to foresee all of the potential changes that may occur during a corporation's life. For example, small corporations that may not have planned for expansion may need to increase their financial resources by issuing more stock; the company may want to expand its business interests (which requires expanding its purpose clause); the duration of the corporation may need to be extended; or the corporation may even elect to change its name. By amending the corporation's articles, any or all of these changes can be made to the structure of the corporation.

In order to avoid the problem of amending the articles when changes, even small changes, are made in the corporation after it is created, articles of incorporation should be kept simple. It is advisable to include only the minimal information required by state statute in the corporation's articles unless there are specific reasons to do otherwise (e.g., provisions designed to protect minority shareholders).

> **Example:** When ABC Productions, Inc. was first formed, the organizers intended to produce feature films for television. Therefore, the corporation's articles of incorporation provided that the purpose of the corporation was to "produce feature films for television." The corporation's films became increasingly popular and several filmmakers approached the company to produce movies for the big screen. The corporation's purpose clause does not allow it to expand its business ventures beyond producing films for television. Therefore, the corporation must amend its purpose clause. The amended purpose clause provides that the corporation is formed "for any lawful purpose."

Merger

Mergers are probably the most well-known and common fundamental change that occurs in a corporation's structure. A **merger** occurs when one or more corporations, known as the **merged corporations,** are absorbed into another corporation, the **surviving corporation,** that continues after the merger. The requirements for the merger of two or more corporations are dictated by statute; thus, mergers are often referred to as **statutory mergers.**

> **Example:** *Merger*
> A Corporation
> **A Corporation**
> B Corporation
>
> Union Airlines, Inc., a Midwestern airlines, wants to expand its market. Therefore, it purchases and merges with Pacific Air, Inc., which flies in the Pacific Northwest. After the two corporations merge, the surviving corporation, Union Airlines, Inc., advertises its new markets in the Pacific Northwest.

Merger Occurs when one or more corporations (merged corporations) are absorbed into another existing corporation (surviving corporation).

Merged corporation Corporation that is absorbed by another corporation.

Surviving corporation Corporation that continues its existence after a merger.

Statutory merger Merger that occurs pursuant to statutory requirements.

Target corporation Corporation subject to takeover by another entity (e.g., corporation) or individual.

Share exchange Merger occurring when a corporation exchanges its shares for those of a target corporation.

Subsidiary Corporation owned by another corporation.

Articles of merger Document notifying the secretary of state of a merger.

Certificate of merger Document issued by the secretary of state approving, and thus effecting, a merger.

Consolidation Merger of two corporations into a newly formed corporation.

The surviving corporation may absorb the merged corporation by purchasing all of its assets (e.g., buildings, accounts, and merchandise), by purchasing its stock, or exchanging its shares for the shares of the **target corporation.** In the latter type of merger, known as a **share exchange,** both corporations survive. The surviving corporation owns the target corporation; the target corporation becomes a **subsidiary,** or branch, of the surviving corporation.

> **Example:** *Share Exchange*
> Bananas, Inc. is a very popular computer hardware manufacturer. Because of its increasing reputation, it decides to branch out and purchase a small software company, Bits & Bites, Inc. Because Bananas has all of its cash invested in research and development, it offers to give shares in its company to the stockholders of Bits & Bites, rather than purchasing their shares for cash. The shareholders of Bits & Bites are happy to exchange their shares because Bananas, Inc. stock has doubled its value every year for the last five years. After the share exchange, Bananas, Inc. owns Bits & Bites, Inc. and both corporations continue to operate basically the same as they did before the share exchange.

In order for a merger to be legally effective, the surviving corporation must file **articles of merger** with the secretary of state. This filing notifies the secretary of state that two or more corporations have merged; once the secretary of state reviews and approves the articles, a **certificate of merger** will be issued, making the merger effective.

Consolidation

The **consolidation** of two or more corporations is substantially the same as a merger; however, unlike a merger, after corporations consolidate, the previous corporations are extinguished and a new corporation is formed. The new corporation acquires everything owned by the consolidated corporations, including its buildings, merchandise, and shareholders.

> **Example:**   *Consolidation*
> A Corporation
>   **C Corporation**
> B Corporation
>
> Movies, Inc. has been plagued by bad publicity since the release of its last movie, *Bomb City*. Despite this release, the company has great potential and learned a great deal from its mistake. Specifically, it learned that it needs more experienced movie makers. Therefore, in order to acquire great movie-making talent, it purchases Cinema, Inc., a small movie company that has consistently produced movie magic for the last fifty years. Because of its great reputation, Cinema, Inc. wants to charge $25,000 for the use of its name. Movies, Inc. does not want to keep its own name and can not raise the extra $25,000 to use Cinema, Inc.'s name. Therefore, they decide to form a new corporation, CineMagic, Inc.

Once a consolidation is approved and the new corporation is formed, the new corporation must notify the secretary of state of the consolidation by filing **articles of consolidation.** The new corporation begins its existence only after the articles are filed and accepted by the secretary of state.

The R.M.B.C.A., as well as many states, refuse to recognize consolidations because some companies attempt consolidations in order to gain control of another corporation while escaping its liabilities. Because neither corporation is continuing, no entity exists to answer for the debts of the extinguished corporations. In order to avoid such fraudulent conduct, and because a merger effectively achieves the same result as a consolidation without the deception, the R.M.B.C.A. provides only for corporate mergers.

Sale of Corporate Assets

One corporation may acquire another corporation by buying all or substantially all of its assets. By purchasing just the assets of the corporation, the surviving corporation is able to acquire the assets of the other corporation but escape its liabilities. In addition, because there is not a fundamental change in the structure of the acquiring corporation, the board of directors of the acquiring corporation is not required to get the approval of its shareholders before the purchase; only the purchased corporation must have its shareholders approve of the sale.

The purchase of all or substantially all of the assets of another corporation is a transaction that looks very much like a merger. Therefore, the board of the corporation selling its assets must generally follow the same standard approval procedures required for any fundamental change: the board of approval must consider and recommend the change to the shareholders, the shareholders must vote on the proposed change, and the state must be notified of the change in the corporate structure.

The sale of all or substantially all of a corporation's assets causes a fundamental change in the corporation only if the sale is not in the ordinary course of the corporation's business. If, for example, a new car dealership sells the majority of its inventory to a used car dealership because it is making room on its lot for next year's models, the sale of its assets is in the ordinary course of business. However, if the car dealership sells its assets to the used car dealer because it is going out of business, the sale results in a fundamental change in the corporation's structure and the board must have shareholder approval before it can liquidate the company's inventory.

Some transactions that occur in the ordinary course of a corporation's business require that the corporation transfer the bulk of its assets (e.g., mortgages). In order to determine if the transfer of a corporation's assets is within the **ordinary course of business,** look at the purpose for which the corporation was formed (e.g., car sales, real estate, shoe manufacturing); this is contained in the corporation's purpose clause in its articles of incorporation.

Articles of consolidation
Document notifying the secretary of state of a consolidation.

Ordinary course of business   The usual and customary dealings of a business.

Hostile Takeovers

Sometimes fundamental changes occur in the structure of a corporation without the approval of its board of directors and/or shareholders. Attempts to take over management and/or ownership of a corporation without its consent are known as **hostile takeovers.** Although hostile takeovers are sensationalized by Hollywood, they are relatively uncommon, in large part because it is very difficult to succeed with a hostile takeover.

In a hostile takeover, an aggressor (usually another company) makes a bid for a target corporation by attempting to buy a majority (more than 50 percent) of the target corporation's stock. Generally, the aggressor attempts to inconspicuously purchase a small block of shares of the target corporation (less than 5 percent). The aggressor may purchase stock in the corporation through various brokers, using various names. Once the aggressor has acquired a block, it will make a public offer to purchase shares of the corporation; this is known as a **tender offer.** If the aggressor acquires a block of a corporation's stock or makes a tender offer, it must comply with the strict reporting and disclosure requirements of the Securities and Exchange Commission.

If a hostile takeover attempt is unsuccessful or infeasible, an aggressor may attempt to gain control of a corporation through a **proxy fight.** In a proxy fight, the aggressor approaches the corporation's shareholders with the intent to obtain the right to vote their shares in a board of directors' election. The intent is to take over the corporation by gaining control of the board, and thus the management of the corporation. In theory, a proxy fight would seem less complicated than a hostile takeover. However, shareholders are reluctant to allow an aggressor, particularly a corporate outsider, to vote on their behalf. They would much rather reap the profit from the sale of their shares during a hostile takeover attempt.

Termination of a Corporation

Most corporations continue to exist until they are expressly dissolved. The termination of a corporation is a two-step process: (1) the corporate form must be dissolved and (2) its assets must be liquidated. The dissolution process terminates the corporate entity; once the corporation is dissolved it will no longer exist as a "person" under the law. After the corporation is dissolved, its assets must be converted into cash ("liquid assets"), its debts must be paid, and any remaining funds and/or assets must be distributed to shareholders.

Dissolution of Corporate Entity

The "dissolution" process refers to the formal proceedings necessary to determine whether the corporation should continue its existence. The actions necessary to terminate the corporation once the dissolution is approved are referred to as the *liquidation* of the corporation.

A corporation cannot be liquidated until the decision has been made to dissolve, or terminate, the corporation. A corporation may be dissolved voluntarily by its directors and shareholders or involuntarily by the state, the corporation's shareholders, or its creditors.

Voluntary Dissolution   The board of directors and shareholders of a corporation may choose to dissolve a corporation for a variety of reasons. They may, for example, vote to dissolve the corporation because its business is no longer profitable, the corporation may merge with another corporation, or the corporation may sell all of its assets or stock to another corporation.

The voluntary dissolution of a corporation is a two-step process: (1) the board must vote on the dissolution and make a recommendation to the shareholders and (2) the shareholders must vote on the dissolution. Once the majority of the board of directors determines that the corporation should be dissolved, the directors recommend the dissolution to the shareholders and call a special shareholders' meeting to allow the shareholders to consider the dissolution.

Traditionally, at least two-thirds of a corporation's shareholders had to vote in favor of dissolving the corporation. However, the R.M.B.C.A. requires that only the majority of shareholders (greater than 50 percent) approve of the dissolution. (See R.M.B.C.A. at §14.01.) Once the shareholders approve the dissolution, the creditors of the corporation

Hostile takeover An attempt to take over management and/or ownership of a corporation without the consent of its directors and shareholders.

Tender offer Public offer by an aggressor to purchase shares of a target corporation.

Proxy fight An aggressor's attempt to gain control of a corporation by soliciting the voting rights (proxies) of its shareholders with the intent to elect its board of directors.

must be notified that the corporation will be terminated and they should, therefore, submit a claim for any amounts due them by the corporation. Some states also require that the corporation notify the secretary of state of its intent to dissolve by filing a *notice of intent to dissolve*. Once the notice of intent to dissolve is filed, the corporation can only continue its business for the purpose of winding up the business.

With most fundamental changes, shareholders who vote against the change have the right to force the corporation to buy its shares. However, shareholders who vote against a dissolution do not have dissenters' rights because they will share in the distribution of the corporation's assets when it is liquidated. If shareholders were given dissenters' rights in a dissolution, the corporation would experience a rush of shareholders who wanted to get top dollar for their shares (since they may not get the full value of their shares in a liquidation).

Involuntary Dissolution   A corporation may be dissolved without the consent of its directors and shareholders because poor or ineffective management is ruining the corporation; this is known as an **involuntary termination.** A corporation may be involuntarily terminated by the state, by its shareholders, or by its creditors. In each of these situations, the court generally orders the corporation to dissolve and makes provisions for its liquidation.

If a corporation is involuntarily terminated by the court, the court will generally appoint a **liquidator** to manage its winding up. The court makes this appointment when it determines that there has been mismanagement or no management of the corporation and it would, therefore, be infeasible to order the board to oversee the liquidation of the corporation.

Dissolution by the state. The state, through the attorney general or the secretary of state, may dissolve a corporation if it fails to follow corporate formalities (e.g., fails to file its annual report with the secretary of state), fails to pay filing fees and/or taxes, or acts fraudulently or with misrepresentation. Although the attorney general has traditionally brought dissolution proceedings for these type of violations in the courts, the R.M.B.C.A. and many states have simplified the process by allowing **administrative dissolutions** through the secretary of state's office.

The R.M.B.C.A. gives the secretary of state the authority to dissolve a noncomplying corporation through its offices, without filing a formal lawsuit against the corporation. Such administrative dissolutions are more cost-effective and efficient for the state. If a corporation fails to comply with the state's administrative regulations, the secretary notifies the corporation of its default and offers it a period of time to correct the problem before the corporation will be involuntarily dissolved by the state.

Dissolution by shareholders. A shareholder may ask the court to dissolve a corporation if the corporation is not being effectively managed. For example, a shareholder may file a suit to dissolve the corporation if the directors are deadlocked in their decision making and cannot, therefore, manage the corporation and its business; if corporate assets are being mismanaged/misused by its board; if the shareholders are deadlocked in the election of directors and have not elected directors for the corporation for two years; or if the directors are acting in an illegal or oppressive manner. In order for shareholders to prevail in a suit to dissolve the corporation (known as a *judicial dissolution*) they must demonstrate that the actions or inactions of the directors and/or shareholders are harming the corporation or its business interests.

Dissolution by corporate creditors. Creditors of the corporation may bring legal action to force the corporation to turn its assets into cash and pay its debts. A court may order a corporation to dissolve at the request of a corporate creditor if the creditor can demonstrate that the corporation owes him or her money and shows that the corporation is *insolvent* (i.e., its debts exceed its assets) and therefore, is not able, or likely, to repay its debts without court intervention. In such a dissolution, the court forces the corporation into liquidation so that it can raise the money to pay its creditors. Although an insolvent corporation will not have the money to pay all of its creditors in full, a judicial dissolution forces the corporation to pay at least a portion of the amounts it owes to its creditors.

Liquidation of Corporate Assets

After a corporation is dissolved, its assets must be turned into cash ("liquid assets"), its creditors must be paid, and any money or assets of the corporation that remain may be

Involuntary Termination
Termination of a corporation without the consent of its board and directors and/or its shareholders.

Liquidator   The individual who manages the liquidation of business assets.

Administrative dissolution
Termination of a corporation by the secretary of state.

distributed to its shareholders. This is known as liquidating the corporation. A corporation does not legally terminate until it is liquidated.

In a voluntary dissolution, the liquidation process starts once the decision to dissolve the corporation is made and the corporation notifies the secretary of state of its intent to dissolve. With an involuntary dissolution, the liquidation process starts when the court enters its order to dissolve the corporation. Once the liquidation process begins, the corporation may not conduct any business except for the purpose of winding up its business. *Winding up* means that the corporation only has the authority to collect and liquidate its assets (e.g., call in its accounts receivables and sell all of its property), complete its contracts, pay its creditors, and distribute any "leftovers" to its shareholders.

Creditors' Claims   After a corporation is dissolved, it must notify its known creditors of its intent to dissolve. This allows the creditors to make a claim against the corporation for any amounts its owes. Once a creditor receives notice of the corporation's intent to dissolve, the creditor has a specified number of days to file a claim against the corporation for payment. (See R.M.B.C.A. at § 14.06—providing a creditor at least 120 days to file a claim.) If the creditor does not file within the time allowed, its claim will be barred and cannot be made at a later time.

Unknown Creditors   Invariably, a corporation is not aware of all of the debts that it may owe. Therefore, most states require that the corporation give unknown creditors notice of its intent to dissolve by publishing an announcement in a newspaper in general circulation in the corporation's principal place of business. After the corporation provides this general announcement, creditors of the corporation who were not known at the time of its liquidation (and therefore did not receive personal notice of its intent to dissolve) have five years to submit a claim for amounts due by the corporation.

If the corporation has already wound up its affairs and distributed its assets to shareholders, the shareholders may be responsible to use any money they received in the liquidation to pay the claim(s). This prohibits the corporate owners from escaping responsibility for debts the corporation owed at the time of its liquidation and does not allow shareholders to keep more of the corporation's assets than they would have received had the corporation paid all of its debts at the time of its liquidation.

Distributions to Shareholders   After the corporation pays its creditors, the shareholders are entitled to share any money or other assets that remain in the corporation. A corporation that is voluntarily dissolved may be able to make sizable distributions to its shareholders, especially if the dissolution is caused by a corporate buyout or other merger. However, a corporation that is involuntarily dissolved typically does not have sufficient assets to pay all of its creditors and still have property left to distribute to its shareholders. Therefore, shareholders may receive little or nothing in an involuntary dissolution.

Even if shareholders receive distributions, those distributions are subject to later claims by creditors of the corporation who were not known to the corporation at the time of its liquidation.

Example: Becky owned stock in ABC, Inc. when the corporation dissolved. In the liquidation process, the corporation published notice of its dissolution, as required by state statute. Two years after the corporation was dissolved and liquidated, a customer filed suit against ABC, Inc. for personal injuries sustained during a slip and fall at the company's store. The customer won a judgment of $100,000. Each of the corporation's 100 shareholders received $1,000 in the corporation's liquidation. Because the corporation distributed all of its money to its shareholders during its liquidation, it has no assets/money to pay the customer. Although the customer cannot, therefore, recover the judgment from the corporation, the customer can sue the shareholders to try to force them to pay the amounts they received from the corporation in its liquidation.

Articles of dissolution
Document notifying the secretary of state of the dissolution of a corporation.

Articles of Dissolution

Once the corporation has formally liquidated, it must file **articles of dissolution** with the secretary of state, thereby notifying the secretary that the corporation has completed the dissolution process. Although many states provide a form for articles of dissolution, most articles include the name and address of the corporation, the date the dissolution was approved, verification that the shareholders approved the dissolution, a statement that all the debts of the corporation have been paid, and whether assets of the corporation have been distributed to shareholders.

In addition to this basic information, the secretary of state will generally require that the corporation provide proof that the corporation does not owe state taxes. Any federal taxes owed by the corporation should also be paid; however, most states do not require the corporation to pay federal taxes in order for the secretary to accept its articles.

Once the articles are accepted and filed by the secretary of state, the corporation formally terminates. If the corporation is authorized to do business in other states, it should notify those states of its termination.

◆ FUNDAMENTAL CHANGES IN CORPORATE STRUCTURE IN REVIEW

Fundamental Changes

Amendment to articles of incorporation
   Changes to corporation's organizing document
Merger
   One or more corporations are absorbed into another corporation
Consolidation
   Two or more corporations merge and form a new corporation
Sale of corporate assets not in the ordinary course of business
   Purchase of all or substantially all of the assets of another corporation
Dissolution
   Termination of a corporation requiring corporation to
   (1) terminate its form and (2) liquidate its assets

Standard Approval Procedure

Two-step approval procedure requiring corporation's board of directors and shareholders to approve fundamental changes in the corporate structure.

◆ KEY TERMS

fundamental corporate change	target corporation	hostile takeover
standard approval procedure	share exchange	tender offer
articles of amendment	subsidiary	proxy fight
dissenters' rights	articles of merger	involuntary termination
merger	certificate of merger	liquidator
merged corporation	consolidation	administrative dissolution
surviving corporation	articles of consolidation	articles of dissolution
statutory merger	ordinary course of business	

◆ STUDY QUESTIONS IN REVIEW

1. What are considered to be fundamental changes to the structure of a corporation?
2. Who must approve fundamental changes before they occur?
3. What is the difference between a merger and a consolidation of two or more corporations?
4. What is a hostile takeover?
5. Why would shareholders ask a court to dissolve their corporation?
6. What is the financial status of a corporation that is insolvent?
7. What happens if a corporation is liquidated?
8. Are shareholders always entitled to receive corporate assets if their corporation is dissolved?

◆ CASE STUDIES IN REVIEW

1. Jim is a shareholder of Ducks Forever, Inc., a duck decoy manufacturer. Ducks Forever, Inc. wants to merge with Plastic Producers, Inc., a plastic manufacturer, and begin to manufacture plastic decoys rather than the wood decoys that they have traditionally made. Jim is upset at the prospect of "cheapening" the products and objects to the merger. If the majority of the shareholders of Ducks Forever, Inc. approve the merger, what right does Jim have as a dissenter?

2. Sally and Joe are the sole shareholders of Right Track, Inc., a running shoe manufacturer. After twenty-five years in business together, Sally and Joe decide to dissolve the corporation and retire. After liquidating their assets, the corporation distributed the remaining profits to Sally and Joe; they each received $500,000. Two months after they liquidate, Polka-Dot Leather, Inc., a leather manufacturer, sues Sally and Joe for $25,000 due on supplies provided to Right Track, Inc. for the manufacture of their shoes. Sally and Joe did not notify their creditors of their intent to dissolve the corporation; therefore, many of their creditors' claims were not paid at the time of their liquidation. Are Sally and Joe liable for the corporation's debt even though they received the distribution from the corporation as shareholders?

◆ PROJECT APPLICATION

Your law firm represents Dizknee, Inc., a California corporation specializing in the production of children's movies. Dizknee, Inc. wants to merge with Movie Fun, Inc., a small movie animation company. Your supervising attorney asks you to research your state's statutes regulating corporate mergers to determine who must approve the merger before it occurs. Prepare a brief memorandum to your attorney explaining the approval procedures required for corporate mergers in your state. Be sure to address the statute's application to Dizknee's proposal.

◆ ENDNOTES

1. See R.M.B.C.A. at §13.01 et. seq.

SECTION FIVE
Limited Liability Companies

CHAPTER 13

LLC: Corporate Liability with Partnership Taxation

Limited liability companies (LLCs) share many of the characteristics of a corporation but are taxed as partnerships. In most respects they are almost identical to limited liability partnerships (LLPs) but lack the aesthetic value of "being partner." LLCs offer all members management rights, limited liability, and the pass-through taxation of a partnership. Since 1988, LLCs have become the entity of choice in many states. However, with the advent of the LLP, they will probably lose this status in the future.

Wyoming was the first state to adopt the LLC in 1977. However, they became increasingly popular after the 1988 ruling by the Internal Revenue Service (IRS) that a properly formed LLC could be treated as a partnership for federal taxation purposes.[1] In 1995, the National Conference of the Commissions on Uniform State Law adopted the Uniform Limited Liability Act to provide states guidance in their legislation. Although only a few states have adopted the act, most states are considering LLC legislation. (See Appendix F.)

LLCs can offer their members the limited liability of corporations, the management rights of general partnerships, and the pass-through taxation of partnerships. They are often compared to S corporations, which offer these same advantages but have the burdensome formation and operational reporting requirements of a corporation as well as ownership restrictions (e.g., an S corporation may have only a limited number of shareholders and their shareholders may only be individuals, not corporations, nonresident aliens, partnerships, or charitable organizations).

More recently, LLCs have also been compared to limited liability partnerships. While LLPs offer most of the advantages of LLCs (limited liability, management rights, and partnership taxation), LLPs offer greater simplicity in creation (to become an LLP, a general partnership simply files a form with the secretary of state) and the traditional image of a partnership; this latter advantage is particularly appealing to professionals. The "aesthetic value" of the partnership form has been explained:

> Tradition dictates that when lawyers and accountants decide to mold a firm, they should form a partnership. Despite the liability exposure, professionals have long cherished the financial reward and status of "making partner." This tradition is a major reason why partnerships prevail in the professional arena.[2]

Although LLPs are often favored over the LLC, they do not offer the same degree of protection to their participants. LLPs generally protect partners from liability only for the negligence and malfeasance of other partners; individual partners remain liable for the contractual obligations of the partnership as well as their own negligence or malfeasance and that which they participated in, supervised, or had knowledge of. In contrast, an LLC generally offers its members absolute immunity for the debts and obligations of the LLC, including those arising from tort. Because of these extensive liability protections, LLCs will continue to remain a strong force in business organizations.

CHARACTERISTICS OF THE LIMITED LIABILITY COMPANY

An LLC is a separate legal entity from its members and is authorized by state statute and its organizing document, the articles of organization. While the operating procedures of LLCs may vary between states and companies, the common characteristics of LLCs are their personal liability protections, shared management rights, finite duration, pass-through taxation, and limited transferability of interests. An LLC is inherently an entity offering limited liability to its owners and may elect to be taxed as either a partnership or a corporation.

Liability

No member of an LLC is personally liable for the debts or other obligations of the LLC. This is an important distinction between an LLC and a limited liability partnership. An LLP generally offers partners protection only from the negligence or malfeasance of other partners, but does not insulate partners from liability for their own negligence or malfeasance nor the contractual obligations of the partnership.

Management

All members of the LLC are allowed to participate in the management and operation of the company, unless the LLC's operating agreement limits these rights. If members of an LLC waive their management rights, a board of managers is generally appointed to oversee the operation and management of the LLC's business.

Duration

Many states limit the duration of an LLC to thirty years, although its operating agreement may provide that it automatically dissolves on the death, insanity, bankruptcy, retirement, expulsion, or resignation of any member. The lack of continuity of life is a disadvantage for many companies, especially if they need to obtain long-term financing (e.g., a physician needs to finance the medical equipment and supplies necessary to begin a practice) or have become large organizational structures at the end of their duration. The limited duration of an LLC may be circumvented by allowing the LLC to continue, by unanimous agreement of the members, after the date of termination. This opportunity for continuity prevents many of the difficulties inherent in the automatic termination of an LLC but does not guarantee its long-term existence.

Taxation

LLCs may elect to receive the pass-through taxation of a partnership as opposed to the double taxation of a corporation. The partnership taxation afforded the LLC is seen as one of its most significant advantages. It is the only entity, other than a corporation, that provides personal liability immunity to managers while offering the tax advantages of a partnership.

Transferability of Shares

Ownership of an LLC is not freely transferable. Members of an LLC generally participate in the management of the LLC; therefore, as in a partnership, changes in membership (share transfers) must be approved by all of the members to ensure some measure of harmony and cooperation in management and to protect the members from unwelcome intruders in the management ranks. If all of the members approve of a proposed share transfer, the purchaser will become a new member of the LLC and be entitled to participate in management decisions.

However, if the members of an LLC do not unanimously consent to a proposed share transfer, the purchaser does not become a member of the LLC and does not have management rights. The unapproved purchaser may still purchase a member's interest in the LLC, but is only entitled to the share of company's profits that the selling member would have been entitled to receive.

FORMATION

All business organizations must comply with the following basic formation requirements:

♦ Registering its business name as an assumed business name/trade name
♦ Obtaining the required business and/or professional licenses and permits
♦ Applying for a sales tax permit, if goods will be sold

♦ Applying for a tax identification number with the IRS and state
♦ Establishing employee withholding accounts
♦ Establishing unemployment and workers' compensation coverage

In addition to these requirements, an LLC must also:

♦ Designate its status as an LLC in its name
♦ File articles of organization with the secretary of state
♦ Draft an operating agreement addressing the formation, operation, management, and termination and/or continuation of the LLC[3]

Once these prerequisites are satisfied, the LLC begins its existence.

Name of the Limited Liability Company

The name of the LLC must contain the designation "Limited Liability Company" or an appropriate abbreviation, such as "L.L.C." or "Ltd. Liability Co." This designation notifies those dealing with the partnership of its status and the limited liability of its members.

Purpose

LLCs commonly have a general purpose clause which allows them to "transact any and all lawful business" associated with their business form (e.g., "Toys, LLC may transact any and all lawful business associated with the sale and distribution of toys"). Such a general purpose is set forth in the articles of organization and/or the operating agreement in order to allow the LLC to expand its business operations without restrictions. The use of the boilerplate "any and all lawful business" also grants the members and managers expansive authority to bind the LLC. The potential liabilities that such unrestrained authority may create must be considered when drafting the purpose clause for an LLC.

Many states protect the public from the lack of accountability that the liability limitations of the LLC form offers its members by restricting the purposes for which LLCs may be formed. Such restrictions generally prohibit businesses that could incur extensive debts and/or liabilities, such as banking and insurance, from organizing as LLCs. In addition, some states have not yet authorized professionals to transact business as an LLC because of the desire to hold them accountable for the services they render. The statutes of the state in which the LLC is organizing must be reviewed before the LLC is recommended as an organizational form for a particular business.

Registration of Limited Liability Company

Articles of organization
Document forming a limited liability company.

An LLC must register with the secretary of state by filing its **articles of organization,** an informational filing notifying the secretary of state of an LLC's intent to do business. The "organizers," who create and establish the LLC, are responsible for filing the articles. Once the articles are accepted by the secretary of state, a certificate of organization will be provided to the LLC, evidencing its authority to transact business.

State statutes often set forth the information that must be provided in an LLC's articles of organization. (See, e.g., Form 13.1, *Articles of Organization for Domestic Limited Liability Company.*) Typically, the articles will contain the following information:

♦ Name of the LLC
♦ Name and address of the organizer(s)
♦ Name and address of the initial registered office for service of process
♦ Name and address of the initial agent for service of process
♦ Duration of the LLC
♦ Name and addresses of the initial managers, if the LLC will be managed by managers, or the name and addresses of the initial members, if the LLC will be managed by members
♦ Statement setting forth the members' liability for any debts or other obligations of the LLC

The articles are intended to (1) notify the secretary of state and the general public of the existence of an LLC and the respective liabilities of its members for obligations of the

State of California

File#_____

Secretary of State

LIMITED LIABILITY COMPANY
ARTICLES OF ORGANIZATION

A $70.00 filing fee must accompany this form.
IMPORTANT – Read instructions before completing this form.

This Space For Filing Use Only

---

1. Name of the limited liability company (end the name with the words "Limited Liability Company," " Ltd. Liability Co.," or the abbreviations "LLC" or "L.L.C.")

2. The purpose of the limited liability company is to engage in any lawful act or activity for which a limited liability company may be organized under the Beverly-Killea limited liability company act.

3. Name the agent for service of process and check the appropriate provision below:

   _____ which is

   [ ] an individual residing in California. Proceed to item 4.

   [ ] a corporation which has filed a certificate pursuant to section 1505. Proceed to item 5.

4. If an individual, California address of the agent for service of process:
   Address:

   City: State: **CA**   Zip Code:

5. The limited liability company will be managed by: **(check one)**

   [ ] one manager   **[ ] more than one manager**   **[ ] limited liability company members**

6. Other matters to be included in this certificate may be set forth on separate attached pages and are made a part of this certificate. Other matters may include the latest date on which the limited liability company is to dissolve.

7. Number of pages attached, if any:

   Type of business of the limited liability company.

DECLARATION: It is hereby declared that I am the person who executed this instrument, which execution is my act and deed.

_____   _____
Signature of Organizer   Type or Print Name of Organizer

_____
Date

SEC/STATE (REV. 1/99)   FORM LLC-1 – FILING FEE $70.00
                                          Approved by Secretary of State

FORM 13.1.
Articles of Organization for Domestic Limited Liability Company

FORM 13.1. *continued*

New York State
Department of State
Division of Corporations, State Records
and Uniform Commercial Code
Albany, NY 12231

(This form must be printed or typed in black ink)

ARTICLES OF ORGANIZATION
OF

_____
(Insert company name)

Under Section 203 of the Limited Liability Company Law

FIRST: The name of the limited liability company is: _____

SECOND: The county within this state in which the office of the limited liability company is to be located is: _____

THIRD: (optional) The latest date on which the limited liability company is to dissolve is:
_____
(month/day/year)

FOURTH: The Secretary of State is designated as agent of the limited liability company upon whom process against it may be served. The post office address within or without this state to which the Secretary of State shall mail a copy of any process against the limited liability company served upon him or her is:

_____
_____
_____

FIFTH: (optional) The name and street address within this state of the registered agent of the limited liability company upon whom and at which process against the limited liability company may be served is:

_____
_____
_____

SIXTH: (optional) The future effective date of the Articles of Organization, which does not exceed 60 days from the date of filing, is: _____
(month/day/year)

SEVENTH: (optional) If all or specified members are to be liable in their capacity as members for all or specified debts, obligations or liabilities of the limited liability company as authorized by Section 609 of the Limited Liability Company Law, an affirmative statement must be made. A statement of such effect is made as follows:

_____
_____

_____   _____
(signature)   *(name and capacity of signer)*

ARTICLES OF ORGANIZATION
OF

Under Section 203 of the Limited Liability Company Law

Filed by:

_____
(Name)

_____
(Mailing address)

_____
(City, State and ZIP code)

NOTE: • This form was prepared by the New York State Department of State for articles of organization. It does not contain all optional provisions under the law. You are not required to use this form. You may draft your own form or use forms available at legal supply stores. The Department of State recommends that legal documents be prepared under the guidance of an attorney. The certificate must be submitted with a $200 filing fee made payable to the Department of State.

• This form may not be accompanied by any riders or attachments except a certificate evidencing reservation of name.

company, (2) provide the information necessary to serve the LLC in the event legal action is brought against it (the name and address of the registered agent), and (3) establish the date of termination for the benefit of the public as well as the records of the secretary of state.

Foreign Registration

If an LLC intends to do business in a state other than the one in which it originated, it generally must apply for the authority to do business in the foreign jurisdiction. Foreign registration not only notifies the foreign jurisdiction of the LLC's intent to do business in the state but also allows the state to collect fees for this privilege. If an LLC fails to properly register in a foreign jurisdiction, it will generally be denied access to the state's courts (i.e., the LLC would lack the ability to enforce its business contracts in the foreign jurisdiction).

Prior to registering in another state, the LLC should first determine if its assumed business name or trade name, if one is being used, is available in the state. If it is not, the LLC will need to modify its name before it may register with the secretary of state of that jurisdiction. The Uniform Limited Liability Company Act allows an LLC to reserve its assumed business name in a foreign jurisdiction for one year before it intends to begin business in the foreign state. However, this takes considerable forethought. Companies often adopt a business name without considering its availability in other jurisdictions, where they may initially have no intent of expanding.

An LLC must register in a foreign jurisdiction only if it intends to "transact business in the state." While most state statutes define what actions constitute "transacting business," the Uniform Limited Liability Company Act provides guidelines for what actions will not result in this determination.

Uniform Limited Liability Company Act

Section 1003. *Activities Not Constituting Transacting Business*

(a) Activities of a foreign limited liability company that do not constitute transacting business within the meaning of this (article) include:

    (1) maintaining, defending, or settling an action or proceeding;

    (2) holding meetings of its members or managers or carrying on any other activity concerning its internal affairs;

    (3) maintaining bank accounts;

    (4) maintaining offices or agencies for the transfer, exchange, and registration of the foreign company's own securities or maintaining trustees or depositories with respect to those securities;

    (5) selling through independent contractors;

    (6) soliciting or obtaining orders, whether by mail or through employees or agents or otherwise, if the orders require acceptance outside this State before they become contracts;

    (7) creating or acquiring indebtedness, mortgages, or security interest in real or personal property;

    (8) securing or collecting debts or enforcing mortgages or other security interests in property securing the debts, and holding, protecting, and maintaining property so acquired;

    (9) conducting an isolated transaction that is completed within thirty days and is not one in the course of similar transactions of a like manner; and

    (10) transacting business in interstate commerce.

(b) For purposes of this (article), the ownership in this State of income-producing real property or tangible personal property, other than property excluded under subsection (a), constitutes transacting business in this State.

(c) This section does not apply in determining the contacts or activities that may subject a foreign limited liability company to service of process, taxation, or regulation under any other law of this State.

LLCs do not enjoy the same flexibility as partnerships and corporations in expanding their businesses into other jurisdictions. Not all states recognize LLCs as an organizational form and there is inconsistency between state laws regulating these companies, in part because the Uniform Limited Liability Company Act became available after most states had already adopted the LLC form. If a state does not recognize LLCs, it may treat the foreign LLC as either a partnership or a corporation, at its option. Companies considering interstate expansion must take these potential jurisdictional limitations into account in choosing their form of business organization.

Professional Limited Liability Companies

In some states, an LLC may be formed to offer professional services (physicians, attorneys, accountants, etc.) if the articles provide that the LLC is a professional limited liability company, a "PLLC." In the event a PLLC is formed, only the licensed professionals can be members, managers, or officers.

Operating Agreement

Operating agreement
Written agreement governing the management and operation of a limited liability company.

The **operating agreement** sets forth the operating procedures of the LLC, as well as the rights and duties of its members. Like a partnership agreement, the operating agreement is crucial to the successful management of the LLC.

The basic form for partnership agreements may be used as a guideline for drafting an LLC operating agreement. (See Appendix G, Model LLC Operating Agreement.) Generally, the operating agreement will set forth, at a minimum, the voting/management rights of the members, the capital contribution of the members, the members' right to share in profits, and the relative distribution rights of the members. Although many requirements for an LLC operating agreement are set by statute, typically, the following provisions should be included:

- ◆ Duration of the LLC
- ◆ Purpose of the LLC
- ◆ Whether the LLC will be managed by member-managers or managers who are not members
- ◆ Capital contributions by each member
- ◆ Voting rights of members
- ◆ Schedule/provisions for meetings of members and managers
- ◆ Allocation of the profits and losses of the LLC
- ◆ Rights and duties of members and managers and members' right to indemnification for unauthorized acts of other members
- ◆ Fiduciary duties owed by members and managers to the LLC and its members
- ◆ Accounting procedures (including tax preparation) and record keeping
- ◆ Right and authority of members to assign or transfer their financial and/or participatory interests, including the right or restrictions on the substitution of new members
- ◆ Events causing a dissolution of the LLC
- ◆ Members' rights to continue the LLC upon the occurrence of an event triggering dissolution
- ◆ Procedures for amending the agreement
- ◆ Any other provisions that the organizers and members choose to include (e.g., the method of repayment of loans made to the LLC by members)

The operating agreement must be signed by all members and must not conflict with the articles of organization. It must be carefully drafted to set forth the rights and duties of its members and managers and generally may only be amended by unanimous vote of the members. Therefore, matters that may change from time to time (e.g., the name and address of the registered agent for service of process) should be placed in the articles of organization, which are more easily amended (by majority vote) than the operating agreement.

Annual Reporting Requirements

The LLC may be required to file annual reports with the secretary of state of the operating jurisdictions (foreign and/or origination jurisdiction). Such reports often simply verify and update the information contained in the original articles and also give the secretary of state the opportunity to collect annual fees from the LLC. However, the required reports generally must be filed in order for an LLC to continue to have the right to operate in the particular jurisdiction.

TAXATION CONSIDERATIONS OF THE LIMITED LIABILITY COMPANY

Initially, the IRS denied LCCs partnership status for purposes of taxation because the IRS considered a business association to be a "partnership" only if at least one member was personally liable for the obligations of the partnership.[4] In 1988, the IRS reconsidered its position and granted partnership status to LLCs for purposes of federal taxation as long as the LLC had more characteristics of a partnership than a corporation.

The IRS identified four characteristics as being unique to corporations:

1. Continuity of life
2. Centralization of management
3. Limited liability
4. Free transferability of interests[5]

If an LLC had more than two of these characteristics, it would be deemed a corporation for taxation purposes and the profits of the LLC would be taxed twice: (1) the LLC would be taxed on its profits and (2) after the profits were distributed to the individual member, the profits would be taxed as the member's personal income.[6]

However, in 1997, the IRS eliminated the uncertainty surrounding the taxable status of LLCs by adopting the "check-the-box regulation." This relatively new approach to the tax classification of LLCs makes the analysis of the four corporate characteristics moot.

The *entity classification election* allows LLCs and other unincorporated entities, such as limited liability partnerships, to choose whether they will be taxed as a partnership or a corporation literally by checking a box declaring their taxable status. (See Form 13.2, *IRS Form 8832, Entity Classification Election.*) If a business does not formally declare its taxable status, the IRS will, by default, generally classify an unincorporated business as a partnership for tax purposes if it has two or more members.

As a partnership, the LLC must conform to the IRS partnership filings and file an informational tax return with the IRS (see Form 13.3, *IRS Form 1065, U.S. Partnership Return of Income*) and provide each member with a schedule of their proportionate share of business income (see Form 13.4, *IRS Form 1065, Schedule K-1, Partner's Share of Income, Credits, Deductions, etc.*). In addition, each member must declare his or her proportionate share of business profits as personal income. (See Form 13.5, *IRS Form 1040, Schedule E, Supplemental Income and Loss.*)

Although the IRS does grant an LLC the benefit of pass-through taxation, some states do not afford LLCs this taxation advantage for state revenue purposes. Thus, a business owner cannot automatically assume that an LLC will offer favorable tax treatment until the state's revenue rulings are reviewed.

MANAGEMENT OF THE LIMITED LIABILITY COMPANY

An LLC may be managed by members or by managers who are not members. All members of an LLC have the inherent right to manage and participate in the operation of the LLC; however, if the members agree to waive these rights, they may vote to elect a board

Form **8832**
(December 1996)
Department of the Treasury
Internal Revenue Service

Entity Classification Election

OMB No. 1545-1516

Please Type or Print	Name of entity	Employer identification number (EIN)
	Number, street, and room or suite no. If a P.O. box, see instructions.	
	City or town, state, and ZIP code. If a foreign address, enter city, province or state, postal code and country.	

1   Type of election (see instructions):

a ☐ Initial classification by a newly-formed entity (or change in current classification of an existing entity to take effect on January 1, 1997)

b ☐ Change in current classification (to take effect later than January 1, 1997)

2   Form of entity (see instructions):

a ☐ A domestic eligible entity electing to be classified as an association taxable as a corporation.

b ☐ A domestic eligible entity electing to be classified as a partnership.

c ☐ A domestic eligible entity with a single owner electing to be disregarded as a separate entity.

d ☐ A foreign eligible entity electing to be classified as an association taxable as a corporation.

e ☐ A foreign eligible entity electing to be classified as a partnership.

f ☐ A foreign eligible entity with a single owner electing to be disregarded as a separate entity.

3 Election is to be effective beginning (month, day, year) (see instructions) . . . . ▶ ___ / ___ / ___

4 Name and title of person whom the IRS may call for more information

5 That person's telephone number

Consent Statement and Signature(s) (see instructions)

Under penalties of perjury, I (we) declare that I (we) consent to the election of the above-named entity to be classified as indicated above, and that I (we) have examined this consent statement, and to the best of my (our) knowledge and belief, it is true, correct, and complete. If I am an officer, manager, or member signing for all members of the entity, I further declare that I am authorized to execute this consent statement on their behalf.

Signature(s)	Date	Title

For **Paperwork Reduction Act Notice, see page 2.**   Cat. No. 22598R   Form **8832** (12-96)

FORM 13.2.

IRS Form 8832, Entity Classification Election

Form **1065**	**U.S. Partnership Return of Income**	OMB No. 1545-0099
Department of the Treasury Internal Revenue Service	For calendar year 1999, or tax year beginning ...., 1999, and ending ...., ... ▶ **See separate instructions.**	19**99**

A Principal business activity	Use the IRS label. Other- wise, please print or type.	Name of partnership	D Employer identification number
B Principal product or service		Number, street, and room or suite no. If a P.O. box, see page 12 of the instructions.	E Date business started
C Business code number		City or town, state, and ZIP code	F Total assets (see page 12 of the instructions) $

G Check applicable boxes: **(1)** ☐ Initial return   **(2)** ☐ Final return   **(3)** ☐ Change in address   **(4)** ☐ Amended return

H Check accounting method: **(1)** ☐ Cash   **(2)** ☐ Accrual   **(3)** ☐ Other (specify) ▶ ....

I Number of Schedules K-1. Attach one for each person who was a partner at any time during the tax year ▶ ....

Caution: *Include **only** trade or business income and expenses on lines 1a through 22 below. See the instructions for more information.*

Income

1a Gross receipts or sales	**1a**		
b Less returns and allowances.	**1b**		**1c**
2 Cost of goods sold (Schedule A, line 8)			**2**
3 Gross profit. Subtract line 2 from line 1c.			**3**
4 Ordinary income (loss) from other partnerships, estates, and trusts *(attach schedule)*. ..			**4**
5 Net farm profit (loss) *(attach Schedule F (Form 1040))*			**5**
6 Net gain (loss) from Form 4797, Part II, line 18.			**6**
7 Other income (loss) *(attach schedule)*			**7**
8 **Total income (loss).** Combine lines 3 through 7			**8**

Deductions (see page 14 of the instructions for limitations)

9 Salaries and wages (other than to partners) (less employment credits)			**9**
10 Guaranteed payments to partners			**10**
11 Repairs and maintenance			**11**
12 Bad debts			**12**
13 Rent			**13**
14 Taxes and licenses			**14**
15 Interest			**15**
16a Depreciation (if required, attach Form 4562)	**16a**		
b Less depreciation reported on Schedule A and elsewhere on return	**16b**		**16c**
17 Depletion **(Do not deduct oil and gas depletion.)**			**17**
18 Retirement plans, etc.			**18**
19 Employee benefit programs			**19**
20 Other deductions *(attach schedule)*			**20**
21 **Total deductions.** Add the amounts shown in the far right column for lines 9 through 20 .			**21**
22 **Ordinary income (loss)** from trade or business activities. Subtract line 21 from line 8 . .			**22**

Please Sign Here

Under penalties of perjury, I declare that I have examined this return, including accompanying schedules and statements, and to the best of my knowledge and belief, it is true, correct, and complete. Declaration of preparer (other than general partner or limited liability company member) is based on all information of which preparer has any knowledge.

▶ _____   ▶ _____
Signature of general partner or limited liability company member   Date

Paid Preparer's Use Only	Preparer's signature ▶	Date	Check if self-employed ▶ ☐	Preparer's SSN or PTIN
	Firm's name (or yours if self-employed) and address ▶		EIN ▶	
			ZIP code ▶	

For Paperwork Reduction Act Notice, see separate instructions.   Cat. No. 11390Z   Form **1065** (1999)

FORM 13.3.

IRS Form 1065, U.S. Partnership Return of Income

| SCHEDULE K-1
(Form 1065)
Department of the Treasury
Internal Revenue Service | Partner's Share of Income, Credits, Deductions, etc.
▶ See separate instructions.
For calendar year 1999 or tax year beginning _____ , 1999, and ending _____ , _____ | OMB No. 1545-0099
1999 |

Partner's identifying number ▶ _____

Partnership's identifying number ▶ _____

Partner's name, address, and ZIP code

Partnership's name, address, and ZIP code

A This partner is a ☐ general partner ☐ limited partner
☐ limited liability company member

B What type of entity is this partner? ▶ _____

C Is this partner a ☐ domestic or a ☐ foreign partner?

D Enter partner's percentage of:
	(i) Before change or termination	(ii) End of year
Profit sharing	_____ %	_____ %
Loss sharing	_____ %	_____ %
Ownership of capital	_____ %	_____ %

E IRS Center where partnership filed return: _____

F Partner's share of liabilities (see instructions):
Nonrecourse . . . . $ _____
Qualified nonrecourse financing . . $ _____
Other . . . . $ _____

G Tax shelter registration number . . ▶ _____

H Check here if this partnership is a publicly traded partnership as defined in section 469(k)(2) . . . . . . ☐

I Check applicable boxes: **(1)** ☐ Final K-1 **(2)** ☐ Amended K-1

J Analysis of partner's capital account:

(a) Capital account at beginning of year	(b) Capital contributed during year	(c) Partner's share of lines 3, 4, and 7, Form 1065, Schedule M-2	(d) Withdrawals and distributions	(e) Capital account at end of year (combine columns (a) through (d))
			( )	

	(a) Distributive share item		(b) Amount	(c) 1040 filers enter the amount in column (b) on:
Income (Loss)	**1** Ordinary income (loss) from trade or business activities . . .	**1**		See page 6 of Partner's Instructions for Schedule K-1 (Form 1065).
	2 Net income (loss) from rental real estate activities	**2**		
	3 Net income (loss) from other rental activities	**3**		
	4 Portfolio income (loss):			
	a Interest	**4a**		Sch. B, Part I, line 1
	b Ordinary dividends	**4b**		Sch. B, Part II, line 5
	c Royalties	**4c**		Sch. E, Part I, line 4
	d Net short-term capital gain (loss)	**4d**		Sch. D, line 5, col. (f)
	e Net long-term capital gain (loss):			
	(1) 28% rate gain (loss)	**e(1)**		Sch. D, line 12, col. (g)
	(2) Total for year	**e(2)**		Sch. D, line 12, col. (f)
	f Other portfolio income (loss) *(attach schedule)*	**4f**		Enter on applicable line of your return.
	5 Guaranteed payments to partner	**5**		See page 6 of Partner's Instructions for Schedule K-1 (Form 1065).
	6 Net section 1231 gain (loss) (other than due to casualty or theft) .	**6**		
	7 Other income (loss) *(attach schedule)*	**7**		Enter on applicable line of your return.
Deductions	**8** Charitable contributions (see instructions) *(attach schedule)* . .	**8**		Sch. A, line 15 or 16
	9 Section 179 expense deduction.	**9**		See pages 7 and 8 of Partner's Instructions for Schedule K-1 (Form 1065).
	10 Deductions related to portfolio income *(attach schedule)* . . .	**10**		
	11 Other deductions *(attach schedule)*.	**11**		
Credits	**12a** Low-income housing credit:			
	(1) From section 42(j)(5) partnerships for property placed in service before 1990	**a(1)**		Form 8586, line 5
	(2) Other than on line 12a(1) for property placed in service before 1990	**a(2)**		
	(3) From section 42(j)(5) partnerships for property placed in service after 1989	**a(3)**		
	(4) Other than on line 12a(3) for property placed in service after 1989	**a(4)**		
	b Qualified rehabilitation expenditures related to rental real estate activities	**12b**		
	c Credits (other than credits shown on lines 12a and 12b) related to rental real estate activities.	**12c**		See page 8 of Partner's Instructions for Schedule K-1 (Form 1065).
	d Credits related to other rental activities	**12d**		
	13 Other credits.	**13**		

For Paperwork Reduction Act Notice, see Instructions for Form 1065.   Cat. No. 11394R   **Schedule K-1 (Form 1065) 1999**

FORM 13.4.

IRS Form 1065, Schedule K-1, Partner's Share of Income, Credits, Deductions, etc

Schedule K-1 (Form 1065) 1999   Page **2**

	(a) Distributive share item		(b) Amount	(c) 1040 filers enter the amount in column (b) on:
Investment Interest	**14a** Interest expense on investment debts	**14a**		Form 4952, line 1
	b (1) Investment income included on lines 4a, 4b, 4c, and 4f . .	**b(1)**		} See page 9 of Partner's Instructions for Schedule K-1 (Form 1065).
	(2) Investment expenses included on line 10.	**b(2)**		
Self-employment	**15a** Net earnings (loss) from self-employment	**15a**		Sch. SE, Section A or B
	b Gross farming or fishing income.	**15b**		} See page 9 of Partner's Instructions for Schedule K-1 (Form 1065).
	c Gross nonfarm income.	**15c**		
Adjustments and Tax Preference Items	**16a** Depreciation adjustment on property placed in service after 1986	**16a**		
	b Adjusted gain or loss	**16b**		
	c Depletion (other than oil and gas)	**16c**		See page 9 of Partner's Instructions for Schedule K-1 (Form 1065) and Instructions for Form 6251.
	d (1) Gross income from oil, gas, and geothermal properties . .	**d(1)**		
	(2) Deductions allocable to oil, gas, and geothermal properties	**d(2)**		
	e Other adjustments and tax preference items *(attach schedule)*	**16e**		
Foreign Taxes	**17a** Type of income ▶			Form 1116, check boxes
	b Name of foreign country or possession ▶			
	c Total gross income from sources outside the United States *(attach schedule)*	**17c**		Form 1116, Part I
	d Total applicable deductions and losses *(attach schedule)*. . .	**17d**		
	e Total foreign taxes (check one): ▶ ☐ Paid ☐ Accrued . .	**17e**		Form 1116, Part II
	f Reduction in taxes available for credit *(attach schedule)* . . .	**17f**		Form 1116, Part III
	g Other foreign tax information *(attach schedule)*	**17g**		See Instructions for Form 1116.
Other	**18** Section 59(e)(2) expenditures: **a** Type ▶			} See page 9 of Partner's Instructions for Schedule K-1 (Form 1065).
	b Amount	**18b**		
	19 Tax-exempt interest income	**19**		Form 1040, line 8b
	20 Other tax-exempt income.	**20**		} See pages 9 and 10 of Partner's Instructions for Schedule K-1 (Form 1065).
	21 Nondeductible expenses	**21**		
	22 Distributions of money (cash and marketable securities) . . .	**22**		
	23 Distributions of property other than money	**23**		
	24 Recapture of low-income housing credit:			
	a From section 42(j)(5) partnerships	**24a**		} Form 8611, line 8
	b Other than on line 24a.	**24b**		

25 Supplemental information required to be reported separately to each partner *(attach additional schedules if more space is needed):*

(Supplemental Information — blank lines)

Schedule K-1 (Form 1065) 1999

FORM 13.4. *continued*

SCHEDULE E
(Form 1040)

Department of the Treasury
Internal Revenue Service   (99)

Supplemental Income and Loss

(From rental real estate, royalties, partnerships,
S corporations, estates, trusts, REMICs, etc.)

▶ Attach to Form 1040 or Form 1041.   ▶ See Instructions for Schedule E (Form 1040).

OMB No. 1545-0074

1999

Attachment
Sequence No. **13**

Name(s) shown on return

Your social security number

Part I   Income or Loss From Rental Real Estate and Royalties   Note: *Report income and expenses from your business of renting personal property on Schedule C or C-EZ (see page E-1). Report farm rental income or loss from Form 4835 on page 2, line 39.*

1 Show the kind and location of each **rental real estate property:**	2 For each rental real estate property listed on line 1, did you or your family use it during the tax year for personal purposes for more than the greater of: • 14 days, **or** • 10% of the total days rented at fair rental value? (See page E-1.)	Yes	No
A	A		
B	B		
C	C		

| Income: | | Properties | | | Totals |
		A	B	C	(Add columns A, B, and C.)
3 Rents received	3				3
4 Royalties received	4				4
Expenses:					
5 Advertising	5				
6 Auto and travel (see page E-2) .	6				
7 Cleaning and maintenance . . .	7				
8 Commissions	8				
9 Insurance	9				
10 Legal and other professional fees	10				
11 Management fees	11				
12 Mortgage interest paid to banks, etc. (see page E-2)	12				12
13 Other interest	13				
14 Repairs	14				
15 Supplies	15				
16 Taxes	16				
17 Utilities	17				
18 Other (list) ▶............	18				
19 Add lines 5 through 18	19				19
20 Depreciation expense or depletion (see page E-3)	20				20
21 Total expenses. Add lines 19 and 20	21				
22 Income or (loss) from rental real estate or royalty properties. Subtract line 21 from line 3 (rents) or line 4 (royalties). If the result is a (loss), see page E-3 to find out if you must file **Form 6198** . .	22				
23 Deductible rental real estate loss. **Caution:** *Your rental real estate loss on line 22 may be limited. See page E-3 to find out if you must file* **Form 8582.** *Real estate professionals must complete line 42 on page 2*	23	( )	( )	( )	
24 **Income.** Add positive amounts shown on line 22. **Do not** include any losses				24	
25 **Losses.** Add royalty losses from line 22 and rental real estate losses from line 23. Enter total losses here				25	( )
26 Total rental real estate and royalty income or (loss). Combine lines 24 and 25. Enter the result here. If Parts II, III, IV, and line 39 on page 2 do not apply to you, also enter this amount on Form 1040, line 17. Otherwise, include this amount in the total on line 40 on page 2				26	

For Paperwork Reduction Act Notice, see Form 1040 instructions.   Cat. No. 11344 .   **Schedule E (Form 1040) 1999**

FORM 13.5.

IRS Form 1040, Schedule E, Supplemental Income and Loss

Schedule E (Form 1040) 1999   Attachment Sequence No. **13**   Page **2**

Name(s) shown on return. Do not enter name and social security number if shown on other side.   **Your social security number**

Note: *If you report amounts from farming or fishing on Schedule E, you must enter your gross income from those activities on line 41 below. Real estate professionals must complete line 42 below.*

Part II   **Income or Loss From Partnerships and S Corporations**   **Note:** *If you report a loss from an at-risk activity, you MUST check either column (e) or (f) on line 27 to describe your investment in the activity. See page E-5. If you check column (f), you must attach Form 6198.*

27	(a) Name	(b) Enter P for partnership; S for S corporation	(c) Check if foreign partnership	(d) Employer identification number	Investment At Risk? (e) All is at risk	(f) Some is not at risk
A						
B						
C						
D						
E						

	Passive Income and Loss		Nonpassive Income and Loss		
	(g) Passive loss allowed (attach Form 8582 if required)	(h) Passive income from Schedule K-1	(i) Nonpassive loss from Schedule K-1	(j) Section 179 expense deduction from Form 4562	(k) Nonpassive income from Schedule K-1
A					
B					
C					
D					
E					
28a Totals					
b Totals					

29	Add columns (h) and (k) of line 28a	29
30	Add columns (g), (i), and (j) of line 28b	30 ( )
31	Total partnership and S corporation income or (loss). Combine lines 29 and 30. Enter the result here and include in the total on line 40 below	31

Part III   **Income or Loss From Estates and Trusts**

32	(a) Name	(b) Employer identification number
A		
B		

	Passive Income and Loss		Nonpassive Income and Loss	
	(c) Passive deduction or loss allowed (attach Form 8582 if required)	(d) Passive income from Schedule K-1	(e) Deduction or loss from Schedule K-1	(f) Other income from Schedule K-1
A				
B				
33a Totals				
b Totals				

34	Add columns (d) and (f) of line 33a	34
35	Add columns (c) and (e) of line 33b	35 ( )
36	Total estate and trust income or (loss). Combine lines 34 and 35. Enter the result here and include in the total on line 40 below	36

Part IV   **Income or Loss From Real Estate Mortgage Investment Conduits (REMICs)—Residual Holder**

37	(a) Name	(b) Employer identification number	(c) Excess inclusion from Schedules Q, line 2c (see page E-6)	(d) Taxable income (net loss) from Schedules Q, line 1b	(e) Income from Schedules Q, line 3b

38	Combine columns (d) and (e) only. Enter the result here and include in the total on line 40 below	38

Part V   **Summary**

39	Net farm rental income or (loss) from **Form 4835**. Also, complete line 41 below	39
40	TOTAL income or (loss). Combine lines 26, 31, 36, 38, and 39. Enter the result here and on Form 1040, line 17 ▶	40
41	**Reconciliation of Farming and Fishing Income.** Enter your **gross** farming and fishing income reported on Form 4835, line 7; Schedule K-1 (Form 1065), line 15b; Schedule K-1 (Form 1120S), line 23; and Schedule K-1 (Form 1041), line 14 (see page E-6)	41
42	**Reconciliation for Real Estate Professionals.** If you were a real estate professional (see page E-4), enter the net income or (loss) you reported anywhere on Form 1040 from all rental real estate activities in which you materially participated under the passive activity loss rules . . .	42

Schedule E (Form 1040) 1999

FORM 13.5. *continued*

of managers. If elected, the board of managers generally holds the exclusive authority to transact the business of the LLC.

Member Management

If an LLC is managed by its members, each member has an equal right to manage and participate in the operation of the LLC, unless the operating agreement otherwise delegates the management rights. Decisions of the LLC are generally made by majority vote, although individual members of the LLC have the power, but not necessarily the right, to bind the LLC without the consent of the other members.

Board of Managers

Board of managers Elected managers of a limited liability company.

If all the members of an LLC agree to waive their management rights, they may elect a **board of managers** to operate the LLC. The elected managers become the only agents of the LLC, whether or not they are members. As an agent, the manager may bind the LLC to contractual obligations unless (1) the manager lacks the authority to bind the partnership to a particular obligation and the individual dealing with the partner is aware of the manager's lack of authority and (2) the manager's act was not within the ordinary course of the LLC's business and the members did not authorize such act.

Examples:
1. Mike, the manager of a local gas station, tells his friend Fred, the owner of a logging truck, that he will provide all the gas that Fred wants at no charge, if Fred will give Mike posts for a fence that he is building for his house. Fred knows that Mike always works these kinds of deals, cheating his company out of its money. Nonetheless, Fred agrees to the deal. If Mike later sends Fred a bill for the gas that he used, Fred cannot force the LLC to give him the benefit of the deal he had with Mike because he knew, at the time of agreeing to the deal, that Mike did not have the right to make such an offer.
2. The manager of Horses Unlimited, LLC, a horse boarding business, agrees to sell one of her hunting dogs to a customer of Horses Unlimited. This sale is not within the ordinary course of the business of Horses Unlimited and if the manager does not complete the sale of the hunting dog, the customer cannot hold the LLC liable for the manager's breach of the contract.

Fiduciary Duties

Whether the LLC is managed by its members or a board of managers, member-managers and manager-managers owe fiduciary duties to one another and the LLC. Most states and the Uniform Limited Liability Company Act impose on LLCs the same duties of loyalty and care due in general partnerships.[7] Even if fiduciary duties are not statutorily imposed on members of an LLC, the operating agreement should require that all members and managers act with loyalty and care toward the LLC and its members; those who do not should be held liable for their improper actions.

Liability

Members and managers of an LLC generally are granted absolute immunity from the obligations of the LLC, with three exceptions:

1. Members are liable for the capital contributions which they agree to make to the LLC, as set forth in the operating agreement.
2. Members, managers, and officers may be held personally liable for violations by the LLC of environmental laws.
3. Members, managers, and officers may be personally accountable for unpaid federal and/or state tax obligations of the LLC.

In addition, if the LLC is formed for an improper or fraudulent purpose, its members may be held personally liable for the obligations of the LLC resulting from improper or fraudulent acts.

> **Example:** Greg and George form Helping Hands Insurance, LLC, a health care provider for high-risk individuals (e.g., people with a poor health history who generally cannot get health insurance). As part of their marketing scheme, Greg and George make phone calls to thousands of people and offer them health care insurance for a fraction of the cost charged by other private insurers. Many high risk individuals, finding the insurance coverage attractive, sign up for Helping Hands' health care insurance plan and pay the initial start-up fee of $400 plus the first month's premium, a fixed $300. Unfortunately, Helping Hands is a scam and Greg and George have no intention to provide any health care insurance for the people who sign up. In fact, after Greg and George collect the start-up fees and premiums from over 500 people, they disconnect their business phone and vacate their business offices. If Greg and George can be found, the victims of their scheme can sue to have the LLC set aside and seek to recover the money they paid Helping Hands from Greg and George personally.

However, absent fraud, or one of the other three enumerated exceptions to the extensive liability protections offered to members of LLCs, LLC members have no personal liability for the debts or other obligations of their company because, it is assumed, the public will be protected from the actions of the LLC and its members by liability insurance.

TERMINATION OF THE LIMITED LIABILITY COMPANY

Dissolution of the Limited Liability Company

An LLC will generally dissolve on the occurrence of one or more of the following events:

♦ The termination date stated in the articles of organization or the operating agreement has passed.
♦ The statutory duration period (generally thirty years) has expired.
♦ The death, bankruptcy, expulsion, or other withdrawal of a member has occurred.
♦ The members have agreed to terminate the LLC.
♦ A court decree dissolves the LLC (e.g., because it is impractical to continue the business, or a partner is incapacitated).

Continuation of the Limited Liability Company

In the event the LLC dissolves, the remaining members may, in accordance with its operating agreement or by unanimous vote, agree to maintain the LLC. The original LLC has dissolved and the "continuing" LLC is a new and different membership association.

Winding Up

If an LLC is not continued by the terms of its operating agreement or subsequent vote of its members, its business must be wound up and the assets of the LLC must be liquidated. Once liquidated, the assets will be distributed to the creditors of the LLC and then if funds remain, to the members of the LLC, pursuant to the operating agreement or, absent such provision, in accordance with the capital contributions of the members.

Once the LLC is wound up, one or more of the members must "cancel" the articles of organization by filing the **articles of termination,** notifying the secretary of state and the general public of the termination of the LLC.

Articles of termination
Document notifying the secretary of state of the termination of a limited liability company.

LIMITED LIABILITY COMPANIES IN REVIEW

Definition
An unincorporated entity that offers its members management rights, limited personal liability, and the pass-through taxation of partnerships

Advantages
♦ Limited liability for all members, including managers
♦ Pass-through taxation
♦ Flexibility of management

Disadvantages
♦ Limited duration
♦ Limited transferability of interests
♦ Lack of interstate uniformity

Key Considerations of the Paralegal:
Formation Procedures
1. Register business name, with "LLP" designation, as an assumed business name with the secretary of state.
2. File articles of organization with the secretary of state.
3. Obtain required business and/or professional licenses and permits.
4. Taxation considerations:
   a. Apply for a sales tax permit, if goods will be sold,
   b. Apply for a tax identification number with the IRS and state, and
   c. File IRS Form 8832 electing partnership or corporate taxation.
5. If employees will be hired:
   a. Establish employee withholding accounts, and
   b. Establish unemployment and workers' compensation coverage.
6. Draft a comprehensive operating agreement.

KEY TERMS

articles of organization   board of managers   articles of termination
operating agreement

STUDY QUESTIONS IN REVIEW

1. What is a limited liability company?
2. Who are the managers of a limited liability company?
3. Do LLCs offer more liability protections than an LLP?
4. What is the disadvantage of including an expansive purpose clause that allows a company to transact "any and all lawful business," in an LLC's articles of organization?
5. How would a professional limited liability company designate its status in its name?
6. What document can be drafted for an LLC that establishes the operating procedures and the rights and duties of LLC members?
7. Is an LLC taxed as a partnership or as a corporation? Explain.
8. Have all states adopted LLCs as a business form?
9. What is centralization of management and do LLCs have centralized management? Under what conditions is a board of directors appointed to manage an LLC?
10. What fiduciary duties do members of an LLC owe to the company and to each other?
11. Members of LLCs are generally granted immunity from personal liability for the obligations of the LLC. What are the exceptions to this general rule?

◆ CASE STUDIES IN REVIEW

1. Cathy, Don, and Steve own "T-shirts a GoGo, LLC." They produce T-shirts with personalized logos for local businesses, sports teams, and other organizations. Steve is in charge of marketing for the company. During one of his recent "rainmaking" trips, he discovered that many businesses want to have their business name and logo imprinted on pencils, pens, and other business-related items. Steve is excited about the prospect of this area of expansion and signs contracts with three companies to provide imprinting of their business name and logo on several business supplies. Steve did not receive Cathy's or Don's approval for the contracts and the business does not have the equipment to produce the products Steve contracted for. The purpose clause of the company's articles of organization allows the company to transact "any and all lawful business" and the operating agreement does not restrict the members' authority. Did Steve have the authority to bind the LLC to the new contracts?

2. The Riley family owns and operates a local religious bookstore for profit. The bookstore is an LLC and all the members of the family participate in management of the business, including the parents and eleven children. Although the family generally works well together, it is difficult for everyone to meet for the weekly management meetings. Everyone is offered the opportunity to speak on the management issues at each meeting; thus, the meetings usually take two to three hours. The family finally decides that it makes sense to appoint a board of managers, which they do. What are the advantages and disadvantages to appointing a board of managers?

◆ PROJECT APPLICATIONS

1. Does your state impose annual reporting requirements on LLCs? (Hint: Contact the secretary of state to research this issue).

2. Obtain the documents necessary to register an LLC with the secretary of state of your state. Prepare the documents for the following company:

Joann and Melissa have been partners in an accounting firm for five years. They work mainly with small businesses. They recently received a letter from their attorney notifying them that the state has adopted a new business form, limited liability companies. Joann and Melissa like the extensive liability protections of the LLC. They ask the firm to draft the registration documents.

Their file contains the following relevant information:

Joann Dollars
100 South West
Somewhere, (your state)
55555

Melissa Cents
340 Bend Drive #6
Florence, (your state)
55555

Business Address:　Dollars and Cents
400 Brooks Street
Somewhere, (your state) 55555
County: Missoula County

◆ ENDNOTES

1. See IRS Revenue Ruling 88-76.
2. See VanDyke and Porter, *Limited Liability Partnerships: The Next Generation,* 63 Kansas Bar Association 16 at 18. Cited in Murphy, "It's Nothing Personal: The Public Costs of Limited Liability Partnerships," 71 *Indiana Law Journal* 201 (1995).
3. Although an operating agreement is not mandatory, it is highly desirable and should be drafted.
4. See Classification of Limited Liability Companies: Notice of Proposed Rulemaking, 45 Fed. Reg. 75,709 (1980)
5. See Treasury Regulation § 301.7701–2.
6. See id. § 301.7701–2(1)(3).
7. See Uniform Limited Liability Company Act (1995) § 409.

APPENDIX A
SECRETARIES OF STATE

Alabama
Secretary of State
P.O. Box 5616
Montgomery, AL 36103-5616
(334) 242-5324
www.sos.state.al.us

Alaska
Dept. of Commerce & Economic Development
Division of Banking, Securities & Corporations
State Office Building, Ninth Floor
P.O. Box 110800
Juneau, AK 99811-0800
(907) 465-2500
www.commerce.state.ak.us

Arizona
Secretary of State
State Capitol, West Wing
1700 West Washington, Seventh Floor
Phoenix, AZ 85007
(602) 542-4285
www.sos.az.com
Arizona Department of Commerce
(602) 280-1480
www.state.az.us/commerce (business forms)

Arkansas
Secretary of State
256 State Capitol Building
Little Rock, AR 72201
(501) 682-1010
www.sosweb.state.ar.us/index.html

California
Secretary of State
1500 11th Street, Third Floor
Sacramento, CA 95814-5701
(916) 653-5448
www.ss.ca.gov/

Colorado
Secretary of State
1560 Broadway, Suite 200
Denver, CO 80202
(303) 894-2251
www.state.co.us/gov_dir/sos/index.html

Connecticut
Secretary of State
104 State Capitol
210 Capitol Avenue
Hartford, CT 06106
(203) 566-2739
www.state.ct.us/sots/index.html

Delaware
Delaware Division of Corporations
Townsend Building
P.O. Box 898
Dover, DE 19903
(302) 739-3073
www.state.de.us/corp/index.htm

District of Columbia
The Corporations Office
614 H Street NW, Room 407
Washington, DC 20001
(202) 727-7278
www.dcra.org

Florida
Secretary of State
Division of Corporations
P.O. Box 6327
Tallahassee, FL 32314
(904) 487-6052
www.dos.state.fl.us/doc/index.html

Georgia
Secretary of State
214 State Capitol
Atlanta, GA 30334
(404) 656-2881
www.sos.state.ga.us

Hawaii
Commerce and Consumer Affairs Dept.
Business Registration Division
P.O. Box 40
Honolulu, HI 96810
(808) 586-2727
www.hawaii.state.hi.us/dbedt/start.html

Idaho
Secretary of State
700 West Jefferson, Basement West
P.O. Box 83720
Boise, ID 83720-0080
(208) 334-2300
www.idsos.state.id.us

Illinois
Secretary of State
213 State Capitol Building
Springfield, IL 62576
(217) 782-6961
www.sos.state.il.us

Indiana
Secretary of State
201 State House
Indianapolis, IN 46204
(317) 232-6587
www.state.in.us/sos/index.html

Iowa
Secretary of State
Hoover Building, Second Floor
Des Moines, IA 50319
(515) 281-5204
www.sos.state.ia.us

Kansas
Kansas Corporation Commission
State Capitol, Second Floor
Topeka, KS 66612-1594
(913) 296-7456
www.kcc.state.ks.us/

Kentucky
Secretary of State
700 Capitol Avenue
Suite 152, State Capitol
Frankfort, KY 40601
(502) 564-2848
www.sos.state.ky.us/

Louisiana
Secretary of State
P.O. Box 94125
Baton Rouge, LA 70804-9125
(504) 922-2675
www.sec.state.la.us

Maine
Secretary of State
Corporations, Elections, and Commissions Bureau
101 State House Station
Augusta, ME 04333-0101
(207) 287-3676
www.state.me.us at *state agency,* go to Corporations, Elections, and Commissions

Maryland
Corporate Charter Division
301 West Preston Street, Room 809
Baltimore, MD 21201
(410) 767-1340
www.dat.state.md.us/

Massachusetts
Corporation Division
17th Floor Ashburton Place
Boston, MA 02108
(617) 727-9640
www.state.ma.us/sec/cor/

Michigan
Corporation and Securities Bureau
P.O. Box 30054
Lansing, MI 48909-7554
(517) 334-6327
www.sos.state.mi.us/

Minnesota
Secretary of State
180 State Office Building
100 Constitution Avenue
St. Paul, MN 55155-1299
(612) 296-3266
www.state.mn.us/ebranch/sos/index.html

Mississippi
Secretary of State
Attn: Corporate Division
P.O. Box 136
Jackson, MS 39205-0136
(601) 359-1350
www.sos.state.ms.us

Missouri
Secretary of State
P.O. Box 778
Jefferson City, MO 65102
(573) 751-4936
www.mosl.sos.state.mo.us/

Montana
Secretary of State
225 State Capitol
Helena, MT 59620
(406) 444-2034
www.state.mt.us/sos/

Nebraska
Secretary of State, Corporations
1305 State Capitol
P.O. Box 94608
Lincoln, NE 68509-4608
(402) 471-4079
www.nol.org/home/sos/

Nevada
Secretary of State
101 North Carson Street, Suite 3
Carson City, NV 89701
(702) 684-5708
http://sos.state.nv.us/

New Hampshire
Secretary of State
107 North Main Street
Concord, NH 03301
(603) 271-3242
www.state.nh.us

New Jersey
Secretary of State
Division of Commercial Recording
125 West State Street, CN 300
Trenton, NJ 08625-0300
(609) 530-6400
Fax on Demand: (609) 530-4992
www.state.nj.us/

New Mexico
Public Regulation Commission
P.O. Drawer 1269
Santa Fe, NM 86504-1269
(505) 827-4500
www.state.nm.us/sec/sccfind.html

New York
New York Department of State
Division of Corporations
41 State Street
Albany, NY 12231-0001
(518) 473- 2492
www.dos.state.ny.us/

North Carolina
Secretary of State
300 North Salisbury Street
Raleigh, NC 27603
(919) 733-4201 or (888) 246-7636
www.state.nc.us/secstate/

North Dakota
Secretary of State
State Capitol
600 East Boulevard Ave. Dept. 108
Bismarck, ND 58505-0500
(701) 328-4284
www.state.nd.us/sec.

Ohio
Secretary of State
30 East Broad Street, 14th Floor
Columbus, OH 43266-0418
1-877-SOS-FILE
www.state.oh.us/sos/

Oklahoma
Secretary of State
2300 N. Lincoln Blvd. Rm. 101
Oklahoma City, OK 73105-4897
(405) 521-3911
www.sos.state.ok.us/

Oregon
Secretary of State
Corporation Division
151 Public Service Building
255 Capitol Street NE
Salem, OR 97310
(503) 986-2200
www.sos.state.or.us/corporation/corphp.htm

Pennsylvania
Secretary of the Commonwealth
Department of State
302 North Capitol Building
Harrisburg, PA 17120
(717) 787-7630
FAX: (717) 787-1734
www.state.pa.us/PA_ExecState

Rhode Island
Secretary of State
218 State House
Providence, RI 02903
(401) 222-3040
www.sec.state.ri.us

South Carolina
Secretary of State
Wade Hampton Building
P.O. Box 11350
Columbia, SC 29211
(803) 734-2155
FAX: (803) 734-2164
www.docauto.com/SCsos.htm

South Dakota
Secretary of State
State Capitol, Suite 204
500 East Capitol Avenue
Pierre, SD 57501-5070
(605) 773-4845
www.state.sd.us/sos/sos.htm

Tennessee
Secretary of State
State Capitol, First Floor
Nashville, TN 37243-0305
(615) 741-2819
www.state.tn.us/sos

Texas
Secretary of State
P.O. Box 12887
1019 Brazos
Austin, TX 78711
(512) 463-5702
Business forms division: (512) 463-5555
www.sos.state.tx.us

Utah
Division of Corporations & Commercial Code
P.O. Box 146705
Salt Lake City, UT 84114-6705
(801) 530-6027
www.commerce.state.ut.us

Vermont
Secretary of State
26 Terrace St., Drawer 09
Montpelier, VT 05609-1101
(802) 828-2363
www.sec.state.vt.us/

Virginia
Secretary of the Commonwealth
P.O. Box 2454
Richmond, VA 23218-2454
(804) 371-0017
FAX: (804) 371-0017
www.soc.vipnet.org/index.htm

Washington
Secretary of State
Corporations Division
505 East Union, 2d Floor
P.O. Box 40234
Olympia, WA 98504-0234
(360) 753-7119
www.wa.gov/corps

West Virginia
Secretary of State
State Capitol Complex
Building 1, Suite 157K
1900 Kanawha Boulevard
Charleston, WV 25305-0770
Corporations: (304) 558-8000
Other Divisions: (304) 558-6000
www.state.wv.us/sos

Wisconsin
Department of Financial Institutions
Corporation Section
30 West Mifflin
P.O. Box 7848
Madison, WI 53707-7848
(608) 261-7577
www.wdfl.org

Wyoming
Secretary of State
State Capitol
Cheyenne, WY 82002-0020
(307) 777-7311
http://soswy.state.wy.us

INTERNAL REVENUE SERVICE FORMS
www.irs.ustreas.gov/prod/cover.html

WEST PUBLISHING FORMS
www.westlegalstudies.com

UNIFORM PARTNERSHIP ACT
1914 ACT

Table of Jurisdictions Adopting Act

Jurisdiction	Statutory Source
Alabama	Code 1975, §§ 10-8-1 to 10-8-103
Alaska	AS 32.05.010 to 32.05.860
Arizona	A.R.S. §§ 29-201 to 29-270
Arkansas	A.C.A. §§ 4-42-101 to 4-42-706
Colorado	West's C.R.S.A. §§ 7-60-101 to 7-60-154
Delaware	6 Del.C. §§ 1501 to 1553
Georgia	O.C.G.A. §§ 14-8-1 to 14-8-61
Hawaii	HRS §§ 425-101 to 425-143, 425-191
Idaho	I.C. §§ 53-301 to 53-343C
Illinois	S.H.A. 805 ILCS 205/1 to 205/52
Indiana	West's A.I.C. 23-4-1-1 to 23-4-1-43
Iowa	I.C.A. §§ 486.1 to 487.47
Kansas	K.S.A. 56-301 to 56-347
Kentucky	KRS 362.150 to 362.360
Maine	31 M.R.S.A. §§ 281 to 323
Massachusetts	M.G.L.A. c. 108A, §§ 1 to 49
Michigan	M.C.L.A. §§ 449.1 to 449.48
Minnesota	M.S.A. §§ 323.01 to 323.49
Mississippi	Code 1972, §§ 79-12-1 to 79-12-119

Jurisdiction	Statutory Source
Missouri	V.A.M.S. §§ 358.010 to 358.520
Nebraska	R.R.S. 1943, §§ 67-301 to 67-346
Nevada	N.R.S. 87.010 to 87.560
New Hampshire	RSA 304-A:1 to 304-A:55
New Jersey	N.J.S.A. 42:1-1 to 42:1-49
New York	McKinney's Partnership Law, §§ 1 to 74, 121-1500 to 121-1504
North Carolina	G.S. §§ 59-31 to 59-73
Ohio	R.C. §§ 1775.01 to 1775.42, 1775.61 to 1775.65
Oregon	ORS 68.010 to 68.790
Pennsylvania	15 Pa.C.S.A. §§ 8301 to 8365
Rhode Island	Gen. Laws 1956, §§ 7-12-12 to 7-12-59
South Carolina	Code 1976, §§ 33-41-10 to 33-41-1220
South Dakota	SDCL 48-1-1 to 48-5-56
Tennessee	West's Tenn. Code §§ 61-1-101 to 61-1-148
Utah	U.C.A. 1953, 48-1-1 to 48-1-48
Virginia	Code 1950, §§ 50-1 to 50-43.12
Wisconsin	W.S.A. 178.01 to 178.53

UNIFORM PARTNERSHIP ACT
1997 ACT

Table of Jurisdictions Adopting Act

Jurisdiction	Statutory Source	Jurisdiction	Statutory Source
Alabama	Code 1975, §§ 10-8A-101 to 10-8A-1109	Minnesota	M.S.A. §§ 323A.1-01 to 323A.12-03
Arizona	A.R.S. §§ 29-1001 to 29-1111	Montana	M.C.A. §§ 35-10-101 to 35-10-710
California	West's Ann. Cal. Corp. Code, §§ 16100 to 16962	Nebraska	R.R.S. 1943, §§ 67-401 to 67-467
		New Mexico	NMSA 1978, §§ 54-1-47 to 54-1A-101 to 54-1A-1206
Colorado	West's C.R.S.A. §§ 7-64-101 to 7-64-1206	North Dakota	NDCC 45-13-01 to 45-21-08
Connecticut	C.G.S.A. §§ 34-300 to 34-434	Oklahoma	54 Okl. St.Ann. §§ 1-100 to 1-1207
Dist. of Columbia	D.C. Code 1981 §§ 41-151.1 to 41-162.3	Oregon	ORS 67.005 to 67.815
		Texas	Vernon's Ann. Texas Civ. St. art. 6132b-1.01 to 6132b-11.04
Florida	West's F.S.A. §§ 620.81001 to 620.91	Vermont	11 V.S.A. §§ 3201 to 3313
Idaho	I.C. §§ 53-3-101 to 53-3-1205	Virginia	Code 1950, §§ 50-73.79 to 50-73.149
Iowa	I.C.A. §§ 486A.101 to 486A.1302	Washington	West's RCWA 25.05.005 to 25.05.907
Kansas	K.S.A. 56a-101 to 56a-1305	West Virginia	Code, 47B-1-1 to 47B-11-5
Maryland	Code, Corporations and Associations, §§ 9A-101 to 9A-1205	Wyoming	W.S. 1977, §§ 17-21-101 to 17-21-1003

MODEL PARTNERSHIP AGREEMENT

THIS AGREEMENT IS SUBJECT TO ARBITRATION
UNDER THE GENERAL PARTNERSHIP AGREEMENT
of ~ Partnership

SECTION 1 NAME, PLACE OF BUSINESS, TERM, INITIAL PARTNERS

1.1 Name. The name of the Partnership is ~.

1.2 Principal Place of Business. The principal place of business of the Partnership is (city), (state)

1.3 Term. The Partnership begins on ~, and continues until dissolved by an act specified in Section 9 of this Agreement.

1.4 Initial Partners. The initial Partners of the Partnership are ~, ~, and ~. The initial Partnership Percentages of the Initial Partners are set forth in Exhibit A.

SECTION 2 PURPOSES OF THE BUSINESS

The Partnership may engage in the business of ~ and in any other business upon which the Partners owning _____ percentages of the Partnership Percentages agree.

SECTION 3 CONTRIBUTIONS TO CAPITAL AND ASSUMPTION OF LIABILITIES

3.1 Capital Accounts.

(a) *Contribution of Assets.* Each Initial Partner contributed the cash or other property listed in Exhibit A to the Partnership.

(b) *Individual Capital Account.* Each Partner has an individual Capital Account. The amount of the initial Capital Account of each Partner is set forth in Exhibit A.

3.2 Assumption of Liabilities.

(a) The Partnership assumes the liabilities of the initial Partners described in Exhibit A.

(b) Neither the Partnership nor the Partners assume any liabilities of Partners not described in Exhibit A.

3.3 Warranty of Partners. Each Partner represents and warrants to the Partnership and to each that the Partnership has good and marketable title to the property contributed pursuant to Section 3.1(a) and described in Exhibit A and that the property is free and clear from all encumbrances at the time of contribution, except for those encumbrances relating to those liabilities specifically described in Exhibit A.

3.4 Limitation on Withdrawal. Except by unanimous vote of the Partners, Partners may not withdraw from their Capital Accounts. Except by unanimous vote of the Partners or pursuant to Section 3.5, Partners may not add to their Capital Accounts.

3.5 Additional Capital Contributions.

(a) *Ordering Additional Capital Contributions.* By vote of Partners owning _____ percent of the Partnership Percentages, the Partners may determine the amount of any Additional Capital Contributions necessary to acquire or retain capital assets of the Partnership or to pay its operating expenses. However, no Partner may be required by this Section to make total Additional Capital Contributions exceeding $ _____ per Partnership Percentage owned.

(b) *Time of Payment.* The amount of an Additional Capital Contribution must be paid in cash and, unless otherwise agreed upon, is due 30 days from the date of the decision to require it.

(c) *Interest Payable on Amount of Contribution-in-Default.* If a Partner (hereinafter Defaulting Partner) fails to make the required Additional Capital Contribution (hereinafter Contribution-in-Default), the amount of the Contribution-in-Default is payable, upon demand, to the Partnership with interest at the prime rate as stated in the *Wall Street Journal* then in effect, plus 6 percent, adjusted as of the first business day of each quarter. So long as such debt is owing, the Defaulting Partner may not withdraw any funds from the Partnership, and Profits otherwise allocated to the Partner shall reduce the amount of the Contribution-in-Default.

(d) *Optional Adjustment of Partnership Percentages.* Partners who do not have any Contributions-in-Default may, at any time, elect to adjust the Partnership Percentages for all purposes. Such election shall be made by those partners owning a majority of the Partnership Percentage entitled to vote. Only those Partners who do not have Contributions-in-Default shall be entitled to vote on this matter. If this election is made, each Partner's Partnership Percentage shall equal the sum of the Partner's initial Capital Account plus the Additional Capital Contributions actually paid divided by the sum of all the Partner's initial Capital Accounts plus all Additional Capital Contributions actually paid by the Partners. The election shall be effective immediately and the Defaulting Partner shall be notified in writing of this election. The debt of Defaulting Partner created by section 3.5(c) shall be forgiven if this election is made but the Defaulting Partner's Capital Account shall not be increased by the amount of the Defaulted Contribution. Interest accrued prior to the date of the election on the debt created by section 3.5(c) will continue to be due and owing.

SECTION 4   PROFITS AND LOSSES

4.1   Income Account. There is an Income Account for each Partner. The amount of the Initial Income Accounts of the initial Partners are set forth in Exhibit A.

4.2   Allocation of Net Profits and Losses. In accordance with generally accepted accounting principles, the Partnership's accountant or bookkeeper shall determine Net Profits or Losses of the Partnership as of the close of each fiscal year. The Partnership's accountant or bookkeeper shall allocate the Net Profits and losses to each Partner's Income Account in accordance with their Partnership Percentages as of the close of each fiscal year.

4.3   Withdrawal from Income Accounts. Withdrawals from the Income Accounts are limited to an amount determined by the Partners owning a majority of the Partnership Percentages. The Partners owning a majority of the Partnership Percentages may determine an amount of Required Balance Partnership Percentage. Any amount in a Partner's Income Account below the Required Balance may not be withdrawn except by unanimous vote of the Partners.

4.4   Interest. As of the first day of each year, the Partnership's accountant or bookkeeper shall credit the balance in each Partner's Income Account with interest at the prime rate stated in the *Wall Street Journal* on the last business day of the prior year.

4.5   Inadequate Income Account.
(a) *Election to Require Restoration.* If a Partner's Income Account drops below the Required Balance, Partners who have a balance in their Income Account above the Required Balance may demand in writing that the Partner with the inadequate Income Account increase the balance in that Account to the Required Balance. A Partner required to increase an Income Account shall do so by contributing the required additional cash within sixty days of the demand.
(b) *Consequences of Failure to Restore.* Failure to pay the required additional cash demanded in Section 4.5(a) creates a debt of the defaulting partner to the Partnership with interest accruing from the date of the demand with interest at the prime rate stated in the *Wall Street Journal* then in effect plus 6 percent, adjusted as of the first business day of each quarter.

SECTION 5   MANAGEMENT

5.1   Conduct of Partnership Business. Each Partner has a vote in the management and conduct of the Partnership business.

5.2   Vote Required. If this Agreement does not specify the amount of the vote of the Partnership Percentages that is needed to make a decision, the decision may be made by an affirmative vote of the Partners owning a majority of the Partnership Percentages entitled to vote.

5.3   Managing Partner. The initial Managing Partner is ~. The Managing Member shall devote such time on the day-to-day business of the Partnership as is reasonably necessary. Unless otherwise restricted by Partners owning a majority of the Partnership Percentages, the Managing Partner will manage the day-to-day business of the Partnership.

5.4   Termination of Management Powers. The Partners may terminate the powers of the Managing Partner or appoint a new Managing Partner by a vote of Partners owning a majority of the Partnership Percentages.

5.5   Salary. Each Partner may receive a salary. The amount of such salary must be approved by Partners owning a majority of the Partnership Percentages. The Partnership shall treat the Salaries of Partners as a Partnership expense in determining Net Profits or Losses.

SECTION 6   DEADLOCK

6.1   General. If the Partners are equally divided, on the basis of Partnership Percentages, on any aspect of the management of the property, business and affairs of the Partnership and the deadlock is preventing action or non-action by the Partnership, then the Partnership may submit the deadlock to mediation in accordance with section 6.2. If the Partners are unable to resolve the deadlock through mediation, the Partners agree to submit the dispute to binding arbitration in accordance with section 6.3.

6.2   Mediation. If the Partners are unable to resolve the deadlock themselves, upon written request of Partners owning 50 percent of the Partnership Percentages, the Partners agree to submit the dispute to mediation and the following guidelines shall apply:
(a) The Partners agree to have the dispute mediated by one of the following people or organizations (in the order listed, circumstances permitting):
   (i)
   (ii)
   (iii)
(b) The Partners agree to follow the mediation procedure selected by the mediator.
(c) Mediation shall terminate upon the written request of the mediator or Partners owning 50 percent of the Partnership Percentages.

6.3   Arbitration. If the Partners are unable to resolve the deadlock through mediation, upon written request of Partners owning 50 percent of the Partnership Percentages, the Partners agree to submit the deadlock to binding arbitration in the following manner:
(a) The Partners agree to have the dispute arbitrated by one of the following people or organizations (in the order listed), circumstances permitting.
   (i)
   (ii)
   (iii)
(b) The arbitrator shall resolve the deadlock, if the arbitrator determines the arbitrator's resolution is in the best interests of the Partnership. The arbitrator may decide whether matters have been properly submitted to the arbitrator for decision, whether there exists a deadlock, and whether this section and the arbitration provisions provided here were properly invoked by the Partnership or applicable. The arbitrator may

act until all questions, disputes, and controversies are determined, adjudged, and resolved.

(c) The arbitrator shall conduct the arbitration proceedings in accordance with the rules of the American Arbitration Association, then in effect, except where this Agreement makes a special provision.

(d) If the arbitrator finds that (i) there have been successive arbitrations, (ii) it is likely that there will be successive arbitrations in the future to resolve most major Partnership decisions, and (iii) it is in the best interest of the Partnership that the Partnership or a group of Partners buys the interest of one or more Partners or that there be a dissolution, then the arbitrator may decree a dissolution or may decree that the Partnership buy out one or more of the Partners.

(e) The arbitrator's decision shall be conclusive and binding upon the Partners and Partnership. The Partnership may not revoke, amend, or overrule the decision, except by an action of Partners owning a majority of the Partnership Percentages.

SECTION 7   DISSOCIATION

7.1   Events of Dissociation.   A Partner ceases to be a Partner by virtue of these events of dissociation:

(a) after a Partner reaches the age of ~, receipt by the Partnership of notice of the Partner's express will to retire as a Partner or upon any later date specified in the notice;

(b) after ~ (date), receipt by the Partnership of notice of the Partner's express will to withdraw as a Partner or upon any later date specified in the notice;

(c) receipt by the Partnership of notice of the Partner's express will to withdraw as a Partner on or prior to *(same date as in 7.1(b))*;

(d) the Partner's expulsion by a vote of the remaining Partners owning _____ percent of the Partnership Percentages if:

(i) it is unlawful to carry on the Partnership business with that Partner;

(ii) except as permitted by Section 8, there has been a transfer of that Partner's transferable interest in the Partnership, other than a transfer for the purposes of creating a security interest or a court order charging the Partner's interest which has not been foreclosed;

(iii) within 90 days after the Partnership notifies a corporate Partner that it will be expelled because it has filed a certificate of dissolution or the equivalent, its charter has been revoked, or its right to conduct business has been suspended by the jurisdiction of its incorporation, there is no revocation of the certificate of dissolution or no reinstatement of its charter or its right to conduct business;

(iv) a Partnership that is a Partner has been dissolved and its business is being wound up;

(v) the Partner is convicted of a felony committed against the Partnership or involving the Partnership business;

(vi) the Partner willfully or persistently committed a material breach of this Partnership Agreement or of a

duty owed to the Partnership or the other Partners under the Montana Uniform Partnership Act.

(e) the Partner's:

(i) becoming a debtor in bankruptcy;

(ii) executing an assignment for the benefit of creditors;

(iii) seeking, consenting to, or acquiescing in the appointment of a trustee, receiver, or liquidator of that partner or of all or substantially all of that partner's property; or

(iv) failing, within 90 days after the appointment, to have vacated or stayed the appointment of a trustee, receiver, or liquidator of the partner or of all or substantially all of the partner's property obtained without the partner's consent or acquiescence, or failing within 90 days after the expiration of a stay to have the appointment vacated;

(f) in the case of a Partner who is an individual:

(i) the Partner's death prior to age ~ (same age as in 7.1(a));

(ii) The Partner's death after the Partner has attained the age of ~ (same age as in 7.1(a));

(iii) the appointment of a guardian or general conservator for the Partner; or

(iv) a judicial determination that the Partner has otherwise become incapable of performing the Partner's duties under the Partnership Agreement;

(g) in the case of a Partner that is a trust or is acting as a Partner by virtue of being a trustee of a trust, distribution of the trust's entire transferable interest in the Partnership, but not merely the substitution of a successor trustee;

(h) in the case of a Partner that is an estate or is acting as a Partner by virtue of being a personal representative of an estate, distribution of the estate's entire transferable interest in the Partnership, but not merely the substitution of a successor personal representative; or

(i) termination of a Partner who is not an individual, partnership, corporation, trust, or estate.

7.2   Purchase Price.

(a) *Continuation.* Partners not dissociating (Remaining Partners) may elect that the business of the Partnership be continued by the Remaining Partners. This election must be made within 90 days of the date of dissolution by an affirmative vote of the Remaining Partners owning a majority of the remaining Partnership Percentages. If an election to continue is made, the Partner, or the estate or legal representative of the Partner causing the dissociation (Dissociated Partner) shall be paid the following amount to be determined, unless otherwise stated, as of the date of dissociation.

(i) *Retirement or Death After Retirement Age.* If an individual Partner voluntarily withdraws pursuant to 7.1(a) or dies after reaching age specified in Section 7.1(f) (i), then the purchase price of the Partner's interest shall be:

a. an amount per Partnership Percentage determined to be the purchase price pursuant to this section by the vote of Partners owning _____ percent of the Partnership Percentages at the most recent annual meeting of the Partnership. If no amount was so determined at the last annual meeting, the amount determined at the prior year's annual meeting shall be the amount.

b. If the Partnership did not determine an amount at the most recent annual meeting or the prior year's annual meeting, then the amount shall equal the sum of Dissociated Partner's:

- Capital Account (as of the close of the previous quarter of the fiscal year);
- Income Account (as of the close of the previous quarter of fiscal year);
- Earned and unpaid salary due, if any;
- Proportional share (based on proportional Partnership Percentages) of the Appraised Surplus multiplied by ____.

The amount of Appraisal Surplus equals the Appraised Value of the Partnership minus the sum of all Capital Accounts and Income Accounts (as of the close of the previous quarter of the fiscal year). The Appraised Value of the Partnership shall be determined by an appraiser named by the Partnership's principal bank. If the Partnership's principal bank does not appoint an appraiser within 60 days of a written request (made by either the Dissociated Partner or the Partnership), the Partnership's principal accountant shall appoint the appraiser. The appraiser shall appraise the Partnership as a going concern, with no discount for lack of marketability of the Partnership interests.

(ii) *Permitted Withdrawal After ~ date specified in Section 7.1(b).* If an individual Partner voluntarily withdraws pursuant to Section 7.1(b), the purchase price of the Partner's interest shall be determined by Subsection (i) of Section 7.2 except the proportional share of the Appraisal Surplus shall be multiplied by ____.

(iii) *Withdrawal before (date specified in Section 7.1(c)) or Expulsion.* If the Partner becomes a Dissociated Partner by reason of Sections 7.1(c) or 7.1(d), the purchase price shall be the sum of the Dissociated Partner's

- Capital Account (as of the close of the previous quarter of the fiscal year);
- Income Account (as of the close of the previous quarter of the fiscal year);
- Earned and unpaid salary, if any,

minus (a) if the withdrawal is by reason of Section 7.1(c), the amount of any damages caused by the withdrawal of the Partner before the date stated in Section 7.1(c); or if the withdrawal is by reason of Section 7.1(d) the amount of damages described in subsection (a) above plus the amount of any other damages caused by the Disassociated Partner.

(iv) *Other Dissociations.* If the Partner becomes a Dissociated Partner pursuant to any other section, the purchase price shall be the sum of the Dissociated Partner's

- Capital Account (as of the close of the previous quarter of the fiscal year);

- Income Account (as of the close of the previous quarter of the fiscal year);
- Earned and unpaid salary, if any.

(b) *Repayment of Negative Amount.* If any amount determined under this section is negative, the Dissociated Partner must immediately pay such amount to the Partnership.

7.3 Terms of Payment.

(a) *Terms of Promissory Note.* The purchase price specified in Section 7.2, if positive, will be paid within 180 days of the day of dissociation by a promissory note drawn on the Partnership. The promissory note will provide for equal monthly payment of principal and interest at the rate of 12 percent per annum. Such payments will be paid over a period of 36 months, starting with one month after the date of the promissory note. The promissory note will provide for no prepayment penalty and will be immediately due and payable if there is a failure to make a timely payment of principal or interest and such payment is not made within 20 days of the date written demand to make payment is received.

(b) *Security for Payment.* The promissory note will be secured by a security interest (junior to all security interests existing on the date of disassociation in all the equipment, real estate, accounts receivable, and inventory of the Partnership). The Partnership agrees to take such actions to perfect the security interest as the Dissociated Partner reasonably requests. The Partnership agrees to execute such agreement or documents to perfect such security interest and to specify the rights of the secured party as an attorney to be appointed by the Managing Partner reasonably deems appropriate.

7.4 Indemnification. In the event that the amount determined in accordance with Section 7.2 is positive or in the event that the amount is negative and the Dissociated Partner has paid that negative amount to the Partnership, the Partnership and Remaining Partners agree to indemnify the Dissociated Partner against any and all damages, loss, cost, and expense (including attorney fees) incurred by the Dissociated Partner from any Partnership indebtedness or liability, unless such indebtedness or liability was created by the unauthorized action of the Dissociated Partner or such indebtedness or liability existed at the date of the dissociation and was not taken into account by the Partnership at the time of computation of the purchase price.

7.5 Continuation of Partnership. In the event the Partnership purchases the interest of the Dissociated Partner, then the Remaining Partners agree to continue the Partnership under the terms of this agreement, except that their Partnership Percentages will be increased on a prorata basis as of the date of dissociation. The Dissociated Partner will have no rights, except those specified in this Section 7, as of the date of dissolution if the Remaining Partners elect to continue the business. In the event that the Remaining Partners do not elect to continue the business, then the Partnership will be wound up in accordance with Section 9.

*This provision allows the Partnership to reduce the amount of payment to the retiring or deceased Partner by an amount to reflect a discount for lack of marketability of the interest or a discount for a minority interest. Appropriate discounts might range from 5 percent to 30 percent. If a 5 percent discount is desired the attorney should complete the blank with a ".95."

SECTION 8   ASSIGNMENT

8.1   Definition of "family member." For purposes of this Agreement, "family member" means a lineal descendant of any of the Initial Partners.

8.2   Assignment. Except as provided in Section 8.3, no part of a Partner's interest in the Partnership may be voluntarily or involuntarily assigned or transferred to a nonfamily member without the unanimous consent of the Partners. A Partner may assign all or part of the Partner's ownership interest to a family member. If a Partner assigns full rights to all or part of the Partner's interest to a family member, the family member becomes a Partner and receives the share of distributions, income, and losses to which the assigning Partner would otherwise be entitled.

SECTION 9   DISSOLUTION

9.1   Events of Dissolution. The Partnership is dissolved upon the happening of one of the following events:
(a) a dissociation pursuant to Section 7.1 and no election has been made by the Remaining Partners to continue the business pursuant to Section 7.2;
(b) all of the Partners consent to a dissolution;
(c) an event that makes it unlawful for all or substantially all of the business of the Partnership to be continued, but any cure of illegality within 90 days after notice to the Partnership of the event is effective retroactively to the date of the event for purposes of this section;
(d) on application by a Partner, a judicial decree that:
  (i) the economic purpose of the Partnership is likely to be unreasonably frustrated;
  (ii) another Partner has engaged in conduct relating to the Partnership business that makes it not reasonably practicable to carry on the business in partnership with that partner; or
  (iii) another Partner has engaged in conduct relating to the Partnership business that makes it not reasonably practicable to carry on the business in partnership with that Partner; or
  (iv) it is not otherwise reasonably practicable to carry on the Partnership business in conformity with the partnership agreement.

9.2   Procedure. Upon dissolution, the affairs of the Partnership will be wound up by liquidating the assets of the Partnership. The liabilities of the Partnership will rank in order of payment as follows:
(a) Those owing to creditors other than the Partners.
(b) Those owing to the Partners other than for capital and profits.
(c) Those owing to the Partners in respect of the Partner's Capital Accounts.
(d) Those owing to the Partners in respect of the Partner's Income Accounts.
Any remaining funds or assets will be then distributed to the Partners in accordance with their Partnership Percentages.

9.3   Additional Contributions to Provide for Liabilities. If additional contributions are necessary to fully pay the liabilities set forth in 9.2 through (d) above, those Partners with a negative combined sum in their Capital and Income Accounts shall contribute such sum to the Partnership. If additional contributions are still needed, those contributions shall be made by the Partners according to their Partnership Percentages to the extent necessary to fully pay the liabilities set forth in 9.2(a) through (d) above.

SECTION 10   PARTNER'S POWERS AND LIMITATIONS

10.1   Bank Accounts—Checks. The Partnership may maintain a bank account in such bank as the Managing Partner selects. Checks may be drawn on the Partnership bank account for Partnership purposes only and must be signed by the Managing Partner.

10.2   Acts Beyond Powers of Partner. No Partner may, without unanimous consent:
(a) dispose of the goodwill of the Partnership or convey, encumber, or lease any other asset of the business outside the ordinary course of business;
(b) cause the Partnership to be converted to another form of business entity;
(c) do any act which would make it impossible to carry on the ordinary business of a Partnership; or
(d) cause the Partnership to be merged with another business;
(e) except as provided in Section 8, cause the admission of a new Partner.

10.3   Statements of Authority. By vote of Partners owning a majority of the Partnership Percentages, the Partnership may expand or restrict the authority of a Partner or Partners by executing and filing the appropriate statements with the Secretary of State. Any statement filed with the Secretary of State must be executed by at least two Partners.

SECTION 11   MISCELLANEOUS

11.1   Books of Account. The Partnership shall cause proper and complete books of account to be kept at all times. The Partnership shall keep its books and records at its chief executive office. Such books of account are open to inspection by any Partner or the Partner's accredited representative at any reasonable time during business hours.

11.2   Annual Meeting. The Partners shall meet annually at noon on the (first, second, etc.) of each (month) at the principal place of business of the Partnership. They may meet at such other times as the Partners owning one-third of the Partnership Percentages specify in a written notice mailed or personally delivered to each Partner at least five days before the meeting.

11.3   Amendment. The Partners may amend this Agreement and Exhibit A upon execution of a written amendment signed by all of the Partners.

11.4   Fiscal Year. The Partnership's fiscal year shall commence on _____ of each year.

11.5   Governing Law. This Agreement is governed by the laws of the State of _____.

Signed on this _____ day of _____, 20__.

_____

_____

_____

_____

EXHIBIT A

Initial Partnership Percentages (Section 1.4):
    Partner A
    Partner B
    Partner C
Description of Initial Property Contributed (Section 3.1(a)):
    Partner A
    Partner B
    Partner C
Value of Initial Capital Accounts (Section 3.1(b)):
    Partner A
    Partner B
    Partner C
Description of Liabilities Assumed (Section 3.2):
    Partner A
    Partner B
    Partner C
Value of Initial Income Accounts (Section 4.1):
    Partner A
    Partner B
    Partner C

UNIFORM LIMITED PARTNERSHIP ACT
1916 ACT

Table of Jurisdictions Adopting Act

*Enacted Revised Limited Partnership Act of 1976 without repealing the 1916 Limited Partnership Act.

REVISED UNIFORM LIMITED PARTNERSHIP ACT (1976) WITH 1985 AMENDMENTS

Table of Jurisdictions Adopting Act

Jurisdiction	Statutory Source	Jurisdiction	Statutory Source
Alabama	Code 1975, §§ 10-9B-101 to 10-9B-1206	Montana	M.C.A. §§ 35-12-501 to 35-12-1404
Alaska	AS 32.11.010 to 32.11.990	Nebraska	R.R.S. 1943, §§ 67-233 to 67-296
Arizona	A.R.S. §§ 29-301 to 29-376	Nevada	N.R.S. 88.315 to 88.645
Arkansas	A.C.A. §§ 4-43-101 to 4-43-1110	New Hampshire	RSA 304-B:1 to 304-B:64
California	West's Ann. Cal. Corp. Code, §§ 15611 to 15723	New Jersey	N.J.S.A. 42:2A-1 to 42:2A-73
		New Mexico	NMSA 1978, §§ 54-2-1 to 54-2-63
Colorado *	West's C.R.S.A. §§ 7-62-101 to 7-62-1201	New York *	McKinney's Partnership Law, §§ 121-101 to 121-1300
Connecticut	C.G.S.A. §§ 34-9 to 34-38r	North Carolina	G.S. §§ 59-101 to 59-1106
Delaware	6 Del.C. §§ 17-101 to 17-1111	North Dakota	NDCC 45-10.1-01 to 45-10.1-62, 45-12-01
Dist. of Columbia	D.C. Code 1981 §§ 41-401 to 41-499.25	Ohio	R.C. §§ 1782.01 to 1782.63
Florida	West's F.S.A. §§ 620.101 to 620.186	Oklahoma *	54 Okl. St.Ann. §§ 301 to 365
Georgia *	O.C.G.A. §§ 14-9-100 to 14-9-1204	Oregon	ORS 70.005 to 70.490
Hawaii	HRS §§ 425D-101 to 425D-1109	Pennsylvania	15 Pa.C.S.A. §§ 8501 to 8594
Idaho	I.C. §§ 53-201 to 53-268	Rhode Island	Gen. Laws 1956, §§ 7-13-1 to 7-13-65
Illinois	S.H.A. 805 ILCS 210/100 to 210/1205	South Carolina	Code 1976, §§ 33-42-10 to 33-42-2040
Indiana	West's A.I.C. 23-16-1-1 to 23-16-12-6	South Dakota	SDCL 48-7-101 to 48-7-1105
Iowa	I.C.A. §§ 487.101 to 487.1106	Tennessee	West's Tenn. Code §§ 61-2-101 to 61-2-1208
Kansas	K.S.A. 56-1a101 to 56-1a609		
Kentucky	KRS 362.401 to 362.527	Texas	Vernon's Ann. Texas Civ. St. art. 6132a-1
Maine	31 M.R.S.A. §§ 401 to 530		
Maryland	Code, Corporations and Associations, §§ 10-101 to 10-1105	Utah	U.C.A. 1953, 48-2a-101 to 48-2a-1107
		Vermont	11 V.S.A. §§ 3401 to 3503
Massachusetts	M.G.L.A. c. 109, §§ 1 to 62	Virgin Islands	26 V.I.C. §§ 321 to 575
Michigan	M.C.L.A. §§ 449.1101 to 449.2108	Virginia	Code 1950, §§ 50-73.1 to 50-73.78
Minnesota *	M.S.A. §§ 322A.01 to 322A.88	Washington	West's RCWA 25.10.010 to 25.1.690
Mississippi	Code 1972, §§ 79-14-101 to 79-14-1107	West Virginia	Code, 47-9-1 to 47-9-63
		Wisconsin	W.S.A. 179.01 to 179.94
Missouri	V.A.M.S. §§ 359.011 to 359.691	Wyoming	W.S. 1977, §§ 17-14-201 to 17-14-1104

*Enacted Revised Limited Partnership Act of 1976 without repealing the 1916 Limited Partnership Act.
Reprinted as adapted from *Uniform Laws Annotated.* Copyright © West Group.

BYLAWS OF _____

ARTICLE I. OFFICES

SECTION 1.1 BUSINESS OFFICE.

The corporation's principal office shall be located either within or outside of (state), the state of incorporation. The company's most current Annual Report, filed with the (state) Secretary of State, shall identify the location of the principal office. The corporation may have other offices, either within or outside of (state). The board of directors may designate the location of these other offices. The secretary of the corporation shall maintain a copy of the records required by Section 2.15 of Article II at the principal office.

SECTION 1.2 REGISTERED OFFICE.

The corporation's registered office shall be located within (state). The location of the registered office may be, but need not be, identical with that of the principal office if the latter is located within (state). The board of directors may change the address of the registered office from time to time.

ARTICLE II. SHAREHOLDERS

SECTION 2.1 ANNUAL SHAREHOLDER MEETING.

The shareholders shall convene their annual meeting on the [first/second/third/fourth] [day of week] of [month], beginning with the year 19__, at the hour of ____ o'clock _.M., or at another time on another day within the month that the board of directors agree upon. The shareholders will gather at the annual meeting to elect directors and to transact any other business. If the date of the annual meeting is a legal holiday (state), the meeting shall be held on the next succeeding business day.

If the shareholders do not elect directors at the annual meeting, or at any continuation of the meeting after adjournment, the board of directors shall cause the shareholders to elect directors at a special shareholder meeting as soon as possible. A corporation may hold an annual meeting by phone if the corporation has fifty or fewer shareholders and the board so authorizes.

SECTION 2.2 SPECIAL SHAREHOLDER MEETINGS.

The president or the board of directors may call a special shareholder meeting for any purpose or purposes described in the meeting notice. If eligible shareholders request a special meeting, the president shall call one. For the purposes of this section, eligible shareholder means those shareholders who own not less than one-tenth of all of the corporation's outstanding votes that are entitled to be cast on any issue at the meeting. A corporation may hold a special meeting by phone if the corporation has fifty or fewer shareholders and the board so authorizes

SECTION 2.3 SHAREHOLDER MEETINGS BY CONFERENCE TELEPHONE.

If the corporation has 50 or fewer shareholders and the board of directors so authorizes, shareholders of the corporation may participate in a shareholder meeting by means of a conference telephone or similar communications equipment, provided all persons entitled to participate in the meeting received proper notice of the telephone meeting (see section 2.5), and provided all persons participating in the meeting can hear each other at the same time. A shareholder participating in a conference telephone meeting is deemed present in person at the meeting. The chairperson of the meeting may establish reasonable rules as to conducting business at any meeting by phone.

SECTION 2.4 PLACE OF SHAREHOLDER MEETING.

The board of directors may designate any place within the county in (state) where the principal office is located as the meeting place for any annual or special meeting of the shareholders. The shareholders may change the meeting place if all the shareholders entitled to vote at the meeting agree by written consents to another location. The written consents may be in the form of waiver of notice or otherwise. The new location may be either within or outside the State of (state). If the board of directors do not designate a meeting place, then the shareholders shall meet at the principal office of the corporation.

SECTION 2.5 NOTICE OF SHAREHOLDER MEETING.

1. *Required notice.* At the direction of the president, the board of directors, or other persons calling the meeting, the secretary of the corporation shall deliver written notice of the shareholder meeting to each record share-

holder entitled to vote at the meeting. The secretary shall also deliver written notice of the meeting to any other shareholder entitled by the (state) Business Corporation Act to receive notice of the meeting. The written notice shall state the place, day, and hour of any annual or special shareholder meeting, and if the meeting is to be held by conference telephone, the notice shall indicate instructions for participating in the telephone meeting. The secretary shall deliver the notice, either personally or by mail, not less than ten nor more than 60 days before the date of the meeting. Notice shall be deemed to be effective at the earlier of the following: (1) the date when the notice was deposited in the United States mail, if mailed postpaid and correctly addressed to the shareholder at the shareholder's address as it appears on the corporation's stock transfer books; (2) the date shown on the return receipt (if sent by registered or certified mail, return receipt requested, and the receipt is signed by or on behalf of the addressee); (3) the date when received; or (4) the date 5 days after deposit in the United States mail, if mailed postpaid and correctly addressed to an address other than that shown in the corporation's current record of shareholders.

2. *Adjourned Meeting.* If the shareholders adjourned any shareholder meeting to a different date, time, or place, the secretary need not give notice of the new date, time, and place, if the new date, time, and place is announced at the meeting before adjournment. But if the board of directors fix a new record date for the adjourned meeting, or must fix one (*see* section 2.7 of Article II), then the secretary must give notice, in accordance with the requirements of paragraph (a) of this section, to those persons who are shareholders as of the new record date.

3. *Waiver of Notice.* A shareholder entitled to a notice may waive notice of the meeting (or any announcement required by the Act, articles of incorporation, or bylaws), by a writing signed by the shareholder. The shareholder must send the notice of waiver to the corporation (either before or after the date and time stated in the notice) for inclusion in the minutes or filing with the corporate records.

   A shareholder's attendance at a meeting:

   a. waives the shareholder's right to object to lack of notice or defective notice of the meeting, unless the shareholder at the beginning of the meeting objects to holding the meeting or transacting business at the meeting.

   b. waives the shareholder's right to object to consideration of a particular matter at the meeting that is not within the purpose or purposes described in the meeting notice, unless the shareholder objects to considering the matter when it is presented.

4. *Contents of Notice.* Unless Section 2.5(d), the corporation's articles, or the (state) Business Corporation Act require it, the notice of an annual shareholder meeting need not include a description of the meeting's purpose or purposes.

   However the notice of each special shareholder meeting shall include a description of the meeting's purpose or purposes.

   Regardless of whether the notice is of an annual or special shareholder meeting, if a purpose of the meeting is for the shareholders to consider either:

   a. a proposed amendment to the articles of incorporation (including any restated articles requiring shareholder approval); of all, or substantially all

   b. a plan of merger or share exchange;

   c. the sale, lease, exchange, or other disposition of the corporation's property;

   d. the dissolution of the corporation; or

   e. the removal of a director,

   then the notice must state this purpose and be accompanied, if applicable, by a copy or summary of the:

   f. articles of amendment;

   g. plan of merger or share exchange; and

   h. transaction for disposition of all the corporation's property.

If the proposed corporate action creates dissenters' rights, then the notice of the shareholder meeting must state that shareholders are, or may be, entitled to assert dissenters' rights; in addition, the notice must be accompanied by a copy of the sections of the (state) Business Corporation Act governing dissenters' rights.

If the president issues or the board of directors authorize the issuance of shares for promissory notes or for promises to render services in the future, the corporation shall report in writing to all the shareholders the number of shares issued or authorized, and the amount of consideration that the corporation received in the exchange; the secretary must send this information with or before the notice of the next shareholder meeting.

Likewise, if the corporation indemnifies or advances expenses to a director as defined by the (state) Business Corporation Act the secretary shall report this information in writing to all the shareholders with or before notice of the next shareholder meeting.

SECTION 2.6   CONDUCT OF SHAREHOLDER MEETINGS.

1. *Conduct of Meeting.* The president, or in the president's absence, the vice-president, or in their absence, any person chosen by the shareholders present shall call the meeting of the shareholders to order and shall act as the chairperson of the meeting. The chairperson shall establish rules of the meeting that will freely facilitate debate and decision making. The chairperson will indicate who may speak when and when a vote

will be taken. The secretary of the corporation shall act as the secretary of all meetings of the shareholders, but in the secretary's absence, the presiding officer may appoint any other person to act as the secretary of the meeting.

2. *Order of Business.* The order of business at a shareholder meeting shall be as follows:
   a. call to order,
   b. reading of prior minutes,
   c. report of officers,
   d. election of directors, if that is the purpose of the meeting,
   e. unfinished business,
   f. new business,
   g. adjournment.

SECTION 2.7   FIXING OF RECORD DATE.

1. *Purpose of Fixing a Record Date.* The board of directors may fix in advance a date, referred to as the record date, for the purpose of determining which shareholders of any voting group, as of a certain date, are entitled to receive notice of a shareholder meeting. The board of directors may also fix this record date for the purpose of determining which shareholders of any voting group are entitled to vote at any meeting of shareholders, or to determine which shareholders are entitled to receive payment of any distribution or dividend, or to determine which shareholders belong in a group for any other proper purpose. The record date shall not be more than 70 days prior to the date on which the particular action, requiring a determination of shareholders, is to be taken.

2. *If No Record Date Is Fixed.* If the board of directors does not fix a record date for the purposes described in paragraph (a) of this section, then the record date for determination of the shareholders shall be at the close of business on one of the following:
   a. With respect to an annual shareholder meeting or any special shareholder meeting properly called, the day before the secretary of the corporation delivers the first notice to the shareholders;
   b. With respect to a special shareholder meeting demanded by the shareholders, the date the first shareholder signs the demand;
   c. With respect to the payment of a share dividend, the date the board authorizes the share dividend;
   d. With respect to actions taken without a meeting (pursuant to Article II, 2.13), the date the first shareholder signs a consent;
   e. And with respect to a distribution to shareholders (other than one involving a repurchase or reacquisition of shares), the date the board authorizes the distribution.

3. *Fixed Record Dates and Adjournment.* When the board of directors set a record date to determine which share-

holders are entitled to vote at any shareholder meeting, as provided in this section, the determination shall apply to any adjournment; this shall be true, unless the board of directors fixes a new record date, which it must do if the meeting is adjourned to a date more than 120 days after the date fixed for the original meeting.

SECTION 2.8   SHAREHOLDER LIST.

The officer or agent maintaining the stock transfer books for shares of the corporation shall make a complete record of the shareholders entitled to vote at each shareholder meeting. The record shall include the address of and the number of shares held by each shareholder, as well as the date of issue. The shareholder list must be available for inspection by any shareholder, beginning two business days after the secretary gives notice of the meeting for which the list was prepared. The list will continue to be available throughout the meeting. The list shall be located for inspection at the corporation's principal office or at a place identified in the meeting notice in the city where the meeting is to be held. A shareholder, the shareholder's agent, or attorney is entitled on written demand to inspect and, subject to the requirements of Section 2.15 of Article II, to copy the list during regular business hours. The shareholder shall be responsible for any reasonable inspection and copying expenses. The corporation shall maintain the shareholder list in written form or in another form capable of conversion into written form within a reasonable time.

SECTION 2.9   SHAREHOLDER QUORUM AND VOTING REQUIREMENTS.

A majority of the votes entitled to be cast on the matter constitute a quorum of the shareholders for action on that matter.

Once a share is represented for any purpose at a meeting, it is deemed present for quorum purposes for the remainder of the meeting and for any adjournment of the meeting unless a new record date is or must be set for that adjourned meeting.

If a quorum exists, action on a matter (other than the election of directors) is approved if the votes cast favoring the action exceed the votes cast opposing the action, unless the (state) Business Corporation Act requires a greater number of affirmative votes.

SECTION 2.10   PROXIES.

At all shareholder meetings, a shareholder may vote in person, or by proxy. The shareholder or the shareholder's attorney shall make the proxy vote in writing and file it with the secretary of the corporation before or at the time of the meeting. No proxy shall be valid after 11 months from the date it was made, unless otherwise provided in the proxy.

SECTION 2.11 VOTING OF SHARES.

Except as otherwise provided by these bylaws or the provisions of the (state) Business Corporation Act, each outstanding share entitled to vote shall be entitled to one vote upon each matter submitted to a vote at a meeting of shareholders.

Except as provided by specific court order, no shares held by another corporation, if a majority of the shares entitled to vote for the election of directors of such other corporation are held by the corporation, shall be voted at any meeting or counted in determining the total number of outstanding shares at any given time for purposes of any meeting. Provided, however, the prior sentence shall not limit the power of the corporation to vote any shares, including its own shares, held by it in a fiduciary capacity.

Redeemable shares are not entitled to vote after notice or redemption is mailed to the holders and a sum sufficient to redeem the shares has been deposited with a bank, trust company, or other financial institution under an irrevocable obligation to pay the holders the redemption price on surrender of the shares.

SECTION 2.12 CORPORATION'S ACCEPTANCE OF VOTES.

1. If the name signed on a vote, consent, waiver, or proxy appointment corresponds to the name of a shareholder, the corporation if acting in good faith is entitled to accept the vote, consent, waiver, or proxy appointment and give it effect as the act of the shareholder.

2. If the name signed on a vote, consent, waiver, or proxy appointment does not correspond to the name of its shareholder, the corporation if acting in good faith is nevertheless entitled to accept the vote, consent, waiver, or proxy appointment and give it effect as the act of the shareholder if:

   a. the shareholder is an entity as defined in the (state) Business Corporation Act and the name signed purports to be that of an officer or agent of the entity;

   b. the name signed purports to be that of an administrator, executor, guardian, or conservator representing the shareholder and, if the corporation requests, evidence of fiduciary status acceptable to the corporation has been presented with respect to the vote, consent, waiver, or proxy appointment;

   c. the name signed purports to be that of a receiver or trustee in bankruptcy of the shareholder and, if the corporation requests, evidence of this status acceptable to the corporation has been presented with respect to the vote, consent, waiver, or proxy appointment;

   d. the name signed purports to be that of a pledgee, beneficial owner, or attorney-in-fact of the shareholder and, if the corporation requests, evidence acceptable to the corporation of the signatory's authority to sign for the shareholder has been presented with respect to the vote, consent, waiver, or proxy appointment.

   e. two or more persons are the shareholder as co-tenants or fiduciaries and the name signed purports to be the name of at least one of the co-owners and the person signing appears to be acting on behalf of all the co-owners.

3. The corporation is entitled to reject a vote, consent, waiver, or proxy appointment if the secretary or other officer or agent authorized to tabulate votes, acting in good faith, has reasonable basis for doubt about the validity of the signature on it or about the signatory's authority to sign for the shareholder.

4. The corporation and its officer or agent who accepts or rejects a vote, consent, waiver, or proxy appointment in good faith and in accordance with the standards of this section are not liable in damages to the shareholder for the consequences of the acceptance or rejection.

5. Corporate action based on the acceptance or rejection of a vote, consent, waiver, or proxy appointment under this section is valid unless a court of competent jurisdiction determines otherwise.

SECTION 2.13 INFORMAL ACTION BY SHAREHOLDERS.

The shareholders may act on any matter generally required or permitted at a shareholder meeting, without actually meeting, if all shareholders entitled to vote on the subject matter sign one or more written consent(s) to the action; the shareholders must deliver the consent(s) to the corporation for inclusion in the minute book.

SECTION 2.14 VOTING FOR DIRECTORS' CUMULATIVE VOTING.

1. *General Provisions.* In all election of directors, each shareholder shall be entitled to as many votes as shall equal the number of the shareholder's shares multiplied times the number of directors to be elected, and the shareholders may cast all of such votes for a single director or may distribute them among the number to be voted for, any two or more of them, as the shareholders may desire. If the articles of incorporation provide for a method of voting inconsistent with this section, the articles of incorporation shall control.

2. *Plurality.* Directors are elected by a plurality of the votes cast by the shares entitled to vote in the election at a meeting at which a quorum is present.

SECTION 2.15 SHAREHOLDER'S RIGHTS TO INSPECT CORPORATE RECORDS.

1. *Minutes and Accounting Records.* The corporation shall keep a permanent record of the minutes of all meetings of its shareholders and board of directors, a record of all actions taken by the shareholders or board of directors without a meeting, and a record of all actions taken by a committee of the board of directors acting in place of the board and on behalf of the corporation. The corporation shall maintain appropriate accounting records.

2. *Absolute Inspection Rights of Records Required at Principal Office.* At least five business days before the date on which the shareholder wishes to inspect and copy records, the shareholder must give the corporation written notice of the shareholder's demand to inspect. If the shareholder gives proper notice (as required by this section), the shareholder (or the shareholder's agent or attorney) has the right to inspect and copy, during regular business hours, any of the following records, all of which the corporation is required to keep at its principal office:
   a. its articles or restated articles of incorporation and all amendments to them currently in effect;
   b. its bylaws or restated bylaws and all amendments to them currently in effect;
   c. resolutions adopted by its board of directors creating one or more classes or series of shares, and fixing their relative rights, preferences, and limitation, if shares issued pursuant to those resolutions are outstanding;
   d. the minutes of all shareholders' meetings, and records of all action taken by shareholders without a meeting, for the past three years;
   e. the financial statement required by the (state) Business Corporation Act to be available to shareholders for the past three years to the shareholders;
   f. a list of the names and business addresses of its current directors and officers; and,
   g. its most recent annual report delivered to the Secretary of State.

3. *Conditional Inspection Right.* (1) The shareholder (or the shareholder's agent or attorney) may inspect and copy, during regular business hours, and at a reasonable location specified by the corporation, additional records (listed below) if the shareholder meets the following criteria:
   a. the shareholder must have been a shareholder of record for at least six months preceding the demand or own at least five percent of all outstanding shares of the corporation when making the demand; and,
   b. the shareholder must give the corporation a written demand to inspect made in good faith and for a proper purpose at least five business days before the date on which the shareholder wishes to inspect and copy; and

   c. the shareholder must describe with reasonable particularity: (a) the shareholder's purpose and (b) the records that the shareholder desires to inspect; and meet the corporation's approval (which shall not be unreasonably withheld) that the records are directly connected with the shareholder's proper purpose.

4. If the shareholder meets the above criteria, the shareholder may inspect and copy:
   a. excerpts from minutes of any meeting of the board of directors, records of any action of a committee of the board of directors acting on behalf of the corporation, minutes of any meeting of the shareholders, and records of action taken by the shareholders without a meeting, to the extent not subject to inspection under paragraph (a) of this section;
   b. accounting records of the corporation; and
   c. the record of shareholders (compiled no earlier than the date of the shareholder's demand).

5. *Copy Costs.* The right to copy includes, if reasonable, the right to photocopy, or copy by other reasonable means. The corporation may impose a reasonable charge, covering the costs of labor and material, for copies of any documents provided to the shareholder. The charge may not exceed the estimated cost of production or reproduction of the records.

6. *Shareholder Includes Beneficial Owner.* For purposes of section 2.15, the term "shareholder" shall include a beneficial owner whose shares are held in a voting trust or by a nominee on the shareholder's behalf.

ARTICLE III. BOARD OF DIRECTORS

SECTION 3.1   GENERAL POWERS.

All corporate powers shall be exercised by or under the authority of, and the business and affairs of the corporation shall be managed under the direction of the board of directors.

SECTION 3.2   NUMBER, TENURE, AND QUALIFICATIONS OF DIRECTORS.

The number of directors of the corporation shall be _____. Each director shall hold office until the next annual shareholder meeting or until the director dies, resigns, or is removed. However, if the director's term expires, the director shall continue to serve until the shareholders have elected and qualified a successor or until there is a decrease in the number of directors. Directors need not be residents of (state) or shareholders of the corporation.

SECTION 3.3   REGULAR MEETINGS OF THE BOARD OF DIRECTORS.

The board of directors shall hold a regular meeting immediately after, and at the same place as, the annual shareholder meeting. No notice of the meeting other than this bylaw is required. The board of directors may provide, by resolution, the date, time, and place (which shall be within the county where the company's principal office is located) of additional regular meetings. Regular board of director meetings may be held by conference telephone, if convened in accordance with section 3.5.

SECTION 3.4   SPECIAL MEETINGS OF THE BOARD OF DIRECTORS.

The president or any one director may call or request special meetings of the board of directors. The person authorized to call special board meetings may fix any place within the county where the corporation has its principal office as the special meeting place. Special board of director meetings may be held by conference telephone, if convened in accordance with section 3.5.

SECTION 3.5   BOARD OF DIRECTOR MEETINGS BY CONFERENCE TELEPHONE.

The board of directors or any designated committee of the corporation may participate in a board or committee meeting by means of a conference telephone or similar communications equipment, provided all persons entitled to participate in the meeting received proper notice of the telephone meeting (see section 3.6), and provided all persons participating in the meeting can hear each other at the same time. A director participating in a conference telephone meeting is deemed present in person at the meeting. The chairperson of the meeting may establish reasonable rules as to conducting the meeting by phone.

SECTION 3.6   NOTICE OF, AND WAIVER OF NOTICE FOR, SPECIAL DIRECTOR MEETINGS.

1. *Notice.* The corporation's secretary shall give either oral or written notice of any special director meeting at least two days before the meeting. The notice shall include the meeting place, day, and hour. Generally regular meetings do not require notice other than the notice provided by section 3.3; however, if the meeting is to be held by conference telephone (regardless of whether it is regular or special), the secretary must provide instructions for participating in the telephone meeting. If mailed, notice of any director meeting shall be deemed to be effective at the earlier of: (1) when received; (2) five days after deposited in the United States mail, addressed to the director's business office, with postage prepaid; or (3) the date shown on the

return receipt (if sent by registered or certified mail, return receipt requested, and the receipt is signed by or on behalf of the director).

2. *Waiver of Notice.* Any director may waive notice of any meeting. The waiver must be in writing, signed by the director entitled to the notice, and filed with the minutes or corporate records.

A director's attendance at a meeting waives the director's right to object to lack of notice or defective notice of the meeting; this shall be true unless the director, at the beginning of the meeting (or promptly upon arrival), objects to holding the meeting or transacting business at the meeting, and does not vote for or assent to action taken at the meeting.

Neither the secretary nor director needs to specify in the notice or waiver of notice the business to be transacted at, or the purpose of, any special board meeting.

SECTION 3.7   DIRECTOR QUORUM.

A majority of the number of directors shall constitute a quorum for the transaction of business at any board of director meeting, unless the articles require a greater number.

SECTION 3.8   DIRECTORS, MANNER OF ACTING.

The act of a majority of the directors present at a meeting at which a quorum is present (when the vote is taken) shall be the act of the board of directors.

The corporation shall deem a director to have assented to the action taken if the director is present at a meeting of the board or a committee of the board unless: (1) the director objects at the beginning of the meeting (or promptly upon arrival) to holding it or transacting business at the meeting; or (2) the director's dissent or abstention from the action taken is entered in the minutes of the meeting; or (3) the director delivers written notice of dissent or abstention to the presiding officer of the meeting before its adjournment or to the corporation immediately after adjournment of the meeting. The right of dissent or abstention is not available to a director who votes in favor of the action taken.

SECTION 3.9   CONDUCT OF BOARD OF DIRECTOR MEETINGS.

The president, or in the president's absence, the vice-president, or in their absence, any person chosen by the directors present shall call the meeting of the directors to order and shall act as the chairperson of the meeting. The chairperson shall preside over the meeting and establish rules of the meeting that will freely facilitate debate and decision making. The chairperson will indicate who may speak when and when a vote will be taken. The secretary of the corporation shall act as the secretary of all meetings of the directors, but in the secretary's absence, the presiding officer may appoint any other person to act as the secretary of the meeting.

SECTION 3.10 MEDIATION, ARBITRATION IF BOARD DEADLOCKED.

1. *General.* If the board of directors is equally divided on any aspect of the management of the property, business and affairs of the corporation, or corporation transactions, or if the board is equally divided on any question, dispute, or controversy, and the deadlock is preventing action or non-action by the board, then the board shall submit the deadlock to mediation in accordance with section 3.10(b). If the directors are unable to resolve the deadlock through mediation, the directors agree to submit the dispute to binding arbitration in accordance with section 3.10(c).
2. *Mediation.* If the board of directors is unable to resolve the deadlock itself, upon written request of any one director, the directors agree to submit the dispute to mediation and the following guidelines shall apply:
   a. The directors agree to have the dispute mediated by a mediator chosen by a majority of the board.
   b. The directors agree to follow the mediation procedure selected by the mediator.
   c. Mediation shall terminate upon the written request of the mediator or 30 percent of the directors.
3. *Arbitration.* If the board of directors are unable to resolve the deadlock through mediation, upon written request of 30 percent of the directors, the directors agree to submit the deadlock to binding arbitration in the following manner:
   a. At a duly held board meeting, directors shall submit written requests for an arbitrator; the board shall then vote on which arbitrator to select. If the majority of board members agree on a single arbitrator, then the board shall contact that individual with a request for arbitration. If a majority of the board members can not agree on a single arbitrator, then the board shall select two arbitrators, each director having, in the selection, a number of votes equal to the number of directors under a system of cumulative voting; after the members appoint two arbitrators, those two arbitrators shall select a third arbitrator to be the professional who actually arbitrates for the board. If the initial two arbitrators are unable to agree within 15 days upon a third arbitrator, the Panels of Arbitrators of the American Arbitration Association shall appoint the third arbitrator and do so in accordance with it rules then in effect.
   b. The arbitrator shall determine, decide on, and help resolve the matters that are equally dividing the board of directors. The arbitrator's scope of responsibility will be to decide on matters including (but not limited to) whether the subject before the board is a proper subject for action by the board; the arbitrator may decide whether matters have been properly submitted to the board for decision, whether the board is actually divided, and whether this section and the arbitration provisions provided here were properly invoked by the board or applicable. The arbitrator may act until all questions, disputes, and controversies are determined, adjudged, and resolved.
   c. The arbitrator shall conduct the arbitration proceedings in accordance with the rules of the American Arbitration Association, then in effect, except where these bylaws make a special provision.
   d. The arbitrator's decision shall be conclusive and binding upon the board of directors, the corporation, and the parties on all matters that the board submits to the arbitrator. The arbitrator's decision shall be the equivalent of a resolution unanimously passed by the full board at an organized meeting. The board of directors or the shareholders may not revoke, amend, or overrule the decision, except by a majority action of either body. The arbitrator's decision shall be filed with the secretary of the corporation; and the arbitrator may enter judgment on the decision in the highest court of the forum having jurisdiction.

SECTION 3.11 DIRECTOR ACTION WITHOUT A MEETING.

The directors may act on any matter generally required or permitted at a board meeting, without actually meeting, if: all the directors take the action, each one signs a written consent describing the action taken, and the directors file all the consents with the records of the corporation. Action taken by consents is effective when the last director signs the consent, unless the consent specifies a different effective date. A signed consent has the effect of a meeting vote and may be referred to as a meeting vote in any document.

SECTION 3.12 REMOVAL OF DIRECTORS.

The shareholders may remove one or more directors at a meeting called for that purpose if the secretary has given notice to all shareholders entitled to vote. The removal may be with or without cause. If less than the entire board is to be removed, a director may not be removed if (a) the number of votes sufficient to elect him or her under cumulative voting is voted against his or her removal, or (b) the number of votes cast for removal is less than two-thirds of the number of votes entitled to vote. The entire board of directors may be removed only by a vote of a majority of the shares entitled to vote. Notwithstanding the previous sentence, if the corporation has 100 or more shareholders, the entire board of directors of a corporation may be removed only by a vote of the holders of two-thirds of the shares entitled to vote.

SECTION 3.13 BOARD OF DIRECTOR VACANCIES.

If a vacancy occurs on the board of directors, including a vacancy resulting from an increase in the number of directors, the shareholders may fill the vacancy. During the time that the shareholders fail or are unable to fill the vacancies, then and until the shareholders act:

1. the board of directors may fill the vacancy; or
2. if the directors remaining in office constitute fewer than a quorum of the board, they may fill the vacancy by the affirmative vote of a majority of all the directors remaining in office.

If a voting group of shareholders elected the director who held the now vacant office, only the holders of shares of that voting group are entitled to vote to fill the vacancy, if it is to be filled by the shareholders.

If a director resigns effective at a specific later date, the shareholders may fill the vacancy, before the vacancy occurs, but the new director may not take office until the vacancy actually occurs.

When the shareholders elect a director to fill a vacancy, the director's term expires at the next shareholders' meeting at which shareholders elect directors. However, if the director's term expires prior to the next shareholders' meeting to elect directors, the director shall continue to serve until the board of directors elect and qualify a successor (in accordance with section 3.13 (1) & (2)) or until there is a decrease in the number of directors.

SECTION 3.14 DIRECTOR COMMITTEES.

1. *Creation of Committees.* The board of directors may create one or more committees and appoint members of the board to serve on them. Each committee must have two or more members, who serve at the pleasure of the board of directors.
2. *Selection of Members.* To create a committee and appoint members to it, the board must acquire approval by the greater of (1) a majority of all the directors in office when the action is taken or (2) the number of directors required by the articles of incorporation to take action, (or if not specified in the articles, the numbers required by section 3.8 of Article III to take action).
3. *Required Procedures.* Sections 3.3, 3.4, 3.5, 3.6, 3.7, 3.8, and 3.9, of this Article III, which govern meetings, action without meetings, notice and waiver of notice, quorum and voting requirements, and conduct of the board of directors, apply to committees and their members. The committees are subject to all the procedural rules governing the operation of the board itself.
4. *Authority.* Unless limited by the articles of incorporation, each committee may exercise the specific board authority (including appointment of officers) which the board of directors confers upon the committee in the resolution creating the committee. Provided, however, a committee may not:
   a. authorize distributions;
   b. approve or propose to shareholders action that the (state) Business Corporation Act requires be approved by shareholders;
   c. fill vacancies on the board of directors or on any of its committees;
   d. amend the articles of incorporation pursuant to the authority of directors, as provided in the (state) Business Corporation Act;
   e. adopt, amend, or repeal bylaws;
   f. approve a plan of merger not requiring shareholder approval;
   g. authorize or approve reacquisition of shares, except according to a formula or method prescribed by the board of directors; or
   h. authorize or approve the issuance or sale or contract for sale of shares or determine the designation and relative rights, preferences, and limitations of a class or series of shares, except that the board of directors may authorize a committee (or a senior executive officer of the corporation) to do so within limits specifically prescribed by the board of directors.

SECTION 3.15 DIRECTOR COMPENSATION.

The board of directors may agree by resolution to pay each director expenses, if any, of attendance at each board meeting. As well, the corporation may pay directors a stated salary or a fixed sum for attendance at each board meeting or both. No payment shall preclude any director from serving the corporation in any other capacity and receiving compensation.

ARTICLE IV. OFFICERS

SECTION 4.1 NUMBER OF OFFICERS.

The officers of the corporation shall be a president, a secretary, and a treasurer. The board of directors shall appoint each of these officers. The board may appoint other officers and assistant officers, including a vice-president, if it deems it necessary. If the board of directors specifically authorizes an officer to appoint one or more officers or assistant officers, the officer may do so. The same individual may simultaneously hold more than one office in the corporation.

SECTION 4.2 APPOINTMENT AND TERM OF OFFICE.

The officers of the corporation shall be appointed by the board of directors for a term as determined by the board of directors. If no term is specified, they shall hold office until they resign, die, or until they are removed in a manner provided in Section 4.3 of this Article IV.

The designation of a specified term does not grant to the officer any contract rights, and the board can remove the officer at any time prior to the termination of such term.

SECTION 4.3 REMOVAL OF OFFICERS.

The board of directors may remove any officer or agent any time, with or without cause. The removal shall be without prejudice to the contract rights, if any, of the person removed. A board's appointment of an officer or agent shall not of itself create contract rights.

SECTION 4.4 PRESIDENT.

The president shall be the principal executive officer of the corporation. The president shall be subject to the control of the board of directors, and shall in general supervise and control all of the business and affairs of the corporation. The president shall, when present, preside at all meetings of the shareholders and of the board of directors. The president may sign and issue, with the secretary or any other officer of the corporation that the board has authorized, certificates for shares of the corporation and deeds, mortgages, bonds, contracts, or other board authorized instruments; and exception will exist when the board or these bylaws expressly delegate the signing and execution to some other officer or agent of the corporation; another exception to the president's signing will exist if the law requires a certain signature other than that of the president. In general, the president shall perform all duties incident to the office of president and any other duties that the board prescribes.

SECTION 4.5 VICE-PRESIDENT.

If the board of directors appoints a vice-president, the vice-president shall perform the president's duties if the president is absent, dies, or is unable to act. If the vice-president acts in the absence of the president, the vice-president shall have all presidential powers and be subject to all the restrictions upon the president. (If there is no vice-president, then the treasurer shall perform the presidential duties.) Any vice-president may sign and issue, with the secretary or an assistant secretary, certificates for shares of the corporation that have been authorized by board resolution. The vice-president shall perform any other duties that the president or board may assign to the vice-president.

SECTION 4.6 SECRETARY.

The secretary shall: (a) create and maintain one or more books for the minutes of the proceedings of the shareholders and of the board of directors; (b) provide notices to be given in accordance with these bylaws or as required by law; (c) be custodian of the corporate records and of any seal of the corporation and if there is a seal of the corporation, see that it is affixed to all authorized and executed documents; (d) when requested or required, authenticate any records of the corporation; (e) keep a current register of the post office address of each shareholder; (f) have general charge of the stock transfer books of the corporation; and (g) in general perform all duties incident to the office of secretary and any other duties that the president or the board may assign to the secretary.

SECTION 4.7 TREASURER.

The treasurer shall: (a) have charge and custody of and be responsible for all funds and securities of the corporation; (b) receive and give receipts for moneys due and payable to the corporation from any source, and deposit all moneys in the corporation's name in banks, trust companies, or other depositaries that the board shall select; and (c) in general perform all of the duties incident to the office of treasurer and any other duties that the president or board may assign to the treasurer. If required by the board of directors, the treasurer shall give a bond for the faithful performance of the treasurer's duties and as insurance against the misappropriation of funds; the bond shall be in a sum and with the surety or sureties that the board of directors shall determine.

SECTION 4.8 ASSISTANT SECRETARIES AND ASSISTANT TREASURERS.

The assistant secretaries, when authorized by the board of directors, may sign and issue with the president or vice-president certificates for shares of the corporation that have been authorized by board resolution. The assistant treasurers shall, if required by the board, give bonds for the faithful performance of their duties and as insurance against the misappropriation of funds; the bond shall be in sums and with the sureties that the board of directors shall determine. The assistant secretaries and assistant treasurers, in general, shall perform the duties that the secretary or treasurer, respectively, or the president or board may assign to them.

SECTION 4.9 SALARIES.

The board of directors shall fix and or adjust salaries of the officers from time to time.

ARTICLE V. INDEMNIFICATION OF DIRECTORS, OFFICERS, AGENTS, AND EMPLOYEES

SECTION 5.1 INDEMNIFICATION OF DIRECTORS.

The corporation shall indemnify any individual made a party to a proceeding because he is or was a director of the corporation, against liability incurred in the proceeding, but only if such indemnification is both (i) determined permissible and (ii) authorized, as defined in subsection (a) of this § 5.1. (Such indemnification is further subject to the limitation specified in subsection (c).)

1. *Determination and Authorization.*

    The corporation shall not indemnify a director under the § 5.1 of Article V unless

    a. *Determination.* A determination has been made in accordance with the procedures set forth in (state) Business Corporation Act that the director met the standard of conduct set forth in subsection (b) below, and

    b. *Authorization.* Payment has been authorized in accordance with the procedures set forth in the (state) Business Corporation Act based on a conclusion that the expenses are reasonable, the corporation has the financial ability to make the payment, and the financial resources of the corporation should be devoted to this use rather than some other use by the corporation.

2. *Standard of Conduct*

    The individual shall demonstrate that:

    a. the individual acted in good faith; and

    b. the individual reasonably believed:

        i. in acting in an official capacity with the corporation, that the individual's conduct was in the corporation's best interests;

        ii. in all other cases, that the individual's conduct was at least not opposed to the corporation's best interests; and

        iii. in the case of any criminal proceeding, that the individual had no reasonable cause to believe that the conduct was unlawful.

    c. *No Indemnification Permitted in Certain Circumstances.* The corporation shall not indemnify an individual under Section 5.1 of Article V if:

        i. the individual was adjudged liable to the corporation in a proceeding by or in the right of the corporation; or

        ii. the individual was adjudged liable in any other proceeding charging that the director improperly received personal benefit, whether or not the individual acted in an official capacity.

    d. *Indemnification in Derivation Actions Limited.* Indemnification permitted under section 5.1 of Article V in connection with a proceeding by the corporation or in the right of the corporation is limited to the reasonable expenses incurred in connection with the proceeding.

SECTION 5.2 ADVANCE EXPENSES FOR DIRECTORS.

The company shall pay for or reimburse, in advance of final disposition of the proceeding, the reasonable expenses incurred by a director who is a party to a proceeding if:

1. by following the procedures of the (state) Code Annotated, the board of directors determined that the director met requirements (c)–(e) listed below; and

2. by following the procedures and standards set forth in the (state) Code Annotated, the board of directors authorized an advance payment to a director; and

3. the director has furnished the corporation with a written affirmation of the director's good faith belief that the director has met the standard of conduct described in Section 5.1 of Article V; and

4. the director has provided the corporation with a written undertaking, executed personally or on the director's behalf, to repay the advance if it is ultimately determined that the director did not meet the standard of conduct; the director's undertaking must be an unlimited general obligation, but need not be secured, and the corporation may accept the undertaking without reference to financial ability to make repayment; and

5. the board of directors determines that the facts then known to it would not preclude indemnification under Section 5.1 of this Article V or the (state) Business Corporation Act.

SECTION 5.3 INDEMNIFICATION OF OFFICERS, AGENTS, AND EMPLOYEES.

The board of directors, by board resolution, may elect to indemnify and advance expenses to any officer, employee, or agent of the corporation, who is not a director of the corporation, to any extent consistent with public policy.

SECTION 5.4 MANDATORY INDEMNIFICATION.

Notwithstanding any other provisions of these bylaws, the corporation shall indemnify a director or officer who was wholly successful, on the merits or otherwise, in the defense of any proceeding to which the director was a party because he or she is or was a director or officer of the corporation, against reasonable expenses incurred by the directors or officers in connection with the proceeding.

ARTICLE VI. CERTIFICATES FOR SHARES AND THEIR TRANSFER

SECTION 6.1 CERTIFICATES FOR SHARES.

1. *Content.* Certificates representing shares of the corporation shall at minimum, state on their face: (a) the name of the issuing corporation; (b) that the corporation is formed under the laws of (state); (c) the name of the person to whom issued; and (d) the number and class of shares and the designation of the series, if any, that the certificate represents. The board of directors shall determine the exact form of the certificate. The president shall sign the certificates (either manually or by facsimile) and may seal them with a corporate seal or a facsimile. The secretary shall consecutively number or otherwise identify each certificate for shares.

2. *Shareholder List.* The secretary shall maintain a shareholder list in the corporation's stock transfer books. The list shall include: the name and address of the person to whom the shares represented are issued, the number of shares, and date of issue.

3. *Transferring Shares.* The secretary of the corporation shall cancel all certificates that an individual surrenders to the corporation for transfer. The president and secretary shall only issue a new certificate for a like number of shares when an individual surrenders and cancels the former certificate; one exception to this exists: in case of a lost, destroyed, or mutilated certificate, the corporation may issue a new one upon the terms and indemnity to the corporation as the board of directors may prescribe.

SECTION 6.2   REGISTRATION OF THE TRANSFER OF SHARES.

The corporation shall register the transfer of shares of the corporation only on the corporation's stock transfer books. To register a transfer, the record owner and appropriate persons shall properly endorse the shares and then the record owner shall surrender the shares to the corporation for cancellation. Unless the corporation has established a procedure by which it recognizes a beneficial owner of shares held by a nominee as the owner, the corporation shall deem the person in whose name shares stand on the books of the corporation to be the owner for all purposes.

SECTION 6.3   RESTRICTIONS ON TRANSFER.

~Optional language No present or future shareholder of the corporation, or shareholder's personal representative, executor, or administrator, shall encumber or dispose of the stock of the corporation which the shareholder now owns or may acquire, except that a sharseholder may transfer all or part of the stock owned subject to the restrictions set forth in this section.

1. *Sale of Stock.* A shareholder who desires to sell all or part of the stock owned shall first offer such stock for sale in writing to the corporation at the same price and upon the same terms offered to the shareholder by a bona fide prospective purchaser of the shares. The corporation shall have the option for 20 days after its receipt of the written offer to accept the offer. If, within the 20-day period, the corporation fails to accept the offer in its entirety, its option shall terminate. Immediately following the termination of the offer as to the corporation, the same offer shall be deemed, without further writing, to have been made to the other shareholders of the corporation. Such shareholders shall then have the option for 30 days to purchase part or all of the stock which the offering shareholder desires to sell, at

the same price and upon the same terms offered to the shareholder by a bona fide prospective purchaser of such shares. If more than one shareholder owns stock in the corporation, the shareholders may exercise this option in the proportion among themselves as they may agree. If they do not agree on the proportionate shares, then each of them who wishes to purchase shares shall have the right to purchase a portion of the shares as corresponds to a fraction in which the numerator is the number of shares then owned by the shareholder, and the denominator is the total number of shares then owned by all of the then employed shareholders who wish to purchase shares. No shareholder, however, shall have the right to purchase any part of the shares so offered for sale unless all of the shares so offered for sale are purchased, pursuant to such option, by one or more of the shareholders.

If the option is not exercised within the 30-day period, then the shareholder desiring to sell all or part of the shareholder's stock shall have the right for a period ending on the sixtieth day after the expiration of the aforesaid 30-day period, to sell such stock to, and only to, the bona fide prospective purchaser in the same quantity, at the same price, and upon the same terms as were offered to the corporation and/or the shareholders. Upon the expiration of such 60-day period, if the shareholder does not sell such stock, then all of the restrictions imposed by this section apply to all of the stock owned by the shareholder.

Death of a Shareholder.

1. *Mandatory Purchase of Shares.* Upon the death of a shareholder, the corporation must purchase, and the legal representative of the deceased shareholder must sell to the corporation, all of the shares of stock of the corporation held by the shareholder immediately prior to death. Such sale shall be made at the purchase price determined as of the date of death of the deceased shareholder, in accordance with the provisions below. In no event shall any shares be transferable on or after the death of such shareholder by will or by operation of law or in any other manner, except as herein provided.

2. *Purchase Price.* The purchase price of the shares required to be purchased and sold hereunder shall be the book value thereof as of the close of business on the last day of the month in which the death of the shareholder occurs. The book value shall be determined by the certified public accountant who is then servicing the account of the corporation, and shall be made in accordance with sound and accepted accounting principles and practices consistently applied; provided, however, that the following directions shall be followed in all events: (i) all life insurance proceeds payable to the corporation on account of a shareholder's death shall be taken into account in making the determination, whether or not such proceeds have been paid to the cor-

poration as of the valuation date; and (ii) readily marketable securities owned by the corporation as of the valuation date shall be taken into account at their fair market value.

3. *Delivery of and Payment for Shares.* Within 90 days after the corporation has notice of the death of a shareholder, it shall give written notice to the legal representative of the deceased shareholder stating (i) the number of shares of the corporation which the deceased shareholder held of record immediately prior to death and (ii) that it will purchase the shares in accordance with the terms hereof. The legal representative, within 30 days after the determination date, shall deliver to the corporation the certificate or certificates representing the shares required to be sold hereunder (duly endorsed in blank or accompanied by proper instruments of transfer duly executed in blank with all necessary stock transfer stamps affixed), and against such delivery the corporation shall pay the legal representative the price required to be paid. Upon the surrender to the corporation of the certificates for shares purchased by the corporation, the corporation shall deliver to the representative of the deceased shareholder the purchase price as follows: Twenty-five percent in cash and the balance with a promissory note which shall (i) be dated as of the date of delivery of the last of the certificates required to be delivered hereunder; (ii) be due and payable as to principal in 60 equal monthly installments commencing 30 days from the date of the note; and (iii) shall bear interest on the unpaid principal balance at the rate of 10 percent per year.

The corporation shall have the right without penalty to prepay, in whole or in part, any balance owing by it to a shareholder under the terms of this section.

4. *Legend to be placed on certificates.* The following notation shall be placed upon all stock certificates:

"The transfer of the shares of the corporation is restricted by the By-laws, a copy of which is on file at the office of the corporation."

SECTION 6.4   STOCK REGULATIONS.

The board of directors shall have the power and authority to make all such further rules and regulations not inconsistent with the statutes of the State of (state) as it may deem expedient concerning lost stock certificates, the issue, transfer, and registration of certificates representing shares of the corporation.

ARTICLE VII. CONTRACTS, LOANS, CHECKS, AND DEPOSITS; SPECIAL CORPORATE ACTS

SECTION 7.1   CONTRACTS.

The board of directors may authorize any officer(s) or agent(s) to enter into any contract or to execute or deliver any instrument in the name of and on behalf of the corporation. The authorization may be general or specific. In the absence of another designation, the president and the secretary shall make all corporate deeds, mortgages, and instruments of assignment or pledge.

SECTION 7.2   LOANS.

The corporation shall not allow anyone to contract on behalf of it for indebtedness for borrowed money unless the board of directors authorizes such a contract by resolution. The corporation shall not allow anyone to issue evidence of the corporation's indebtedness unless the board of directors authorizes the issuance by resolution. The authorization may be general or specific.

SECTION 7.3   CHECKS, DRAFTS, ETC.

The board of directors shall authorize by resolution which officer(s) or agent(s) may sign and issue all corporation checks, drafts, or other orders for payment of money, and notes or other evidence of indebtedness. The board of directors shall also determine by resolution the manner in which these documents will be signed and issued.

SECTION 7.4   DEPOSITS.

The treasurer of the corporation shall deposit all funds of the corporation, that are not being used, in banks and other depositories; the board of directors shall authorize by board resolution the exact location of the banks and depositories.

SECTION 7.5   VOTING OF SECURITIES OWNED BY THIS CORPORATION.

Subject to the specific directions of the board of directors, (a) any shares or other securities issued by any other corporation and owned or controlled by this corporation may be voted at any meeting of security holders of such other corporation by the president of this corporation who may be present, and (b) whenever, in the judgment of the president, or in the president's absence, of the vice-president, it is desirable for this corporation to execute a proxy or written consent in respect to any shares or other securities issued by any other corporation and owned by this corporation, such proxy or consent shall be executed in the name of this corporation by the president or vice-president of this corporation, without necessity of any authorization by the board of directors, affixation of corporate seal or countersignature or attestation by another officer. Any person or persons designated in the manner above stated as the proxy or proxies of this corporation shall have full right power and authority to vote the shares or other securities issued by such other corporation and owned by this corporation the same as such shares or other securities might be voted by this corporation.

ARTICLE VIII. CORPORATE SEAL

SECTION 8.1   CORPORATE SEAL.

The board of directors may provide a corporate seal. The seal may be circular in form and be inscribed with any designation including the corporation's name, (state) as the state of incorporation, and the words "Corporate Seal."

ARTICLE IX. EMERGENCY BYLAWS

SECTION 9.1   EMERGENCY BYLAWS.

Unless the articles of incorporation provide otherwise, the following provisions of this Article IX, Section 9.1 "Emergency Bylaws" shall be effective during an emergency which is defined as when a quorum of the corporation's directors cannot be readily assembled because of some catastrophic event.

During such emergency:

1. *Notice of Board Meetings.* Any one member of the board of directors or any one of the following officers: president, any vice-president, secretary, or treasurer, may call a meeting of the board of directors. Notice of such meeting need be given only to those directors and officers whom it is practicable to reach, and may be given in any practical manner, including by publication and radio. Such notice shall be given at least six hours prior to commencement of the meeting.
2. *Temporary-Directors and Quorum.* One or more officers of the corporation present at the emergency board meeting, as is necessary to achieve a quorum, shall be considered to be temporary directors for the meeting, and shall so serve in order of rank, and within the same rank, in order of seniority. In the event that less than a quorum (as determined by Article III, Section 3.6) of the directors are present (including any officers who are to serve as directors for the meeting), those directors present (including the officers serving as directors) shall constitute a quorum.
3. *Actions Permitted To Be Taken.* The board as constituted in paragraph (b), and after notice as set forth in paragraph (a) may:
   a. Officers' Powers. Prescribe emergency powers to any officer of the corporation;
   b. Delegation of Any Power. Delegate to any officer or director, any of the powers of directors;
   c. Lines of Succession. Designate lines of succession of officers and agents, in the event that any of them are unable to discharge their duties;
   d. Relocate Principal Place of Business. Relocate the principal place of business, or designate successive or simultaneous principal places of business;
   e. All Other Action. Take any other action, convenient, helpful, or necessary to carry on the business of the corporation.

ARTICLE X. AMENDMENTS

SECTION 10.1   AMENDMENTS.

The corporation's board of directors may amend or repeal the corporation's bylaws unless:

1. The articles of incorporation of the (state) Business Corporation Act reserve this power exclusively to the shareholders in whole or part; or
2. the shareholders in adopting, amending, or repealing a particular bylaw provide expressly that the board of directors may not amend or repeal that bylaw; or
3. the bylaw adopts or amends the quorum or voting requirement for the shareholders.

In the case described in subsections (1), (2), and (3) hereof, the shareholders must approve of the amendment or repeal. The adoption or amendment described in subsection three hereof must meet the same quorum requirement and be adopted by the same vote required to take action under the quorum and voting requirement then in effect or proposed to be adopted, whichever is greater.

The corporation's shareholders may amend or repeal the corporation's bylaws even though the bylaws may also be amended or repealed by its board of directors.

ARTICLE XI. TERM OF CORPORATION AND FISCAL YEAR

SECTION 11.1   THE TERM OF THE CORPORATION.

The term of the corporation shall be perpetual.

SECTION 11.2   FISCAL YEAR.

The fiscal year of the corporation shall be

_____.

Adopted on _____.

_____

Chairperson
Board of Directors

UNIFORM LIMITED LIABILITY COMPANY ACT
1995 ACT

Table of Jurisdictions Adopting Act

Jurisdiction	Statutory Citation
Alabama	Code 1975, §§ 10-12-1 to 10-12-58
Hawaii	HRS §§ 428-101 to 428-1302
South Carolina	Code 1976, §§ 33-44-101 to 33-44-1207
South Dakota	SDCL 47-37A-101 to 47-37A-1207
Vermont	11 V.S.A. §§ 3001 to 3162
West Virginia	Code, 31B-1-101 to 31B-13-1306

LIMITED LIABILITY COMPANY OPERATING AGREEMENT

THIS AGREEMENT IS SUBJECT TO ARBITRATION
UNDER THE UNIFORM ARBITRATION ACT
OPERATING AGREEMENT
OF
~ Limited Liability Company

SECTION 1 NAME, PLACE OF BUSINESS, TERM, INITIAL MEMBERS

1.1 Name. The name of the limited liability company is ~.

1.2 Principal Place of Business. The principal place of business of the limited liability company is ~.

1.3 Term. The limited liability company begins on the date of filing its Articles of Organization with the Secretary of State, and continues until dissolved by an act specified in Section 9 of this Agreement or a date or act specified by the limited liability company's Articles of Organization.

1.4 Initial Members. The initial members of the limited liability company are ~, ~, and ~. The Initial limited liability company Percentages of the initial members are set forth in Exhibit A.

SECTION 2 PURPOSES OF THE BUSINESS

The limited liability company may engage in the business of ~ and in any other lawful business upon which members owning a majority of the limited liability company Percentages may agree.

SECTION 3 CONTRIBUTIONS TO CAPITAL AND ASSUMPTION OF LIABILITIES

3.1 Capital Accounts.
(a) Each initial member shall contribute the property listed in Exhibit A to the limited liability company.
(b) Each member has an individual Capital Account. The amount of the Initial Capital Account of each member is set forth in Exhibit A.

3.2 Assumption of Liabilities.
(a) The Limited Liability company assumes the liabilities of the initial members described in Exhibit A.
(b) Neither the limited liability company nor the members assume any liabilities not described in Exhibit A.

3.3 Warranty of Members. Each member represents and warrants to the limited liability company and to each other that the limited liability company has good and marketable title to the property contributed pursuant to Section 3.1 (a) and described in Exhibit A and that the property is free and clear from all encumbrances at the time of contribution, except for those encumbrances relating to those liabilities specifically described in Exhibit A.

3.4 Limitation on Withdrawal. Except by unanimous vote of the members, members may not withdraw from the Capital Accounts or add to their Capital Accounts.

3.5 Additional Contributions. No member shall be obligated to make any additional contributions to the limited liability company members.

SECTION 4 PROFITS AND LOSSES

4.1 Income Account. There is an Income Account for each member. The amount of the Initial Income Accounts of the initial members are set forth in Exhibit A.

4.2 Allocation of Net Profits and Losses. In accordance with generally accepted accounting principles, the limited liability company's accountant or bookkeeper shall determine Net Profits or Losses of the limited liability company as of the close of each fiscal year. The limited liability company's accountant or bookkeeper shall allocate the Net Profits and Losses to each member's Income Account in accordance with their limited liability company Percentages as of the close of each fiscal year.

4.3 Withdrawal from Income Accounts. Withdrawals from the Income Accounts are limited to an amount determined by the members owning a majority of the limited liability company Percentages. The members owning a majority of the limited liability company Percentages may determine an amount of Required Balance per limited liability company Percentage. Any amount in a member's Income Account below the Required Balance may not be withdrawn except by unanimous vote of the members.

4.4 Interest. As of the first day of each fiscal year, the limited liability company's accountant or bookkeeper shall credit the balance in each member's Income Account with interest at the prime rate stated in the *Wall Street Journal* on the last business day of the prior year.

SECTION 5 MANAGEMENT

5.1 Management. Each member has a vote in the management and conduct of the limited liability company business.

5.2 Vote Required. If this Agreement does not specify the amount of the vote of the limited liability company Percentages that is needed to make a decision, the decision may be made by an affirmative vote of the members owning a majority of the limited liability company Percentages entitled to vote.

5.3 Salary. Each member may receive a salary. The amount of such salary must be approved by members owning a majority of the limited liability company Percentages. The limited liability company shall treat the salaries of members as a limited liability company expense in determining Net Profits or Losses.

SECTION 6   DEADLOCK

6.1 General. If the members are equally divided on the basis of limited liability company Percentages on any aspect of the management of the property, business, and affairs, and the deadlock is preventing action or nonaction by the limited liability company, then the limited liability company may submit the deadlock to mediation in accordance with section 6.2. If the members are unable to resolve the deadlock through mediation, the members agree to submit the dispute to binding arbitration in accordance with section 6.3.

6.2 Mediation. If the members are unable to resolve the deadlock itself, upon written request of members owning 50% of the limited liability company Percentages, the members agree to submit the dispute to mediation and the following guidelines shall apply:

(a) The members agree to have the dispute mediated by one of the following people or organizations (in the order listed, circumstances permitting):

(i)

(ii)

(iii)

(b) The members agree to follow the mediation procedure selected by the mediator.

(c) Mediation shall terminate upon the written request of the mediator or Members owning 50% of the limited liability company Percentages.

6.3 Arbitration. If the members are unable to resolve the deadlock through mediation, upon written request of Members owning 50% of the limited liability company Percentages, the Members agree to submit the deadlock to binding arbitration in the following manner:

(a) The Members agree to have the dispute arbitrated by one of the following people or organizations (in the order listed), circumstances permitting.

(i)

(ii)

(iii)

(b) The arbitrator shall resolve the deadlock, if the arbitrator determines the arbitrator's resolution of the deadlock is in the best interests of the limited liability company. The arbitrator may decide whether matters have been properly submitted to the arbitrator for decision, whether there exists a deadlock, and whether this section and the arbitration provisions provided here were properly invoked by the limited liability company or applicable. The arbitrator may act until all questions, disputes, and controversies are determined, adjudged, and resolved.

(c) The arbitrator shall conduct the arbitration proceedings in accordance with the rules of the American Arbitration Association, then in effect, except where this Operating Agreement makes a special provision.

(d) If the arbitrator finds that (i) there have been successive arbitrations, (ii) it is likely that there will be successive arbitrations in the future to resolve most major limited liability company decisions, (iii) it is in the best interest of all Members that the limited liability company or a group of Members buys the interest of one or more Members or that there be a dissolution, then the arbitrator may decree a dissolution or may decree that the limited liability company buy out one or more of the Members. If the arbitrator decrees a buyout, the arbitrator shall decree the terms of the buyout.

(e) The arbitrator's decision shall be conclusive and binding upon the Members and limited liability company. The limited liability company may not revoke, amend, or overrule the decision, except by an action of Members owning a majority of the limited liability company Percentages.

SECTION 7   DISSOCIATION

7.1 Events of Dissociation. A Member ceases to be a Member of the limited liability company upon the happening of one of these events of dissociation:

(a) after a Member reaches the age of _____, receipt by the Limited Liability Company of notice of the Member's express will to retire as a Member or upon any later date specified in the notice;

(b) after ~ (date), receipt by the limited liability company of notice of the Member's express will to withdraw as a Member or upon any later date specified in the notice;

(c) receipt by the limited liability company of notice of the Member's express will to withdraw as a Member on or prior to ~ (same date as in 7.1(b));

(d) subject to the contrary written consent of all Members, the Member:

(i) makes an assignment for the benefit of creditors;

(ii) files a voluntary petition in bankruptcy;

(iii) is adjudicated a bankrupt or insolvent;

(iv) files a petition or answer seeking a reorganization, arrangement, composition, readjustment, liquidation, dissolution, or similar relief under any statute, law, or regulation;

(v) files an answer or other pleading admitting or failing to contest the material allegations of a petition filed against the Member in any proceeding under subsection (d); or

(vi) seeks, consents to, or acquiesces in the appointment of a trustee, receiver, or liquidator of the Member or of all or any substantial part of the Member's properties;

(e) subject to the contrary written consent of all Members at the time if

(i) 120 days after the commencement of any proceeding against the Member seeking reorganization, arrangement, composition, readjustment, liquidation, dissolution,

(ii) similar relief under any statute, law, or regulation, the proceeding has not been dismissed, within 90 days after the appointment without the Member's consent or acquiescence of a trustee, receiver, or liquidator of the Member or of all or any substantial part of the Member's properties, the appointment is not vacated or stayed; or

(iii) within 90 days after the expiration of any stay, the appointment is not vacated;

(f) in the case of a Member who is an individual:

(i) the Member's death prior to age ~ (same age as in 7.1(a)); or

(ii) the Member's death after the Member has attained the age of ~ (same age as in 7.1(a)); or

(iii) the entry of an order by a court of component jurisdiction adjudicating the member incompetent to manage the Member's person or estate;

(g) subject to the contrary written consent of all Members at the time, in the case of a Member who is a trustee or is acting as a Member by virtue of being a trustee of a trust, the termination of the trust, but not merely the substitution of a new trustee;

(h) subject to the contrary written consent of all members at the time, in the case of a Member that is a separate limited liability company, the dissolution and commencement of winding up of the separate limited liability company;

(i) subject to the contrary written consent of all members at the time, in the case of a Member that is an estate, the distribution by the fiduciary of the estate's entire interest in the limited liability company; or

(j) the Member's expulsion by a vote of the remaining Members owning _____% of the limited liability company Percentages if:

(i) it is unlawful to carry on the limited liability company business with that Member;

(ii) the Member is convicted of a felony committed against the limited liability company or involving the limited liability company business;

(k) Subject to the contrary written consent of all members at the time, a Member voluntarily or involuntarily transfers that Member's Membership Interest in the limited liability company in violation of this Agreement or the (state) limited liability company Act.

7.2   Purchase Price.

(a) *Continuation.* Members not dissociating (Remaining Members) may elect that the business of the limited liability company be continued by the Remaining Members. This election must be made within 90 days of the date of dissolution by a unanimous vote of all of the Remaining Members. If an election to continue is made, the Member or the estate or legal representative of the Member causing the dissociation (Dissociated Member) shall be paid the following amount to be determined, unless otherwise stated, as of the date of dissociation.

(i) *Retirement or Death After Retirement Age.* If an individual Member voluntarily withdraws pursuant to 7.1(a) or dies after reaching age specified in Section 7.1(f)(i), then the purchase price of the Member's interest shall be:

a. an amount per limited liability company Percentage determined to be the purchase price pursuant to this section by the vote of Members owning _____% of the Percentages at the most recent annual meeting of the limited liability company. If no amount was so determined at the last annual meeting, the amount determined at the prior recent annual meeting shall be the amount.

b. if the limited liability company did not determine an amount at the most recent annual meeting or the prior year's annual meeting, then the amount shall equal the sum of Dissociated Member's:

- Capital Account (as of the close of the previous quarter of the fiscal year);
- Income Account (as of the close of the previous quarter of the fiscal year);
- Earned and unpaid salary due, if any;
- Proportional share (based on proportional Partnership Percentages) of the Appraised Surplus multiplied by _____.*

The amount of Appraisal Surplus equals the Appraised Value of the limited liability company minus the sum of all Capital Accounts and Income Accounts (as of close of the previous quarter of the fiscal year). The Appraised Value of the limited liability company shall be determined by an appraiser named by the limited liability company's principal bank. If the limited liability company's principal bank does not appoint an appraiser within sixty days of a written request (made by either Dissociated Partner or the Partnership), the Partnership's principal accountant shall appoint the appraiser. The appraiser shall appraise the limited liability company as a going concern, with no discount for lack of marketability of the limited liability company interests.

(ii) *Permitted Withdrawal After ~ (date specified in Section 7.1(b)).* If an individual Member voluntarily withdraws pursuant to Section 7.1(b), the purchase price of the Member's interest shall be determined by Subsection (i) of Section 7.2 except the proportional share of the Appraisal Surplus shall be multiplied by _____.*

(iii) *Withdrawal before ~(date specified in Section 7.1(c)) or Expulsion.* If the Member becomes a Dissociated Member by reason of Sections 7.1(c), 7.1(j), or 7.1(k), the purchase price shall be the sum of the Dissociated Member's

- Capital Account (as of the close of the previous quarter of the fiscal year);
- Income Account (as of the close of the previous quarter of the fiscal year);
- Earned and unpaid salary, if any,

---

*This provision allows the Limited liability company to reduce the amount of payment to the retiring or deceased Member by an amount to reflect a discount for lack of marketability of the interest or a discount for a minority interest. Appropriate discounts might range from 5% to 50%. If a 5% discount is desired the attorney should complete the blank with a ".95."

minus (a) if the withdrawal is by reason of Section 7.1(c), the amount of any damages caused by the withdrawal of the Member before the date stated in Section 7.1(c); or (b) if the withdrawal is by reason of Section 7.1(j) or 7.1(k), the amount of damages described in subsection (a) of this paragraph plus the amount of other damages caused by the Dissociated Partner or the amount caused by the expelled Member.

(iv) *Other Dissociations.* If the Member becomes a Dissociated Member pursuant to any other Section, the purchase price shall be the sum of the Dissociated Members'

- Capital Account (as of the close of the previous quarter of the fiscal year);
- Income Account (as of the close of the previous quarter of the fiscal year);
- Earned and unpaid salary, if any.

7.3   Terms of Payment.

(a) *Terms of Promissory Note.* The purchase price specified in Section 7.2, if positive, will be paid within 120 days of dissociation by a promissory note drawn on the limited liability company. The promissory note will provide for equal monthly payment of principal and interest at the rate of 12% per annum. Such payments will be paid over a period of 36 months, starting with one month after the date of the promissory note. The promissory note will provide for no prepayment penalty and will be immediately due and payable if there is a failure to make a timely payment of principal or interest and such payment is not made within 20 days of the date written demand to make payment is received.

(b) *Security for Payment.* The promissory note will be secured by a security interest (junior to all security interests existing on the date of dissociation) in all the equipment, real estate, accounts receivable, and inventory of the limited liability company. The limited liability company agrees to take such actions to perfect the security interest as the Dissociated Member reasonably requests. The limited liability company agrees to execute such agreement or documents to perfect such security interest and to specify the rights of the secured party as an attorney to be appointed by the limited liability company reasonably deems appropriate.

7.4   Continuation of limited liability company. In the event the limited liability company purchases the interest of the Dissociating Member pursuant to the unanimous vote of the Members, then the Remaining Members agree to continue the limited liability company under the terms of this agreement, except that their limited liability company Percentages will be increased on a pro-rata basis as of the date of dissociation. The Dissociated Member will have no rights, except those specified in this Section, as of the date of dissolution if the Remaining Members elect to continue the business. In the event that the Remaining Members do not unanimously elect to continue the limited liability company, then the limited liability company will be wound up in accordance with Section 9.

SECTION 8   ASSIGNMENT

8.1   General Rules Regarding Assignment. The rules in this Section govern the assignment of a Member Interest.
(a) a Membership Interest is assignable in whole or in part;
(b) an assignment entitles the assignee to receive, to the extent assigned, only the distributions to which the assignor would be entitled;
(c) an assignment of a Membership Interest does not entitle the assignee to participate in the management and affairs of the limited liability company or to become or to exercise any rights of a member;
(d) an assignee may not become a member, except upon the unanimous consent of all members.
(e) until the assignee of a limited liability company Interest becomes a member, the assignor continues to be a member and to have the power to exercise rights of a member, subject to the members' or limited liability company's right to remove the assignor pursuant to this Operating Agreement.

8.2   Pledge of Membership Interest. The pledge or granting of a security interest, lien, or other encumbrance in or against any of the Membership Interests of a member is not an assignment and may not cause the member to cease to be a member or to cease to have the power to exercise any rights or powers of a member.

SECTION 9   DISSOLUTION

9.1   Events of Dissolution. The limited liability company is dissolved upon the happening of one of the following events:
(a) at the time or upon the occasion of events specified in the limited liability company's Article of Organization;
(b) a dissociation pursuant to Section 7.1 and no election has been made by the remaining members to continue the business pursuant to Section 7.2;
(c) all of the members consent to a dissolution;
(d) the entry of a decree of judicial dissolution.

9.2   Articles of Dissolution. Upon the dissolution and the commencement of winding up of the limited liability company, the limited liability company shall file Articles of Dissolution with the Secretary of State.

9.3   Procedure. Upon dissolution, the affairs of the limited liability company will be wound up upon dissolution by liquidating the assets of the limited liability company. The liabilities of the limited liability company will rank in order of payment as follows:
(a) Those owing to creditors including members, other than liabilities to members for distributions pursuant to Section 7.
(b) Those owing to the member pursuant to Section 7.
(c) Those owing to the members in respect of the member's capital accounts.
(d) Those owing to the members in respect of the member's income accounts.

Any remaining funds or assets will be then distributed to the members in accordance with their limited liability company Percentages.

SECTION 10   MEMBERS' POWERS AND LIMITATIONS

10.1   Bank accounts—checks. The limited liability company may maintain a bank account in such bank as it selects.

10.2   Acts Beyond Powers of Member. No Member may, without unanimous consent:

(a) dispose of the goodwill of the limited liability company or convey, encumber, or lease any other asset of the business outside the ordinary course of business;

(b) cause the limited liability company to be converted to another form of business entity;

(c) do any act which would make it impossible to carry on the ordinary business of a limited liability company; or

(d) cause the limited liability company to be merged with another business; and

(e) cause the admission of a new Member.

SECTION 11   INDEMNIFICATION

11.1   Mandatory Indemnification. Subject to Section 11.2, the limited liability company shall indemnify a Member for judgments, settlements, penalties, fines, or expenses incurred in a proceeding to which an individual is a party because the individual is or was a Member.

11.2   Limitations on Indemnification. The limited liability company may not indemnify a Member from liability for

(a) the amount of a financial benefit received by a Member to which the Member is not entitled;

(b) an intentional infliction of harm by the Member on the limited liability company or its Members;

(c) an intentional violation of criminal law by the Member; or

(d) an unlawful distribution by the Member.

SECTION 12   MISCELLANEOUS

12.1   Books and Records. The limited liability company shall keep at its principal place of business:

(a) a current list in alphabetical order of the full name and last known business street address of each Member;

(b) a copy of the Articles of Organization and all certificates of amendment to them, together with executed copies of any powers of attorney pursuant to which any certificate of amendment has been executed;

(c) copies of the limited liability company's federal, state, and local income tax returns and reports, if any, for the three most recent years;

(d) copies of any financial statements of the limited liability company, if any, for the three most recent years; and

(e) a copy of this Operating Agreement and any amendments thereto.

12.2   Annual Meeting. The Members shall meet annually at noon on the (first, second, etc.) (day of week) of each (month) at the principal place of business of the limited liability company. They may meet at such other times as the Members owning 20% of the Membership Percentages specify in a written notice mailed or personally delivered to each Member at least five days before the meeting.

12.3   Amendment. The Members may amend this Agreement and Exhibit A upon execution of a written amendment signed by all of the Members.

12.4   Fiscal Year. The limited liability company's fiscal year shall be a calendar year.

12.5   Governing Law. This Agreement is governed by the laws of the State of

This Operating Agreement is signed on (date)

_____

EXHIBIT A

Initial limited liability company Percentages: (Section 1.4):
   Member A
   Member B
   Member C
Description of Initial Property Contributed (Section 3.1(a)):
   Member A
   Member B
   Member C
Value of Initial Capital Accounts (Section 3.1(b)):
   Member A
   Member B
   Member C
Description of Liabilities Assumed (Section 3.2):
   Member A
   Member B
   Member C
Value of Initial Income Accounts (Section 4.1):
   Member A
   Member B
   Member C

GLOSSARY

Actual authority   Authority granted to an agent when a principal directs an agent to perform a task.

Administrative dissolution   Termination of a corporation by the secretary of state.

Agency   Relationship in which one person, an agent, acts on behalf of another, the principal.

Agent   One who acts for the benefit of another.

Alter ego   Literally "the other self"; when shareholders do not treat a corporation as a separate entity and use it to conduct private business, they may be held personally liable for the obligations of the corporation under the *alter ego* doctrine.

Annual meeting   Yearly meeting of corporate shareholders to elect directors and/or conduct other corporate business.

Apparent authority   When the principal's conduct makes it appear to a third party than an agent is authorized to act on behalf of the principal.

Appraisal rights   Rights of dissenting shareholders to have their shares appraised (valued) at a fair market price and purchased by the corporation.

Articles of amendment   Document notifying the secretary of state of a fundamental corporate change.

Articles of consolidation   Document notifying the secretary of state of a consolidation.

Articles of dissolution   Document notifying the secretary of state of the dissolution of a corporation.

Articles of incorporation   Document that creates a corporation.

Articles of merger   Document notifying the secretary of state of a merger.

Articles of organization   Document forming a limited liability company.

Articles of partnership   Partnership agreement.

Articles of termination   Document notifying the secretary of state of the termination of a limited liability.

Assignment of interest   Transfer of ownership interest to another.

Assumed business name   A name, other than the owner's name, under which a business operates.

Attachment   Taking of property for the payment of debts.

Board of directors   The group elected to manage a corporation.

Board of managers   The group elected to manage a limited liability company.

Bonding   Guarantee that an act will be performed.

Business corporation   A legal entity created to conduct business.

Business judgment rule   General rule adopted by courts immunizing directors from liability for their actions if due care is used (e.g., seeking the opinion of an expert, etc.).

Bylaws   Written guidelines and procedures for the operation and management of a corporation.

Capital   Money or other property.

Capital contribution   The initial investment of property or money by a partner to a partnership.

Centralization of management   Core group of individuals who manage a corporation.

Certificate of limited partnership   Document filed with the secretary of state registering for limited partnership status.

Certificate of merger   Document issued by the secretary of state approving, and thus effecting, a merger.

Close corporation   *See* Statutory close corporation.

Commingling of assets   Combining personal assets with business assets.

Consolidation   Merger of two corporations into a newly formed corporation [Corporation A + Corporation B = Corporation C].

Continuity of life   Perpetual existence.

Corporation   A legal business entity owned by shareholders and managed by an elected board of directors and appointed officers.

Cumulative voting   A voting mechanism that allows each shareholder to cast as many votes as there are vacancies on a board of directors.

Deferred dissolution   Ninety-day grace period allowing partnership business to continue when a partner withdraws.

De jure corporation   A corporation properly formed in accordance with state law.

De facto corporation   A business that has not strictly complied with the state's statutory incorporation process but conducts business in good faith as though it were a corporation.

Derivative action   Lawsuit filed by shareholders on behalf of the corporation to protect corporate interests.

Dissenters' rights   Rights of shareholders who object to a fundamental corporate change to force the corporation to buy their shares at a fair market price.

Dissolution   Termination of business association.

Dividends   Distribution of corporate profits to shareholders.

Domestic corporation   A corporation operating in the state in which it was incorporated.

Double taxation   Taxation of corporate income at two levels: (1) the corporate level (the corporation itself pays taxes on its profits) and (2) the shareholder level (shareholders pay personal taxes due on distributions of corporate income [dividends]).

Duty of care   The care a reasonably prudent person would use in similar circumstances.

Duty of loyalty   Responsibility of an agent to act for the benefit of the principal.

Entity classification election   Allows unincorporated entities to elect to be taxed as a partnership or a corporation.

Exhaustion rule   Requires that business assets be used to pay partnership debts before a creditor can look to partners' personal assets.

Express authority   Direction by a principal to an agent to perform specified tasks.

Express implied authority   The authority necessary for an agent to carry out the express directives of a principal.

Extraordinary corporate matter   An action that will affect the organization of the corporation.

Fiduciaries   Those in a relationship of trust.

Fiduciary relationship   A relationship of trust creating a duty to act in good faith.

Foreign jurisdiction   A state other than the one in which a business is registered.

Foreign corporation   A corporation operating in a state other than the state in which it was incorporated.

Foreign partnership   A partnership organized and/or registered in another state.

Formalities   Requirements for creating and maintaining a business.

Forum shopping   Selection of a jurisdiction in which to do business.

Fundamental corporate change   Change that significantly affects the basic foundation of a corporation.

General partner   An individual or entity that manages a general or limited partnership.

General partnership   An association of two or more persons or entities who operate a business as co-owners for profit and allow all partners the right to manage business affairs.

General proxy   A proxy allowing a proxy holder to vote at his or her discretion.

Goodwill   Reputation of a business and its goods and services.

Hostile takeover   An attempt to take over management and/or ownership of a corporation without the consent of its directors and shareholders.

Implied authority   The authority necessary for an agent to carry out the express directives of a principal.

Inadequate capitalization   Insufficient funding for corporate ventures.

Incorporater   The individual who signs and files the corporation's articles of incorporation.

Incorporation by estoppel   A business that is not properly incorporated but may be extended the liability protections of corporation in a contract dispute.

Indemnification   Reimbursement for payment of another's debt.

Insider trading   Transaction by a corporate insider who has information that is not available to the general public; prohibited by SEC Rule 10b-5.

Insurance   Protection from unforeseen losses.

Interested director   A director who has a personal interest in a corporate transaction.

Involuntary termination   Termination of a corporation without the consent of its board and directors and/or its shareholders.

Joint and several liability   Doctrine of shared responsibility allowing creditors to sue individuals separately (severally) or together (jointly) to satisfy a debt.

Joint liability   Shared responsibility; requires that all individuals be sued together to recover a debt.

Joint venture   Partnership for a limited duration.

Liability   An individual's responsibility for the debts and obligations of a business.

Liability insurance   Insurance coverage intended to compensate third parties for losses.

Limited liability   Investors' responsibility for the debts and obligations of a business is limited to the amount of their investment; when an investor is not responsible for paying the debts and obligations of a business from his or her personal assets.

Limited liability company   An unincorporated entity that offers its members management rights, limited personal liability, and the "pass through" taxation of partnerships.

Limited liability partnership   A general or limited partnership that registers as a limited liability partnership and protects its partners from vicarious liability for the negligence or malfeasance of other partners.

Limited partner   An investor in a limited partnership who has no management rights.

Limited partnership   An association of two or more persons or entities who operate a business as co-owners for profit with one or more general partners (managers) and one or more limited partners (investors).

Limited proxy   A proxy directing a proxy holder how to vote on a particular issue.

Liquidation   Process of turning assets into cash ("liquid assets").

Liquidator   The individual who manages the liquidation of business assets.

Merger   Occurs when one or more corporations (merged corporations) are absorbed into another existing corporation (surviving corporation) [Corporation A » Corporation B = Corporation B].

Merged corporation   Corporation that is absorbed by another corporation.

Minutes   Written summary of proceedings of shareholders' or directors' meetings.

Nonprofit corporation   Corporation formed for charitable purposes.

Officer   Individual appointed by the board of directors to manage the daily operations of a corporation.

Operating agreement   Written agreement governing the management and operation of a limited liability company.

Ordinary course of business   The usual and customary dealings of a business.

Partnership   An association of two or more persons or entities who operate a business as co-owners "for profit."

Partnership agreement   A contract among partners that addresses the rights, duties, and interests of the partners and governs the operation of the partnership; also known as the *articles of partnership.*

Partnership capital   The contribution of property or money to a partnership.

"Pass-through taxation"   Taxation of business profits and losses as the personal income of business owners.

Personal liability   An individual's responsibility to pay the debts and obligations of a business from personal assets (e.g., home, car, etc.).

Piercing the corporate veil   When individual shareholders are held personally liable for corporate debts to prevent fraud or injustice.

Preemptive rights   The right of a shareholder to purchase newly issued shares of stock in order to maintain their proportionate ownership interest of corporation.

Preincorporation share subscription   An agreement to purchase shares of a business once it is incorporated.

Principal   One who permits or directs another to act on his behalf.

Pro bono   Work performed without charge (literally, "for the public good").

Professional corporation   A corporation formed by one or more professionals to conduct business.

Promoter   The individual who organizes and forms a corporation.

Proprietor   Owner.

Proxy   Written authorization for another person to vote on behalf of a shareholder.

Proxy fight   An aggressor's attempt gain control of a corporation by soliciting the voting rights (proxies) of its shareholders with the intent to elect its board of directors.

Purpose clause   Describes the intended purpose(s) of a corporation.

Quorum   The minimum number of shares or directors that must be present at a meeting for an action by shareholders or directors.

Ratification   Retroactive acceptance/approval of an obligation created by an agent who did not have authority to act on behalf of the principal at the time of the transaction.

Record date   The date set for determining shareholders entitled to notice of a shareholders' meeting.

Respondeat superior   The doctrine that holds a master/superior responsible for the acts of a servant or agent.

S corporation   Tax designation available to qualifying small corporations allowing corporate income to pass through the corporation to be taxed as personal income of the shareholders.

Sales tax permit   Registration that allows state and local governments to impose and collect taxes assessed on the sale of goods.

Securities and Exchange Commission   Federal agency that regulates securities.

Securities Exchange Act of 1933   Federal law regulating the issuance of securities to the public.

Securities Exchange Act of 1934   Federal law regulating the disclosure of information in the sale or exchange of securities.

Share exchange   Merger occurring when a corporation exchanges its shares for those of a target corporation.

Shareholders   Owners of a corporation.

Share subscription   An agreement to purchase shares of a business once it is incorporated.

Share transfer restriction   *See* Stock transfer restriction.

Short swing profits   Profits made by directors, officers, or 10 percent shareholders from the purchase and sale of a corporation's shares within a six-month period.

Sole proprietorship   A business owned by one person.

Special meeting   A shareholders' meeting held between annual meetings or a directors' meeting held between regular meetings.

Standard approval procedure   Two-step process for approval of fundamental corporate change requiring (1) board of directors approval and recommendation and (2) shareholder approval.

Statement of partnership authority   Document filed with the secretary of state that identifies the partners authorized to act for the partnership and describes the extent of the partners' authority.

Statutory close corporation   A corporation owned by a small number of shareholders whose shares are not freely transferable.

Statutory merger   Merger that occurs pursuant to statutory requirements.

Stock transfer restriction   Restrictions on the transfer of ownership (stock) of a corporation.

Subsidiary corporation   Corporation owned by another corporation.

Surviving corporation   Corporation that continues its existence after a merger.

Target corporation   Corporation subject to takeover by another entity (e.g., corporation) or individual.

Tenancy in partnership   Co-ownership of property by partners.

Tender offer   Public offer by an aggressor to purchase shares of a target corporation.

Torts   Wrongful acts.

Trade name   Name used by a business.

***Ultra vires* act**   Actions by a corporation that exceed the corporate purpose and/or powers.

Usurpation of a corporate opportunity   When a director takes advantage of a corporate opportunity for him/herself without first allowing the corporation the opportunity.

Vicarious liability   Responsibility imposed on one person for the acts of another.

Winding up   The process of liquidating assets, paying debts, and distributing surplus to partners.

Written Consent   An action by taken by shareholders or directors without a meeting; written consent generally must be unanimous.

INDEX